FICTION OF THE MODERN GROTESQUE

Also by Bernard Mc Elroy

SHAKESPEARE'S MATURE TRAGEDIES

Fiction of the Modern Grotesque

Bernard Mc Elroy

St. Martin's Press   New York

First published in the United States of America in 1989

Printed in Hong Kong

ISBN 0–312–01340–X

Library of Congress Cataloging-in-Publication Data
Mc Elroy, Bernard.
Fiction of the modern grotesque / by Bernard Mc Elroy.
p. cm.
Bibliography: p.
Includes index.
ISBN 0–312–01340–X : $30.00 (est.)
1. Grotesque in literature.   I. Title.
PN56.G7M36   1989
809'.91—dc19   87–27866
                                                          CIP

The door opened and what entered the room, fat and succulent, its sides voluptuously swelling, footless, pushing itself along on its entire underside, was the green dragon. Formal salutation. I asked him to come right in. He regretted that he could not do that, as he was too long. This meant that the door had to remain open, which was rather awkward. He smiled, half in embarrassment, half cunningly, and began:

'Drawn hither by your longing, I come pushing myself from afar off, and underneath am now quite sore. But I am glad to do it. Gladly do I come, gladly do I offer myself to you.'

Kafka's Journals

Contents

Contents

Preface

What follows is a traditional approach to an impossible subject. The approach is traditional in that my interest is primarily in the works considered rather than in theories of language and criticism. As a phenomenon in art, the grotesque is physical, predominantly visual; its true home is in painting and sculpture, the media studied by John Ruskin in his classic treatise on the subject, *The Stones of Venice*. In literature, it exists in precisely those works that use language to evoke for the reader a vivid visual image which is perceived as grotesque. I am more interested in the image evoked than in the process of the evocation. Primarily, I will be asking what is the *source* of the grotesque. Why does it make its riotous appearance again and again in the work of so many writers who seem to speak with most urgency and power to the modern imagination?

Considering the diversity of the works I am to discuss, the answer to that question will not be simple, or, more exactly, I hope it will not be simplistic. In my opening chapter, I attempt to expand upon and, by way of Freud, to update the basic idea of Ruskin's argument, that the grotesque arises from a peculiar attitude or stance of mind toward the fearsome. But what a particular group of people or what individuals within that group find fearsome will vary greatly from culture to culture and individual to individual. Certainly, there are common concerns in the literature of the modern grotesque that make it characteristically modern, and in the second part of the opening chapter, I attempt to identify them as they emerge in Feodor Dostoyevsky's *Notes From Underground*, a work that brings us to the threshold of our topic. But in the chapters that follow, the most striking thing is that the grotesque arises from a different source in the case of each writer considered. The source of the grotesque in Franz Kafka is a comprehensive view of reality itself, a view that I have characterised as the paranoid vision, for it shares much in common with the clinical descriptions given of the world experienced in paranoia. In James Joyce's *Ulysses*, the assemblage of grotesques that haunt the world of Nighttown all arise from the ambivalent love, hate, shame, fear, and laughter simultaneously directed toward the human body.

Here, as at so many junctures, the grotesque is used to expose in magical, exaggerated terms what has been implicit all along in the 'real' strata of the novel.

In a whole group of works, the narrative has been delivered over to a speaker who is either insane or probably insane. The grotesque arises from the deranged fantasies and delusions which he mingles freely with the 'reality' of his story. But even within this category, there is a wide range of difference among authors. For both Günter Grass and Vladimir Nabokov, the narrator's insanity becomes a way of coping with a world that is otherwise intolerable, and a sense of manic gaiety overlies the basic desperation of his predicament. For Samuel Beckett, however, schizophrenia becomes the embodiment of the bleakest limits of isolation and incoherence.

For both Flannery O'Connor and Nathanael West, the departure of religion and myth from the modern world and the inability of secular culture to supply any comparable conviction on which to base meaning or value is the situation that gives rise to the grotesque. But in West's fiction, the grotesques are the victims; in O'Connor's, they are more likely to be the heroes and saints. Thomas Pynchon uses the grotesque as a symptom of massive failure in the entire enterprise of culture itself. In *V.*, he locates the source of this demise in atrophy of the emotions and the cultivation of illusion to mask the psyche from its own innate cruelty. In *Gravity's Rainbow*, the hallucinating mind of the narrator provides a kind of palimpsest through which the conclusion of World War II is viewed, with the novel's principal grotesque, Captain Blicero, becoming its principal spokesman on the subject of the terminal infection from which Western civilisation is expiring. In Gabriel García Márquez' masterpiece, it is the very nature of man's endeavour to impose culture on a riotous natural world that inevitably turns him into a grotesque.

If there is such diversity, then why try to gather such a disparate group of writers under one heading? The common element among them is their use of the grotesque as a crucial and powerful force in their work. Naturally, an important purpose of this book is to provide a model of the grotesque itself, drawing where possible on previous studies, but attempting to go beyond them in essential respects. I hope to show how the grotesque is a perennial strain in the human imagination, present in the art and literature of diverse cultures, and to demonstrate what the works of a variety of twentieth-century authors share in common with earlier manifestations of the grotesque. At the same time, I hope to suggest fundamental ways in which they differ from those manifestations and are characteristically modern.

A few words are in order about the scope of this study. Exhaustive comprehensiveness was not a possible or desirable goal; a comprehensive book on the grotesque in modern literature would be longer than *The Anatomy of Melancholy*. The present work is largely a study of Kafka, Joyce, Grass, and Pynchon, a selection justified, I believe, by their preeminence in the kind of literature I am discussing. But the final two chapters are organised topically rather than being built exclusively around an individual author. Given the conspicuous use in fiction of the modern grotesque of first person narrators who are possibly insane, and the preoccupation with decline and decadence in Western civilisation, it seemed warranted to include several examples handling the same concerns but with important differences. Other critics might have included other writers, but the objective here has been to strike a balance between offering a representative, if selective, set of examples and rendering the whole undertaking so broad as to be virtually impossible.

A generous grant from the Harry Frank Guggenheim Foundation made it possible for me to go on leave to complete the writing of this book. Earlier, a fellowship from the National Endowment for the Humanities enabled me to get the project started. Loyola University of Chicago provided several grants and other assistance. I would like to express my gratitude to the following institutions for the use of their resources and much help from their staffs: the British Library, the University of London and its Institute for Germanic Studies, the libraries of Loyola University of Chicago and its Rome Center of Liberal Arts, the Newberry Library of Chicago, and the libraries of Cornell University, Northwestern University, and Rice University. Portions of this book in somewhat different form have appeared as articles in *Modern Fiction Studies*, and *Forum for Modern Language Studies*.

Support of a less material but no less valued kind came from the many friends and colleagues who were generous with their time, ideas, and encouragement. In particular, I wish to thank Eileen Baldeshwiler, Kathleen Burke, Anne Callahan, Thomas Gorman, Alan Grob, Joyce Markle, Gene Phillips, Linda Revere, and Elizabeth Wally. Great also is my gratitude to my students, both

graduate and undergraduate, who by their enthusiasm for the
subject, kept me convinced it was worth pursuing; and I recall with
particular fondness a small group of undergraduates at Loyola
University's Rome Center of Liberal Arts some years ago who were
in at the beginning.

Rome   B. Mc E.

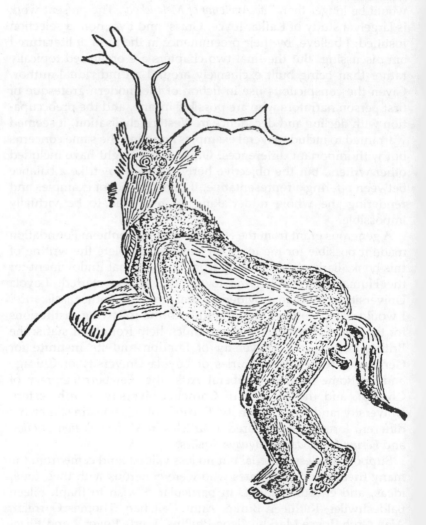

The 'Sorcerer of Trois Frères'

1

The Grotesque and the Modern Grotesque

I

The source of the grotesque in art and literature is man's capacity for finding a unique and powerful fascination in the monstrous. The psychic reasons for this proclivity are far from clear, but the proclivity itself has left its mark on a wide variety of cultures, from prehistory to the present, from the most primitive societies to the most sophisticated. From ice-age cave paintings to modern films, from shaman costumes and devil masks to the paintings of Dali and Picasso, from folk stories and fairy tales to the writings of Kafka, the transmutations of men, beasts, devils, and chimeras have made their bizarre progress, constantly changing with the world-views of the cultures which produced them, yet still retaining the essential qualities by which we may attempt to designate them as grotesques. In few ages has this proclivity been more pronounced than in our own.

Though the phenomenon it designates is older than history, the word itself is of fairly recent origin, having been coined in Renaissance Italy to describe certain droll decorations unearthed in the *grotte* of Nero's House of Gold.[1] In its comparatively short history, the term has meant very different things to different eras, and even in our own day it has a subtly graded series of connotations. In its most limited sense, it refers to a type of decorative art combining human features with lithe beasts and fantastic birds in a filigree of vines and curlicues – the style developed in ancient Rome and imitated by such Renaissance artists as Raphael and Pinturicchio. This, somewhat surprisingly, is the only sense in which the grotesque is discussed in the fifteenth edition of the *Encyclopedia Britannica*. On the other hand, in colloquial usage, it can mean almost anything unseemly, disproportionate, or in bad taste, and the term is routinely applied to everything from a necktie to a relationship.[2] The first problem to

1

face, then, is that, historically and semantically, the word has variable meanings, and the problem is further complicated by a whole skein of more or less related words whose meanings are similar to but, presumably, not synonymous with grotesque: bizarre, macabre, fantastic, weird, Gothic, arabesque – these are but a few, and much effort by previous critics has gone into trying to undo the tangle and delineate where the province of one ends and that of another begins.

I hope to avoid such hair-splitting by recognising from the outset that the limits of definition of the word must be fairly flexible. There can be no precise point at which one says, 'the grotesque stops here; commence using some other term', because the grotesque is not a genre to which a work either does or does not belong. It does not originate in a particular school or artistic theory, but antedates all schools and theories. Nor is it an absolute which is either fully present or not at all. Rather, it is a continuum which may be present in varying degrees in otherwise disparate works.

There have been numerous modern efforts to define the nature of the beast, the most notable being those of Wolfgang Kayser and Mikhail Bakhtin.[3] Still, the most enduring and valuable discussion of the subject remains John Ruskin's *The Stones of Venice*. Its strength is in the simplicity and rightness of its central assertion: 'that the mind, under certain phases of excitement, *plays* with terror'.[4] Though Kayser and Bakhtin in most respects differ from Ruskin as much as they do from each other, both retain that central concept of the grotesque as play. For the former, the grotesque is, among other things, a game with the absurd, while the latter locates the grotesque in the spirit of carnival which distorts and defuses all that is terrible by the peoples' triumphant laughter.

However, there are problems to be solved if Ruskin's concept of the grotesque is to be used as a means of approaching modern literature. His discussion of the grotesque is but a part of his massive treatise on medieval and Renaissance Venetian art and architecture. Moreover, Ruskin's purposes were frankly polemical: to show how the Venetians fell off from a healthy, virile, pious society into vainglory and decadence, and to issue a warning to nineteenth-century England to avoid the pride of vain knowledge and the idleness of vain pleasure. Every part of his exposition is coloured by that polemic, and none more so than his discussion of the grotesque. Moreover, as a man of his time, Ruskin brought to the subject a set of beliefs about nobility and baseness, the soul and sin, God and man, not to mention a whole pack of racial, religious, sexual, and cultural prejudices which are different from those of most moderns. However, his notion of the grotesque as the mind's play with terror can still be useful in a discussion of the modern grotesque if we can reformulate answers to just two questions: What kind of play? What kind of terror?

For Ruskin, the source of the terror of the grotesque is not a specific situation but the human condition itself, '. . . not the sudden, selfish, and contemptible fear of immediate danger, but the fear which arises out of the contemplation of great powers in destructive operation, and generally from the perception of the presence of death' (p. 163). This account is all right as far as it goes, but it leaves a number of important questions unanswered. All people fear cataclysm and death, but is there a special kind of fear that manifests itself in images of the grotesque? In the time since Ruskin, such special fear – the eerie, unsettled feeling, the combination of fascination and revulsion so difficult to define but so unmistakable in our felt response to certain situations and certain kinds of art – has been most effectively dealt with by Freud under the heading of the 'Unheimlich', literally the 'unhomely', but more usually in translation, the 'uncanny'.

In exploring this feeling (to which he claimed to be only very slightly susceptible himself), Freud used as a point of departure E. T. A. Hoffman's story, 'The Sandman'. It narrates the tale of a young man driven to insanity and suicide by a sinister and possibly supernatural figure who appears in various guises, all of them avatars of the Sandman, a childhood bogy that throws sand in the eyes, causing them to pop out.[5] Freud interprets the story as an expression of infantile castration anxiety, and attributes its uncanny effect to the recurrence of repressed emotion.

However, as he surveys other examples of the uncanny in life and literature, he finds that a second psychological stimulus which can induce the strange sensation is a partial reversion to 'the old animistic conception of the universe'.[6] In the world views of many primitive peoples, the external environment is endowed with anthropomorphic consciousness, with intentions, benign or malevolent, toward the individual, and with powers to influence the course of events. 'It seems as if each one of us has been through a phase of individual development corresponding to this animistic stage in primitive men, that none of us has passed through it without preserving certain residues and traces of it which are still capable of manifesting themselves, and that everything which now strikes us as "uncanny" fulfils the condition of touching those residues of animistic mental activity within us and bringing them to expression' ('The "Uncanny"',' p. 240–1).

Thus, there are two kinds of psychological material that, separately or in combination, can produce a sense of the uncanny: repressed infantile anxieties, and surmounted modes of primitive thought. Freud views the latter as more conducive to the sensation, but finds that ultimately the two are not fully separable from each other. 'When we consider that primitive beliefs are most intimately connected with infantile complexes, and are, in fact, based on them, we shall not be greatly astonished that the distinction is often a hazy one' (p. 249).

I suggest that our response to the grotesque, whether in life or in art, has as a fundamental component that sense of the uncanny which arises from the reassertion of the primitive, magical view of the world. It seems to me inescapable that the grotesque is linked definitively to aggression in human nature, both the impulse to commit agression and even more, the fear of being the victim of aggression: and I do not mean merely natural aggression, but aggression by impossible, all-powerful means – which is to say aggression by magic. As Freud explains, our primitive ancestors actually believed in the possibility of magic occurrences, were, in fact, convinced that such things happened routinely. 'Nowadays we no longer believe in them, we have *surmounted* these modes of thought; but we do not feel quite sure of our new beliefs, and the old ones still exist within us ready to seize upon any confirmation. As soon as something *actually happens* in our lives which seems to confirm the old discarded beliefs we get a feeling of the uncanny . . .' (pp. 247–8).

More recently than Freud, Jean Paul Sartre, in his *Sketch for a Theory of the Emotions*, has also discussed the role of magic in psychic phenomena.[7] According to his formulation, a strong emotion quite transcends the object or event which evoked it and transforms the entire world subjectively preceived. The deterministic world, empirically constructed by the rational intellect, disintegrates to be replaced by a magical one shaped by the emotions. 'And-what happens when the superstructures laboriously built up by reason disintegrate, and man finds himself suddenly plunged back into the original magic? That is easily guessed; the consciousness seizes upon magic as magic, and lives it vividly as such. The categories "suspicious and disquieting", etc. designate the magical, in so far as it is being lived by consciousness or tempting consciousness to live it' (p. 86).

Above all, Sartre insists, a fully realised emotion is not a modification in the attitude of a person surrounded by an unchanged world; no apprehension of an object as frightening, irritating, or saddening, etc. can arise except against the background of an alteration of the world, and this is especially true when the object is perceived as horrific. He uses the example of a man who suddenly sees a hideous face staring at him through a window across the room. The window and the distance between it and the horror-stricken man are no longer perceived as usable or necessary, as that which would have to be opened or that which would have to be traversed. They are subsumed into and united with the horror, become part of its context. 'For the horrible is *not possible* in the deterministic world of the usable. The horrible can appear only in a world which is such that all things existing in it are magical by nature and the only defenses against them are magical. This is what we experience often enough in the world of dreams. . . . In a word, to experience any object as horrible is to see it against the background of a world which reveals itself as *already* horrible' (pp. 88–9). Just so, to render and object as grotesque is to situate it in a world which is grotesque. The artist of the grotesque does not merely combine disparate forms or distort surfaces. He creates a context in which such distortion is possible, an implied world where men can and do find themselves metamorphosed into vermin, where playing a child's tin drum can and does have magical efficacy.

This, then, is the first quality of the special kind of terror that discharges itself in images of the grotesque: it is primitive, magical, uncanny. The grotesque transforms the world from what we 'know' it to be to what we fear it might be. It distorts or exaggerates the surface of reality in order to tell a qualitative truth about it. The grotesque does not address the rationalist in us or the scientist in us, but the vestigial primitive in us, the child in us, the potential psychotic in us. This magical, animistic quality prevails in the grotesque art of the most disparate periods and cultures. In primitive art, images that appear to the modern eye grotesque are conjured up by an animistic view of the world and the spirits that control it – fertility figures and gods who are both anthropomorphic and theriomorphic. In the Middle Ages, the demonic provided the material for one of the richest strains in the history of grotesque art, culminating in the fantastic hellscapes of Hieronymus Bosch. The same concern with magic, especially aggression by magic, dominates the work of modern writers of the grotesque. Once the world of familiar surfaces has been transformed into the world of grotesque possibilities, events abound that can only be called magical, and almost invariably they centre around victimisation and efficacy.

It is no accident, I think, that the word 'grotesque' came into currency at exactly the time when rationalism and empiricism were assuming an increasingly important role in Western man's address to the world. A primitive in a demon mask strikes *us* as a grotesque, but he scarcely could seem so to himself or to those who believe what he represents actually exists. The very concept of the grotesque in the modern sense would be impossible, for it implies a differentiation from the norm.[8] For the modern, the grotesque is by nature something exceptional, something set apart or aberrant, and in its most extreme forms, situated in the realm of fantasy, dream, or hallucination – in the realm, that is, of unreality. The primitive makes no such distinction, nor does a very young child, and it is upon the vestige of precisely that mentality in us that the grotesque exerts its power. The word 'grotesque' differentiates that which we want to have separate from our sense of reality, but still powerfully experience as real.

The uncanny in Freud's sense of the term, the magical in Sartre's, are always part of the special kind of terror with which the grotesque plays. However, not everything that is uncanny or magical is grotesque; clearly, there is some other component to that terror, and I believe Ruskin points us toward it when he discusses the role of physical debasement in the art of the grotesque. Noting the relationship between corporeal degradation and the depiction of Satanic evil, he asserts that the twenty-first and twenty-second books of Dante's *Inferno* 'present the most perfect instances with which I am acquainted of the terrible grotesque' (*Stones*, p. 175). By contrast, he finds Milton's Satan a 'smoothed and artistical' conception specifically because it lacks vivid physicality. Of particular interest is his comment that the form of Milton's Satan is not distinct enough to be painted.

As an aesthetic category, the grotesque is physical, predominantly visual. It true habitat is pictorial and plastic art; in literature, it is created by narration and description which evoke scenes and characters that can be visualised as grotesque.[9] There is no such thing as an abstract grotesque, at least not in the sense in which I am using the term in this study.[10] As Ruskin points out, 'It is not as the creating, but as the *seeing* man, that we are here contemplating the master of the true grotesque. It is because the dreadfulness of the universe around him weighs upon his heart that his work is wild; and therefore through the whole of it we shall find the evidence of deep insight into nature. His beasts and birds, however monstrous, will have profound relations with the true' (*Stones*, p. 169).

The relationship between any art work and 'the true' has, of course, become problematic in ways that Ruskin could not have envisioned. Given the direction critical thought has taken in recent years, it was predictable, even inevitable, that theories of post-structuralism and strategies of deconstruction would be brought to bear on the subject of the grotesque. The most elaborate and ambitious attempt at such an application is Geoffrey Harpham's recent study, *On the Grotesque*.[11]

Harpham is no dogmatic post-structuralist, setting out theories in jargon borrowed from linguistics or phenomenology. He brings a variety of approaches to this subject, the most impressive being erudition and sensitivity as a student of art history. The eloquence, indeed the passion, with which he writes of the Renaissance *grottesche* make his the finest discussion of that subject I know. But like a lot of recent critics, he seems most interested in what language and literature do *not* say, and he runs a serious risk of making indeterminacy into a fetish. Given the tendency for all models of the grotesque to wind up as restatements of their own premises, post-structuralism seems to me particularly ill-suited to account for the vividness and impact with which we experience the grotesques of artists like Bosch or writers like Kafka and Grass.

Harpham's approach, like Todorov's earlier study of the fantastic, attempts to account for our response as a non-event.[12] In his very complex formulation, grotesques 'stand at a margin of consciousness between the known and the unknown, the perceived and the unperceived, calling into question the adequacy of our ways of organizing the world, of dividing the continuum of experience into knowable particles' (p. 3). Much of the spirit of his inquiry seems summed up in his exclamation, 'What a paltry thing meaning is, that it can be created *ex nihilo* by a brush stroke – and then wiped

out, or "masked" by another similar brush stroke elsewhere'
(p. 40).

It is certainly neither my concern nor my intention to get involved
here in any abstract and complicated discussion of contemporary
theory. My reservations about post-structuralism as an approach
to the grotesque are really quite specific: for a system which places
so much emphasis on explaining the reactions of readers of
literature or viewers of art, it fails in precisely that area of describing
reactions to the grotesque that we can recognise as even remotely
resembling our own. 'Grotesques confront us as a corrupt or
fragmented text in search of a master principle. . . . Looking at
ourselves looking at the grotesque, we can observe our own
projections, catching ourselves, as it were, in the act of perception'
(p. 43). The puzzlement, as it were, and anxiety of a mind trying
to posit determinate meaning to a maze of signs that may refer to
nothing but themselves can describe our reaction to certain kinds
of art, most of it modern, but it has little to do with the *immediacy*
of our response to one of Bosch's hellscapes, or Gregor's metamorphosis, not to mention Grass's eel-catching expedition.

Moreover, if the grotesque is constituted by contradictory mean-
sings, confused categories, and defeated sign systems, then it
becomes difficult to avoid the situation in which *all* contradiction
or confusion is grotesque. Harpham at times seems to betray an
uneasy sense that his subject is in danger of disappearing into the
endless proliferation invited by his theory. Grotesque art tends to
become virtually any art that recognises its own self-contradiction
and cultivates it as an artistic principle. The weakness of this
conception can be seen in the portions of *On the Grotesque*
which discuss specific works of art and literature. Raphael's *The
Transfiguration* is singled out as the epitome of the grotesque in art
not because it is grotesque by, say, the standards of Bosch or
Breughel (one could, I think, make a better case for it being called
sublime), but because it is indeterminate. The black space at the
centre, by its very blankness, its lack of clear meaning, is what
identifies the painting as grotesque.[13] And in the field of literature,
when we are told that in Poe's 'The Mask of the Red Death', the
plague is the word, language is death-tending, and Poe's idea of
language was really rather like Jacques Derrida's (p. 119), we must
conclude that the critic is merely indulging himself.

The perception of the grotesque in the world need not even
involve the mediation of art. A wide variety of perfectly natural

creatures induce in most people that combination of aversion and fascination that characterises our response to the grotesque. Spiders, bats, and virtually the whole kingdom of reptiles usually make perfectly calm, self-controlled people get quickly out of the way, and the depiction of such beasts is a notable feature of much grotesque art. The reason for this strange reaction to certain perfectly natural and often quite harmless creatures is a mystery. Freud discussed animal phobias among children in terms of sexual symbols and father fears.[14] More recently, physiological psychologists, working mostly with lower animals, have postulated innate releasing mechanisms imprinted in the nervous system and transmitted genetically. A newly hatched chick, for instance, which has never seen a hawk, will react defensively when it does see one or even a properly painted effigy of one; the response cannot have been learned, but is innate.[15] It is conceivable (though just barely) that some defense mechanism, developed who knows where on the evolutionary chain and passed on for who knows how long, remains vestigial in modern man and prompts an instinctive aversion to certain kinds of insects and animals. Whatever the case, an effect of that aversion is that the imagination is readily stimulated to endow such creatures with enormous size and magical powers and then to imagine what it might be like to be at their mercy. Among the more puzzling coincidences of cultural history is that man created in his imaginative dragon lore reptilian monsters strikingly similar to animals that actually lived, completely unknown to man, millions of years before him.[16] On a more mundane level, the common housefly is a pest but not a grotesque – until we see one through a microscope.

In a similar vein, severe deformity in human beings unsettles us in ways that go beyond rational explanation and evoke Freud's sense of the uncanny. 'Monstrous' births have been universally attributed to magic or divine intervention, and such explanations are still evident in the attitudes of many moderns. Such events are more than misfortunes; they seem to resurrect primitive fears about human identity, inexplicable influence, and the possibility of some malign principle at work in the very processes of nature. Leslie Fiedler has characterised the attitude precisely.

The true freak, however, stirs both supernatural terror and natural sympathy, since unlike the fabulous monsters, he is one of us, the human child of human parents, however altered by forces we do not quite understand into something mythic and mysterious, as no mere cripple ever is. Passing either on the street, we may be simultaneously tempted to avert our eyes and to stare; but in the latter case we feel no threat to those desperately maintained boundaries on which any definition of sanity ultimately depends. Only the true Freak challenges the conventional boundaries between male and female, sexed and sexless, animal and human, large and small, self and other, and consequently between reality and illusion, experience and fantasy, fact and myth.[17]

Even in cases in which the deformity is the result of injury or disease rather than a birth defect, the impression can be grotesque when the degree of mutilation seems to alter human identity or to suggest gross violation of the body's physical integrity.

The depiction of gross mutilation or debasement of the human form in art can evoke Freud's sense of the uncanny even when there is no direct resort to magical or animistic explanations. Consider, for example, Bosch's painting *Christ Carrying His Cross* (Ghent, Musée des Beaux Arts). It is a study in normal and abnormal faces; in fact, the painting is made up almost entirely of faces. The view is close-up, no setting is delineated, and the cross is suggested only by a single timber running diagonally from the middle to the upper left-hand corner of the picture. In the centre of the canvas is the face of Christ, very human and strangely tranquil, the expression suggesting at once submission and exhaustion that has gone beyond sensibility to pain. Behind Christ is another figure, perhaps Simon the Cyrenian, who is trying to shift or balance the cross, and, since he is looking straight up at it, his face is not visible except for the chin and nostrils. In the lower left, a tranquil Veronica and her saddened companion are looking at another patient face of Christ reproduced on her veil.

These are the only faces in the painting that could be described as normal; the others, fourteen of them, are those of freaks, a chaos of popping eyes, gaping mouths, snarling lips, bared teeth, greenish complexions, and distorted features completely surrounding the face of Christ. The contrast forced by the circular composition is not one between beauty and ugliness, but between the calm resignation of Christ and the ferocity, indeed animality, of the tormentors. In the lower right, one of the thieves, his bulging head almost hydrocephalic, his nose and chin so protuberant that his face is crescent shaped, is snarling at two popeyed, gap-toothed onlookers who appear to be taunting him. Above this group, a fat soldier with fierce eyes and an enormous, bulbous nose is staring with cruel glee at something ahead, perhaps the summit of Calvary. Above him, in the upper right, two spectators, one hook-nosed and snarling, the other distinctly ape-like, flank the other thief who is literally cadaverous, looking as if he were not only dead but had started to decompose.

Now, it would no doubt be possible to find among real people faces as distorted as any of those in the painting, but how many of us have encountered fourteen of them in one place? Moreover, since ugliness and deformity are the common properties of all the tormentors, a generalisation is obviously being made about the nature of humanity and the predicament of Divinity in its midst. Once again, grotesque art presents us not with the world as we know it to be, but with the world as we fear it might be. The artist of the grotesque does not merely combine surfaces; he creates a context in which such distortion is possible. To imagine a monstrosity is to imagine a world capable of producing that monstrosity. To imagine a world in which the common run of humanity look and behave like Bosch's crowd is to imagine a world that is, literally, *Unheimlich*.[18]

The most pervasive effect of such animalism and corporeal degradation in grotesque art is to direct our attention to the undignified, perilous, even gross physicality of existence, and to emphasise it by exaggeration, distortion, or unexpected combination. The result may be thought of as an arc ranging from the entirely animal, though the human-animal, to the entirely human. A gradation of the continuum might go as follows:

A. The depiction of real or imaginary animals which combine aversive appearance with real or imaginable dangers (dinosaurs, other reptiles, large insects);
B. The combination of disparate animal parts to produce chimeras and mythical beasts, sometimes jovial, but more often ominous (griffins, gargoyles, dragons);
C. The combination of human and animal features and traits to produce a hybrid man-beast (totem masks and figures, anthrotheriomorphic gods, the kinds of demons most often depicted by Bosch);
D. The depiction of humans so deformed as to be astonishingly

ugly and suggest an aberration of nature (gnomes, extreme hydrocephalics, persons with very distorted faces or bodies; in a light vein, some clowns);
E. The depiction of humans is some state so bizarre, macabre, or gross that human dignity is obliterated and even identity is threatened (decomposed corpses, skeletons; cannibalism, some behavior of the insane).

To these examples we may add others less typical but still encountered in the art of the grotesque: animalistic or humanoid plants; the combination of mechanical devices with animal forms (the flying stork-boat and wheeled spire-fish of Bosch's *The Temptation of Saint Anthony*); combinations of machines and humans (some robots, the title character of Pynchon's *V.*); or gruesome machines that take on life of their own (the execution contraption in Kafka's 'In the Penal Colony'). No doubt, many other isolated examples could be cited, but we are here in the area of borderline instances.

A primitive, magical reading of experience, corporeal degradation, and animalism – these are common properties of the kind of terror embodied in the grotesque. I turn now to the other half of Ruskin's formulaton to make a similar inquiry into what kind of play is typical of the creation of the grotesque in art and literature, and typical of our own response to it.

One of the oldest and most frequently encountered remarks about the grotesque in art is that it combines the fearsome with the ludicrous, and if the effect in some cases can be quite gruesome, in others it can be quite droll.[19] Here again, Ruskin's summary of the relationship of the two elements is worth quoting since it has never been bettered. 'First, then, it seems to me that the grotesque is, in almost all cases, composed of two elements, one ludicrous, the other fearful; that as one or the other of these elements prevails, the grotesque falls into two branches, sportive grotesque and terrible grotesque; but that we cannot legitimately consider it under these two aspects, because there are hardly any examples which do not in some degree combine both elements: there are few grotesques so utterly playful as to be overcast with no shade of fearfulness, and few so fearful as absolutely to exclude all idea of jest' (*Stones*, p. 151).

Ruskin's subsequent development of this insight is blurred by his polemical purposes; he obscures the original point by morally dividing the noble play of a great mind at rest and the commendable play of the craftsman disporting himself from the ignominous play of the hedonist indulging himself. The result is on one hand the noble grotesque to be admired, and on the other the ignoble grotesque to be deplored, with most examples after the high Gothic falling into the latter category. But what should be emphasised as we move through the spectrum from the fearsome to the sportive grotesque is not the moral quality of play but the *degree* of play. In the drolleries of Renaissance grotesque decoration, the play of fancy in combining forms, the intricacy of the meandering filigree, the play of bright colour and spirit of joviality are the whole point of the game. In Breughel's *The Triumph of Death*, however, there is moral earnestness and pessimism that lie quite outside the realm of amusement, however bizarre the figures may become. In one case the point of view is detached, distant, unworried; in the other it is committed, didactic, full of dread.

In the time since Ruskin, few human activities have received more study than play, and with recognition of the psychological importance of play has come an awareness that play can subsume the serious. Johan Huizinga, who views play as the very fountainhead of culture, includes in his definition of the term a wide variety of religious rituals as well as some kinds of artistic creation. Our sense of the word itself is instructive: our most serious tragedies are 'plays'; the music of Beethoven is 'played', and Rubinstein 'played' the piano. As Huizinga remarks, 'the consciousness of play being "only pretend" does not by any means prevent it from proceeding with the utmost seriousness, with an absorption, a devotion that passes into rapture and, temporarily at least, completely abolishes that troublesome "only" feeling. Any game can at any time wholly run away with the players. The contrast between play and serious is always fluid'.[20]

The gamut of play might be envisioned as running from the man idly doodling while his mind is on something else, through the casual card player, somewhat intent on the game but really engaged in social activity, through the Olympic athlete or tournament chess player whose mind and body are wholly concentrated on his game, through the great musician who may be so totally immersed in his play that he is only marginally aware of anything else. Beyond this, there is the phenomenon that Campbell has called play seizure, which can be observed sometimes in the play of especially imaginative or suggestible children, and in the ritual play of primitive ceremonies.[21] The boundary between play world and real world has ceased to exist. We have a progression of psychic states from one in which the player is in total control of the play to one in which play has taken total control of him. It is a matter of psychic distance between player and game.

In art of the grotesque, the balance between the fearsome and the playful does not depend upon the subject matter but upon the artist's attitude and the response he seems to be encouraging in the reader or viewer. The fear of death and horrors of madness are serious things, but subject to play – an earnest, even exalted play, or a ludicrous burlesque that subordinates the serious. Thus the grotesque does not arise from or necessarily affiliate itself to a particular theme or complex of ideas. Most subjects that can be handled conventionally can be (and have been at one time or another) rendered grotesque, and vice-versa: death, sin, war, damnation, apocalypse; but also joy, love, feasting, sex, fertility, even salvation. The underlying vision always contains some aware-ness of the monstrous, but the degree of play involved in creating the grotesque – from ribald enjoyment of the perverse to ear-nestness reaching toward a game with desperation and despair – controls the balance between the droll and the fearsome in the finished work of art.

An understanding of the various levels of play may help unravel what has become a Gordian knot in theories of the grotesque since Ruskin. As I noted previously, the two most vigorous and original thinkers on the subject in this century, Wolfgang Kayser and Mikhail Bakhtin, disagree completely about the nature of the grotesque, and the centre of their disagreement is the relation of its comic and fearsome sides.

Kayser, beginning with an apparent existential bias, bases his definition of the grotesque primarily upon the examination of German painting and literature. He concludes that the grotesque is a game with the absurd, and that it conjures up the demonic to exorcise it, and such works depict an alien, estranged, inexplicable world in which comedy has little essential function. Such laughter as there is often originates on the caricatural fringe of the grotesque, is bitter, mocking, and ultimately satanic.[22] Bakhtin, beginning with a Marxist bias, bases his definition mainly on the works of Rabelais, and reaches exactly the opposite conclusion: the grotesque is the peoples' triumphant laughter dethroning the shibboleths of the 'official' world view and substituting in their place the carnival spirit of abundance and renewal, thus defeating fear.[23] Writing a few years after Kayser, Bakhtin criticises him severely, stating that 'fear is the extreme expression of narrow-minded and stupid seriousness, which is defeated by laughter' (p. 47). The Russian critic concedes that the grotesque derives from 'cosmic terror', but that such terror is not mystical but 'the fear of that which is materially huge and cannot be overcome by force' (p. 335). What can overcome terror, however, is laughter, folk laughter grounded in the abundance of life, the indomitableness of the collective human animal, and endless renewal through birth even in the very presence of death. 'All that is frightening in ordinary life is turned into amusing or ludicrous monstrosities' (p. 91).

Both Kayser and Bakhtin commit the same essential error: mistaking the part for the whole.[24] Any broad discussion of the grotesque in art is, of necessity, headed for areas that include both the serious and the comic. The point to bear in mind is that the crucial factor separating these two apprehensions of the grotesque is the level of play involved in a particular work.

The playful side of the grotesque determines a further aspect of our response to it, especially in modern times, an aspect that Ruskin thoroughly disapproved of in the art of the late Middle Ages, but which A. P. Rossiter later perfectly described as 'unholy zest'. Noting that medieval drama often treated the most sacred and serious subjects such as the crucifixion or the slaughter of the innocents with cruel, ribald, mocking humour and physical grotesquerie, Rossiter argues that the spirit of such depiction 'derives from that opposite and antithetic world of the diabolical, in which the shadows of primitive paganism survived, . . . in which the spirit of Negation almost speaks out loud and bold . . . as a kind of opposite to our negation of [the] normal religion. A ritual of defamation, sometimes reaching an adumbration of the undermining negatives which threaten all human values and respects, regards and veneration, is the true basis in the English legacy of the clashing contrasts of Gothic drama'.[25] Rossiter finds that many medieval grotesques, such as Bosch's depictions of Christ in the hands of the mob, 'constantly imply two contradictory schemes of values, two diverse spirits; one standing for reverence, awe, nobility, pathos, sympathy; the other for mockery, blasphemy, baseness, meanness of spite, *Schadenfreude* and derision' (p. 72).

Something similar could, I think, be said about the grotesque art of all sophisticated civilisations, especially our own. In such societies, those attitudes antipathetic to civilisation, though by no means banished from it, are liberated in artistic play, just as the various forms of the grotesque are all the absolute antithesis of the harmony, order, dignity, and serenity that, since the time of classical Greece, have constituted for the West the ideal (or idealised) concept of beauty. The grotesque is an aberration that induces fascination, and that fine flicker of perverse glee identifies it in experience, separating it from the merely ugly or simply ludicrous. The grotesque lures even as it repels, fascinates us with our own irrational dreads, and refuses to let us altogether dismiss the game even after we have played it.

To summarise then: grotesque art, even more than most art, is synthetic, and what it synthesises is magic, animalism, and play fused in the presence of an intuition of the world as monstrous. The world intuited by the grotesque is one in which identity may be wholly or partially lost through transformation of the individual into something subhuman, or in which he is susceptible to aggression by magical, irresistible means. Such an intuition, though essentially primitive, remains perennial and manifests itself in modern times in nightmare, in childhood terror, and in the art of the grotesque. The nature of a particular grotesque art work is governed by the balance of its constituent elements, with play being the most variable. The world of the grotesque may be entered whimsically to produce such creatures as Raphael's drolleries or the carnival monsters of Bakhtin; or it may be entered with urgency and concern, though still in a spirit of heightened artistic play, as in many paintings by Bosch and Breughel or in such modern works as the stories of Kafka.

II

On the eve of the First World War, W. M. Letts complained about a lack of the grotesque in modern art, attributing the dearth to the diminishment of terror in the life of progressive, modern man.[26] Writing in England in 1914, he could scarcely have known what Kafka was up to in Prague at about the same time. But, certainly, the events following 1914 in an unbroken line to our day have put an end to the supposed dearth of the grotesque in twentieth-century art, as well as the notion that modern life is deficient in terror. On the contrary, there seems to be an affinity which makes the grotesque not only typical of our art, but perhaps its most characteristic expression, indeed at times even its obsession, in the same way that tragedy was the definitive mode of fifth-century BC Greece or satirical comedy of eighteenth-century England. In Thomas Mann's view, it was the breakdown of the distinction between tragedy and comedy that made the grotesque the 'most genuine style' of modern art. 'The gaze turned upon the horrible is clear, lively, dry-eyed, almost gratified.'[27]

It is not surprising that grotesque fiction of the twentieth century is concerned mostly with the same issues as non-grotesque modern literature. Man is usually presented as living in a vast, indifferent, meaningless universe in which his actions are without significance beyond his own, limited, personal sphere. The physical world of his immediate surroundings is alien and hostile, directing its energies to overwhelming the individual, denying him a place and identity even remotely commensurate with his needs and aspirations, surrounding him on every side with violence and brutalisation, offering him values that have lost their credibility, manipulating and dehumanising him through vast, faceless institutions, the most ominous of which are science, technology, and the socio-economic organisation. Kayser's description of the grotesque world as alien and absurd, inexplicable in its causation and malicious in its intents, is more applicable to the modern grotesque than to the grotesque in general.

Literature of the modern grotesque usually focuses on the unequal struggle between the self and such a hostile environment, and the most common theme linking the novels discussed here is dominance and submission. In one frequently encountered format, the individual is persecuted by a patently insane world which is capable of overwhelming him by means that go beyond the limits of physical possibility. Kafka's fiction provides example after example. Or, in another format, the individual, aware of what he is up against, endows himself with magical powers by which he is suddenly able to deal brilliantly with his surroundings, though he usually loses in the end. Oskar Matzerath in *The Tin Drum* is a prime example of such a character.

In depicting a vindictive, persecuting world, the grotesque can be put to several uses, separately or in combination. The simplest is radical satire, in which the grotesque world is a caricature of the real world accessible to the senses. More effectively, the grotesque can be used as a heightening device by which the conflict between self and other is intensified by expanding it to magical proportions. The attack on the individual, being magical, is irresistible, and it is also physical. A person is not merely cowed psychologically; his body is attacked, transformed, rendered grotesque – and not by the physically possible means of mutilation or torture, but in uncanny, bizarre, and often magical ways. For example, on the literal level of Ken Kesey's *One Flew Over the Cuckoo's Nest*, an oppressive and bigoted society has reduced Chief Bromden to a state of catatonic withdrawal. But in his own deranged view, which is the viewpoint of the novel, he believes that the Combine has planted machines in his body and has wired up the world with gadgets to control it completely, even to the passage of time. The limits of the actual and the possible have been abolished in order to heighten the conflict between self and other and clarify its nature. Such transformations are frequent in the literature of the modern grotesque. Moreover, such literature, to a greater degree than pervious art, presents a protagonist who is himself grotesque; not St Anthony surrounded by demons or Red Crosse fighting the dragon Errour, but Gregor as insect, Bloom as androgyne, Oskar as lunatic, hunchbacked drummer. The protagonist's grotesqueness may result from the attack made on him by the outside world, or it may be the expression of his inner perversity; more often, it is both.

At its most effective, as in, say, the best stories of Kafka, the modern grotesque serves not only to satirise and to heighten, but to expose. The rationalisations and compensations of everyday life are stripped away to bare the substratum of terror which underlies the seemingly mundane. A widely used phrase coined by Hannah Arendt posits 'the banality of evil' in the modern world. Huge atrocities are perpetrated not by monsters but by mediocrities. The evils of the world arise not from satanic grandeur but from the millionfold repetition of shabby vices, most of which boil down to greed and stupidity. The modern grotesque reverses that banality and portrays modern evil in trappings more dramatically compelling, more commensurate with the terrible outcome.

Jean Paul Sartre's early novel, *Nausea*, proves a particularly clear example of the grotesque unmasking terror beneath seemingly mundane life. Antoine Roquentin is living quietly in Bouville, a commercial city whose drab, bourgeois tedium is catalogued in detail. But underneath the surface, Roquentin intuits an entirely different kind of existence. Since the laws by which we interpret nature are our invention, not nature's, and since there is no necessary connection between the categories we designate by names and the chaotic mass of existence, then literally anything can happen. 'A real panic took hold of me. . . . *Anything* can happen.'[28]

At various points in the novel, this intuition of a hidden reality presents itself to him in images of the grotesque. To see a cork floating on the water is to picture the monsters that may lurk beneath; if others could see him as he truly is, they would see a man-sized crab and be terrified. Such fantasies are introduced not merely to portray a morbid or neurotic state of mind in the narrator, but to evoke a world view upon which the novel itself is based. The diversity of things is merely a veneer which, melting away, reveals soft, monstrous masses, naked and in disorder.

Toward the end of the novel, Roquentin is standing on a hill looking down on the city, observing its symmetry, its technology, its citizens going about their business as if their daily habits were constants that could be depended upon.

What if something were to happen? What if something suddenly started throbbing? . . . For example, the father of a family might go out for a walk, and, across the street, he'll see something like a red rag, blown towards him by the wind. And when the rag has gotten close to him he'll see that it is a side of rotten meat, grimy with dust, dragging itself along by crawling, skipping, a piece of writhing flesh, rolling in the gutter, spasmodically shooting out spurts of blood. Or a mother might look at her child's cheek and ask him: 'What's that – a pimple?' and see the flesh puff out a little, split open, and at the bottom of the split an eye, a laughing eye might appear.
. . . And someone else might feel something scratching in his mouth. He goes to the mirror, opens his mouth: and his tongue is an enormous live centipede, rubbing its legs together and scraping his palate. He'd like to spit it out, but the centipede is part of him, and he will have to tear it out with his own hands. And a crowd of things will appear for which people will have to find new names – stone-eye, great three-cornered arm, toe-crutch, spider-jaw.

(p. 159)

Far from viewing such events with horror, Roquentin envisions himself as elated, for at least the mundane illusion will have evaporated revealing the true state of things and vindicating the intuition of them that he has had all along. 'I'll lean against a wall and when they go by I'll shout: "What's the matter with your science? What have you done with your humanism? Where is your dignity?"' (p. 160).

In *Nausea*, the grotesque is clearly located within the imagination of the protagonist: it interprets what is happening in the 'real' world of the novel, but is separate from it. When we encounter works in which such events as Roquentin imagines are depicted as *actually taking place*, or in which the fantasy of the characters is so intermingled with the action of the story as to be quite inseparable from it, then we are in what I would call the mainstream of the modern grotesque. But the purpose is the same as in *Nausea*: to expose reality by dramatising fantasy, to distort surfaces in order to depict the monstrous existence beneath them, to reject the deterministic, knowable world and replace it with a more primitive, magical intuition of reality, 'a frightful sixth sense brooding heavily over things'.

Closely allied to the use of the grotesque for exposure is the *Schadenfreude* which I mentioned earlier, the spark of the perverse glee that is part of the play element in the grotesque. Its purpose is not merely to titillate by rendering laughable things which we know we really should not laugh at (though some portion of that forbidden pleasure is usually involved); the grim joke in the modern grotesque is often a way of jarring the sensibilities into grasping the terrible or the pathetic by excluding the commonplace sentiments of revulsion and pity. The horrible becomes more vivid precisely because we are *not* being called upon for a conventional response.

To cite just one example: in Günter Grass's *The Tin Drum*, during the bombardment of Danzig, a pediatrician called in to treat Oskar tells the Matzeraths that she arrived at Käsemark with a trainload of 4000 refugee children who were refused passage over the Vistula. 'Four thousand kids. All blown to pieces.'[29] To depict the scene naturalistically would be only to expose us to yet one more atrocity of a kind frequent in this century. Unfortunately, we know all about such things, and after the shock of the first few newsreels has worn off, there is not much more we can know or feel about them. But when incorporated into Oskar's fevered delirium, here is what the scene becomes:

I was riding a merry-go-round, I wanted to get off but I couldn't. I was one of many little children sitting in fire engines and hollowed out swans, on dogs, cats, pigs, and stags, riding round and round. I wanted to get off but I wasn't allowed to. All the little children were crying, like me they wanted to get out of the fire engines and hollowed out swans, down from the backs of the cats, dogs, pigs, and stags, they didn't want to ride on the merry-go-round any more, but they weren't allowed to get off.

(p. 411)

The merry-go-round owner is God our Father, who turns out alternately to be Goethe sober, and Rasputin drunk. 'A bit of madness with Rasputin and a bit of rationality with Goethe.' Both keep producing coins for more rides, until finally the 4000 'dizzy little children' are sent floating across the Vistula to the kingdom of heaven.

The manic humour does not diminish the terror of children entrapped in war but intensifies it, and the comic metaphor makes the chaos and cruelty more vivid than could any realistic description of yet another massacre. The depiction of Mr. Fajngold, the Treblinka survivor with his invisible family and boundless faith in disinfectant, is another example of the way that jaded sensibilities can be taken by surprise, and horror and pity brought in by the back door.

Though some modern writers have used great ingenuity to create grotesque renditions of the external world, even more attention has been lavished in the grotesque inner life of twentieth-century man. In earlier art, the source of the grotesque was usually the external realm, natural or supernatural. In societies where men felt themselves to be at the day to day mercy of potent, malevolent spiritual powers, the grotesque often embodied that which, though invisible, was presumed to exist. But in the modern Western world, deeply aware of the rift between the external, objective world and the internal, subjective interpretation of it, the source of the grotesque has moved inward and is found in the fears, guilts, fantasies, and aberrations of individual psychic life. The modern grotesque is internal, not infernal, and its originator is recognised as neither god nor devil but man himself.

Even in those novels which depict the external world as being grotesque itself, the emphasis is usually not so much upon man's predicament before a powerful and dehumanising world as upon the protagonist's inner reaction to that predicament. Irrational fears and primitive dreads are made actual; fantasies, delusions, and hallucinations often mingle freely with physical existence in the external world. Not supernatural demons or devouring chimeras, but external powerlessness and psychic dissolution are the fears with which the modern grotesque plays, and that is the most modern thing about it. Awareness of the gulf between self and other has become total and obsessive, but if the other is sterile and dehumanising, the self is abject and contemptible; and yet contemptible as it may be, the self is the only thing man has left to fight for if he wishes to retain some semblance of control over his actions and identity. Gregor Samsa, Leopold Bloom, Oskar Matzerath, Botkin/Kinbote, Watt, Benny Profane, and many others are all trying in one way or another to force upon a monstrous world a self which that world holds to be despicable, and which they themselves even feel to be despicable. The central figure of the modern grotesque, then, is not alienated man but *humiliated* man.

It is not possible to say at precisely what point the modern grotesque detaches itself from the supernaturalism and Gothic tradition that permeates the mainstream of the nineteenth century grotesque in the works of such writers as Edgar Allan Poe and E. T. A. Hoffman. First of all, the emergence did not take place in fiction alone; there were analogous developments in painting, poetry, and drama. However, like so many characteristics of twentieth-century fiction, the modern grotesque can be seen gradually emerging in some of the literature of the nineteenth century. Mark Spilka, among others, has studied the relation between Dickens and Kafka.[30] Gogol's stories, 'The Nose' and 'Diary of a Madman' offer especially striking examples of themes and techniques which twentieth-century authors were to elaborate, as do the dream sequences in Dostoyevsky's *Crime and Punishment*. But it is the latter author's novella, *Notes from Underground*, that will, I think, provide the most useful example of the modern grotesque in the process of becoming. Though a borderline case as far as the grotesque is concerned, it dramatises with particular force and clarity the attitudes and obsessions that were to become the mainstream of fiction of the grotesque in this century.

'I am a sick man . . . a mean man. There's nothing attractive about me. I think there's something wrong with my liver.'[31] With this remarkable self-introduction, the modern anti-hero makes his most significant early appearance on the stage of literature. Ostensibly, *Notes* is the rambling, at times almost raving autobiography of a nameless, forty-year-old, nineteenth-century intellectual and former civil servant talking to himself on paper. In effect, it is a brilliant examination of the relationship between self and other in the modern milieu, an environment which, Dostoyevsky tells us in an introductory footnote, was bound by necessity to produce underground men in considerable numbers. Necessity, as it turns out, is a crucial issue in the story, for the fundamental conflict is between a romantic gone rancid and the deterministic, progressive, stultifying society that places total confidence in science, progress, and the perfectability of human institutions. Alienation is not the issue here, at least not the main one; irreconcilability is, and in his furious rejection of a world which attempts to make of him an organ stop, underground man is forced to take his final refuge in perversity, perversity willingly – indeed enthusiastically – embraced and defended with the desperate energy of a man trying to repel a horde from his door.

Underground man's real problem is not that he cannot find a home in the world; in fact, he finds one of sorts: the mousehole. But what makes him writhe in his mousehole is that he can neither accept the self-confident, materialistic world, nor reject the humiliating appraisal that world makes of him. On the contrary, he fully agrees. Having been taught since childhood that he is contemptible, even repugnant, he seizes repugnance as his banner and forces it upon the world with defiance and spite as an act of self-assertion.

But even such a recourse is no real solution to his problem. Whether he likes his era or not, underground man is very much its product. The rational skepticism, the rigorous testing of assertions that characterise scientific thought have thoroughly permeated him. Thus, he finds it impossible to believe in the absolute truth of anything, including his own frantic account of himself. For him, vigorously to assert something is to assert its opposite with equal vigour a moment later. He is aware of the ease with which sincere feeling can coexist with sham, aware that any emotion, however strong, is 'true' only while it is being experienced and may be looked back upon and laughed at a moment later, may sometimes be laughed at *while* it is being felt. He looks upon his own confession as a desperate attempt to tell the truth at any cost, but at the same time a clownish performance. He insists he is writing only for himself, but keeps addressing the world at large and is anxious about what the 'ladies and gentlemen' will think of him or what arguments they might raise against him. Above all, he is never certain whether his rejection of the world is because of its unfitness to live in or because of his unfitness to live at all. Once again, the central figure of the modern grotesque is humiliated man, and his prototype is Dostoyevsky's curdled romantic.

There are other ways in which *Notes from Underground* can be seen as a precursor of the modern grotesque. The narrator's most fundamental assertion, repeated time and again, is that the perverse side of human nature is not only innate but is the dominant force in shaping history, and is even to be preferred over the reasonableness and enlightened self-interest by which men of the world purport to act. The most conspicuous feature in all of underground man's dealings with other characters in the novella – his elaborate preparations to jostle an officer who had brushed him out of the way, his inviting himself to a dinner party honouring a man he despises and who despises him – is the positive gusto with which he deliberately seeks out occasions of pain and humiliation. He insists finally that there is a subtle but unmistakable pleasure in such debasement. 'I reached a point where I felt a secret, unhealthy, base little pleasure in creeping back into my hole after some disgusting night in Petersburg and forcing myself to think that I had again done something filthy, that what was done couldn't be undone. And I inwardly gnawed at myself for it, tore myself and ate myself away, until the bitterness turned to some shameful, accursed sweetishness and, finally, into a great, unquestionable pleasure. Yes, yes, definitely a pleasure! I mean it! And that's why I started out on this subject: I wanted to find out whether others experience this sort of pleasure too' (p. 94).

The ultimate source of such pleasure is man's chronic perversity, which underground man views as humanity's greatest defect, but also its indispensable asset as the weapon of last resort against a society that is trying to regularise, reduce, and manipulate the individual. He vehemently rejects that idea that man is governed by reason and can be depended upon to act in his own best interest once he has been shown what his true interest is in the long run. On the contrary, man will consistently act against his best interest in order to assert his right to act in any way he chooses. The ideal society, the crystal palace, is not worth having if the price is to deny a man the right to stick out his tongue at it if he feels like it –

and someone will always feel like it. 'Now, you may say that this too can be calculated in advance and entered on the timetable – chaos, swearing, and all – and that the very possibility of such a calculation would prevent it, so that sanity would prevail. Oh no! In that case man would go insane on purpose, just to be immune from reason' (p. 115).

The lowest common denominators of the modern grotesque are guilt and fear. One after another, the anti-heroes of grotesque fiction in this century feel they are being called upon in some preposterous way to account for themselves before some ominous, irrational power. More often than not, the charge is not specific, but rests upon something fundamentally and totally objectionable in the protagonist himself, or upon the gratuitous malice of the persecuting force. Moreover, the anti-hero at least partially acquiesces in his arraignment; part of his mind admits that the insane power persecuting him has a perfect right to do so. Once again, underground man provides the prototype: 'And then, I'm also guilty because, even if there had been any forgiveness in me, it would only have increased my torment, because I would have been conscious of its uselessness. I surely would have been unable to do anything with my forgiveness: I wouldn't have been able to forgive because the offender would simply have been obeying the laws of nature in slapping me, and it makes no sense to forgive the laws of nature – but neither could I have forgotten it, because it is humiliating after all' (p. 95).

I have suggested that problems of dominance and submission are crucial to much literature of the modern grotesque, and that issue is spelled out with particular clarity in *Notes*. To prevail over an implacable, persecuting world is impossible for underground man, but to dominate completely another individual might make him feel better. At least he gives it a try. The final chapters of the novella deal with his relations with Liza, a young Petersburg prostitute, relations defined largely by his attempts to gain the upper hand, either by representing himself as better than he is, or, when that fails, by showing her that she is one creature who is even more miserable than he. Their first conversation becomes a contest to determine whether he can get past her detached manner and short-circuit the unreflecting contempt with which she treats her customers. He succeeds initially beyond his own intentions: using his talent for words, he vividly describes the short and terrible future that inevitably is before her in the Petersburg slums.

'It was a game I was playing, and I was altogether absorbed in it – although, perhaps, it wasn't only the game. . . . But now, having attained the effect I sought, I suddenly found I had no stomach for it. The fact is, I'd never, never witnessed such despair' (p. 179).

The possibility is now open to present himself as better than he is, a gentleman of letters and compassion who will become her saviour, and for days after leaving the brothel, he feasts his imagination on sentimental fantasies inspired by the novels of George Sand. But for underground man, to become a saviour is to become nothing less than sole possessor: 'But now you're mine, you're my creation', he tells her in his daydreams (p. 186). Moreover, like underground man's romantic fantasies, this one denies the true facts of his life. Liza discovers the true facts when she pays him a visit and finds him living in squalour, hysterically shrieking at his servant of whom he is secretly afraid. This development completely turns the tables on his struggle to dominate; he had fancied becoming her saviour, but now she is in a likelier position to become his. 'The thought also flashed through the turmoil in my head that we definitely changed places, Liza and I, that she now had the heroic role, and I was the beaten-down, crushed creature she had been that night over there' (p. 198). This is one debasement in which he can take no pleasure at all. Accepting her love and the change it might bring about in his own life is out of the question, because since childhood, he has never been able to think of love as anything except the total submission to total domination: 'for me, loving means bullying and dominating. I have never been able to imagine any other way of loving and have reached a point where, to me, love consists of a voluntary concession by the object of my love of my right to bully it. Even dreaming in my mousehole, I have never visualized love as anything but a struggle, starting with hatred and ending in subjection of the loved object, after which I was unable to think up anything' (p. 199).

To regain the upper hand, to prove his power to humiliate at least one creature worse off than he is, he sexually abuses her and then, to crown the outrage, pays her. '"And isn't it much better", I mused later, back at home, trying to soothe the living pain with my fantasies, "for her to bear this humiliation as long as she lives, because humiliation is purification, because it causes the most corrosive, the most painful awareness?"' (p. 202).

Underground man's conclusion about humiliation illustrates

another way in which *Notes* anticipates the modern grotesque. Not only is there a radical reversal of conventional values so that what is usually thought of as bad is presented as good and vice versa; the conclusion itself is reached by a bizarre process which formally resembles reasonable thought, but whose content, by conventional standards, is outlandish, even outrageous. The narrator seems to get caught up in his own unreason and tries to see how far an idea can be pushed into the preposterous without ever abandoning the form of rational argument.

For example, underground man asserts that it would be better to have a definite, unambiguous quality even if it were a vice than to have no quality at all by which to define himself. 'If only my doing nothing were due to laziness! How I'd respect myself then! Yes, respect, because I would know that I could be lazy at least, that I had at least one definite feature in me, something positive, something I could be sure of. To the question "Who is he?" people would answer, "A lazy man"' (p. 104). The notion is odd, but in its context it makes a certain kind of off-beat sense. But underground man now seizes the idea and, half playfully and half in earnest, dilates it to absurd proportions: being lazy is a calling, a career; a man could become admired and famous for devoting all his energies to it. Fiction of the modern grotesque does not simply negate the logic of a reasonable world; it substitutes a more forceful anti-logic, an internally consistent, imaginatively persuasive un-reasonableness by which the conventional function of reason is subverted. Once the grotesque has set normal perspectives askew, all the rest follows with a zany dream-logic of its own. Kafka was particularly adept at achieving this effect.

Finally, the modern grotesque is not merely an assault upon the idea of a rational world; it is an assault upon the reader himself, upon his sensibilities, upon his ideals, upon his feeling of living in a friendly, familiar world or his desire to live in one. Throughout the novella, underground man addresses an imaginary audience of ladies and gentlemen whom he pictures as alternately incredulous and appalled as his assertions, who may be willing to concede he has some truth, but who find him a moral coward, and who, above all, consider him an abnormal case having nothing to do with their own lives. '"Talk about yourself and about your own miseries in your stinking hole,"' he imagines them shouting at the end of his narrative, '"but don't you dare say *all of us*"' (p. 203).

To this, underground man makes his reply: 'As for me, all I did was carry to the limit what you haven't dared to push even halfway – taking your cowardice for reasonableness, thus making yourselves feel better. So I may still turn out to be more *alive* than you in the end. . . . We even find it painful to be men – real men of flesh and blood, *with our own private bodies*; we're ashamed of it and we long to turn ourselves into something hypothetical called the average man. We're stillborn, and for a long time we've been brought into the world by parents who are dead themselves; and we like it better and better' (p. 203). Such aggressiveness is a constant feature of the modern grotesque. The directness and intensity of the attack vary greatly from one writer to another, being very pronounced in Burroughs but quite muted in Nabokov; but the basic assertion is always that the grotesque is not only a real mode of life but the only real mode once modern life has been correctly perceived, and the grotesqueness includes the average man. While this attack is made in earnest, there is also an element of play, a laughing through clenched teeth, a sense of the book as grim joke. There is perverse glee in the very act of creating the grotesque and serving it up to the reader.

To summarise then: in a variety of ways, *Notes from Underground* anticipates much twentieth-century fiction of the grotesque. A repugnant protagonist, aberrant by all 'normal' standards, is a humiliated man totally engrossed in a losing battle with his external environment, yet forced to concede that the world is right in judging him diseased and contemptible. He insists that perversity, not reason, is the basis of human character and the shaper of history, and that there is pleasure in perversity, that perversity is the weapon with which the individual fights for his autonomy against the stupid conformity of the average man. There is an irrational feeling of guilt at the centre of human experience, guilt based not upon having done something but upon the generally loathsome nature of the individual, a loathsomeness that is discerned by the public, even though the protagonist (sometimes) wants to keep it hidden. Because of his guiltless guilt, the protagonist agrees that the forces persecuting him, though vicious and possibly insane, are in the right. All relationships are predicated upon an obsessive concern with dominance and submission. Logic is replaced by anti-logic, a zany but compelling process in which the forms of reason are used to arrive at absurd or outlandish conclusions. Like *Notes*, fiction of the modern grotesque does not merely attack the possibility of a reasonable world, but attacks the reader and his desire to live in such a world, shocking his sensibility, reversing conventional values, and insisting that supposedly 'normal' people are normal only because they lack the courage, honesty, or intelligence to see themselves as they really are. Such deliberate reversal of the polarities of the familiar world is itself a perverse game, though one played in earnest, since the border between play and seriousness, between clowning and desperation, is vague and often illusory.

What separates *Notes* from the modern grotesque, making it a transitional work rather than a clear example, is that the world it delineates is not magical – which is one reason underground man rejects it. Moreover, the animalism, the physicality which I have argued is a necessary element of grotesque art, is lacking. The grotesque is frequently implied by the imagery: 'I'm suspicious and easily offended, like a dwarf or a hunchback' (p. 95). But metaphors are kept distinct from reality; they are never realised in the narrative, and are always recognised as metaphors by both narrator and reader. 'Now I want to tell you, ladies and gentlemen, whether you like it or not, why I couldn't even become an insect' (p. 93). We are here on the threshold of the modern grotesque, a threshold which Kafka crosses when he gives up a character who not only can become an insect, but *does*.

2

The Paranoid Vision

The basic task of Kafka criticism is not to explicate his work but to *account* for it. How does he bring off time and again, often in just a fragmentary paragraph in his journals, the nearly impossible effects that he achieves? What is the source of the power which his writing exerts over our imaginations, the persuasiveness, even fittingness of the bizarre events that he describes? Why do we enter his world with something like an unsettling sense of recognition? Why do his stories so often seem to point to some broader mythic or allegorical meaning and then refuse to yield it?[1] And why does that refusal make them even more tantalising and profound?

What Kafka has done is to take an intuition of the world, a sense of experience, which is peripheral to the vision of most of us most of the time, and make it central to his fiction. Like many artists of the grotesque, he has replaced the world as we 'know' it to be with the world as we fear it might be. Kafka's fiction appeals to us on a sub-rational basis; he heads unfailingly to certain kinds of response that other writers have only limited access to or restrict to the level of individual character. He short-circuits everyday defences that we are not usually even aware we are employing. He allows us to share his imaginative access to a peculiar, distorted version of the world which is the very basis of his art.

'The tremendous world I have in my head', Kafka wrote in his diary on 21 June 1913.[2] 'But how to free myself and free it without being torn to pieces.' Even more than Dostoyevsky, Kafka at his best had the ability to create a world of his own imagining, clearly distinct from the mundane world as we experience it, but in many ways more intense and vivid.[3] An understanding of that world and its relation to our own is essential, because the grotesques which place his work in a class by itself arise from and in the world-view that lies behind virtually all of his fiction. It is that world-view that I am calling here the paranoid vision.

30

Carl Jaspers, among the founders of modern psychology, was particularly concerned with the personal world that is both a subjective and objective construct.[4] Subjective reaction to an objective world grows into a frame of reference which in turn shapes feelings, opinions, ideas, and states of mind. Though such internal phenomena may have their origins as responses to the external world, they become themselves a network by which the external world is interpreted and even transformed. Human behaviour, then, becomes explainable only when individual thoughts and acts are related to the subject's overall picture of reality. Given such a theory of world-view, a radically alien mental state produces not merely isolated delusions or aberrations, but a total transformation of the content of experience.

Jaspers was particularly intrigued with art produced by mentally disturbed persons, especially in those cases where language and thought sequence remain coherent, but the content is shaped by a radically alien world-view.

It is an extremely impressive fact: this exhibition of fine and subtle understanding, this impossible, shattering piano performance, this masterly creativity (van Gogh, Holderlin), these peculiar experiences of the end of the world or the creation of fresh ones, these spiritual revelations and this grim daily struggle in the transitional periods between health and collapse. Such experiences cannot be grasped simply in terms of the psychosis which is sweeping the victim out of his familiar world, an objective symbol as it were to the radical, destructive events attacking him. Even if we speak of existence or the psyche as disintegrating, we are still only using analogies. We observe that a new world has come into being and so far that is the only fact we have

(p. 284)

Jaspers further notes that art produced under such circumstances is likely to embody 'grotesque, misshapen forms of people and animals', and when produced by persons of genuine artistic talent, such works can achieve great power 'by reason of their primitive, vivid expression, weird urgency and strange significance' (p. 292).

That same world which is sometimes described as Kafkaesque is embodied in much of his personal writing, not only in the fanciful journal entries which were sometimes the raw material of his fiction, but also in his private reflections in his diaries and his anguished self-explanations in letters. In the nearly endless letter that Kafka at the age of thirty-six wrote to his father (and apparently never delivered), he attempted to describe explicitly the world that he experienced as a young man: 'the world was for me divided into three parts: into one in which I, the slave, lived under the laws that had been invented only for me and which I could, I did not know why, never completely comply with; then into a second world, which was infinitely remote from mine, in which you lived, concerned with government, with the issuing of orders and with annoyance about their not being obeyed; and finally into a third world where everybody lived free from orders and having to obey'.[5]

We have to be careful here, for the letter, by Kafka's own admission, was full of self-justifying designs: 'in reading try to understand all the lawyer's tricks, it's a lawyer's letter', he advised Melina when entrusting her with a copy.[6] However, Kafka did embody something like this three-part world in much of his fiction. *The Trial* provides the clearest example. There is the sphere in which Joseph K. lives as the Court's victim, completely under its jurisdiction. He may complain that he is unjustly persecuted, that the Court is shabby, absurd, and without legitimate authority, but at the same time he feels compelled to obey its orders, appears when summoned (and even when not), and cooperates in his own execution. Above him is the 'infinitely remote' sphere of the Court itself, with its unknown rules with which it seems impossible to comply, its arrogant judges, advocates, painters, and priests. Finally, there is a third sphere of those not directly implicated in Joseph K.'s case, but aware that he is under the scrutiny of the Court and apparently not surprised. The role of the third sphere, 'where everybody lived happily and free from orders and having to obey', is diminished in *The Trial* in comparison to *Amerika*, and still further diminished in *The Castle*, where everyone in the village is more or less subject to the irrational authority of the Count's officials. Still, the basic pattern of a three-part world of struggling victim, inexplicable persecutor, and indifferent onlookers is maintained throughout a substantial amount of Kafka's fiction.

One result of this division is to push to the extreme the conflict between self and other, and to render it in terms of a totally isolated individual set upon by an omnipotent force that wills his destruction, the conflict being played out before an impersonal but intensely curious audience which regards that destruction as a predictable, even reasonable outcome. This is the world of the paranoid vision. By that I do not mean that Kafka's protagonists are studies in paranoia. On the contrary, they do not overestimate the hostility or power of the forces that are against them. If anything, they underestimate, and their education in the true direness of their situations is the typical Kafka plot. Kafka's fiction consistently presents us with a world in which the paranoid is right, in which his view of the world and his position in it is correct, in which his morbidity is justified, in which he feels he is being persecuted by implacable and inexplicable forces for the good reason that he *is* being persecuted by implacable and inexplicable forces. The corollary of such a view of reality is that the sound mental health recognised by society is a construct of rationalisations and evasions designed to shield ourselves from an intolerable reality which the paranoiac in the honesty of his desperation accepts as given. Such a rendering of experience is not only a consistent feature of Kafka's fiction, but is its very heart, and accounts for the uncanny power so surely felt but so elusive to define. It also accounts for his very individual handling of the grotesque.

Like 'grotesque', the word 'paranoia' is used so freely in our society that its meaning has become blurred. Much of the clinical literature on the subject sees paranoia as not so much an illness as a way of looking at things, a view of reality. Moreover, the holder of that view may not be a mental case or even a particularly neurotic person; a paranoid reading of experience is more or less available to everyone, though decidedly more present in some people than in others, and more likely to be evident under certain kinds of circumstances.

In their compendious study of the subject, Swanson, Bohnert, and Smith argue this general theory of paranoia, and characterise the paranoid view of reality as combining the following:[7]

1. projective thinking;
2. hostility (i.e. the sense of living in a hostile world);
3. suspiciousness;
4. centrality;
5. delusions;
6. fear of loss of autonomy;
7. grandiosity.

These are also the qualities that prevail in the world of Kafka's fiction. Of course, suspiciousness and the rest can be found the works of many other writers too. But just as in clinical practice it is the coalescence of these characteristics into a cohesive world picture that defines paranoia, so in the work of Kafka, it is the coalescence of these qualities, and *precisely* these qualities, that gives the Kafka world its unique shape and quality.

Projective thinking, which Swanson regards as the *sine qua non* of paranoia, is the basis of Kafka's literary technique.[8] For the paranoiac, internal fears, conflicts, and guilts are experienced as emanating from the outside world; what is ontologically internal is ascribed to the external world as a problem imposed upon the individual by malevolent persons or deliberately arranged circumstances. Psychologists have pointed out that this interpretation of external circumstances is made by all individuals at one time or another, and Swanson has linked it to the thought processes of both infants and primitives, particularly in association with animism, the conviction that external objects lead sentient lives of their own and harbour attitudes and intentions like those of people (Swanson, pp. 12–13).

Kafka himself seems to have been at least in touch with such a way of seeing, and perhaps even convinced by it. In a letter to Milena: 'but to me the office – and so was elementary school, grammar school, university family, everything – but to me the office is a living person who looks at me wherever I am with his innocent eyes, a person with whom I'm connected in some way unknown to myself, although he's stranger to me than the people whom at this moment I hear crossing the Ring in their automobiles. He is strange to me to the point of absurdity . . .' (*Letters*, p. 128).

In average perception, there is room for correcting the mis-interpretations of projective thinking, but in paranoia there is not. In Kafka's fiction, however, there are seldom misinterpretations of that type to be corrected. His characters do indeed find the source of their discomfort in the external world, and they are almost always right, because the world of which they are a part is the projection of a state of mind in which irrational guilts and fear have been embodied in institutions such as the Court, in implacable, irrational authority figures such as Georg Bendeman's father, and in magical events such as Gregor's metamorphosis. Kafka has taken universal psychic intuitions often recognised and depicted by other authors as internal features of characterisation, and has given them specific reality as the external world of his fiction. The projective process of the paranoiac becomes the imaginative process of the artist. Had Kafka, the man, literally believed that the world he lived in could contain a Court such as he depicts in *The Trial*, or that men could be changed into animals and animals into men, he would have been clinically insane. But the basic premise of his art is that such a world does exist in the imagined universe of his fiction, that it is not separated from 'reality' by conventions of fantasy, but is a dimension of the urban, bourgeois world which many of his characters inhabit. The distinction between the real and the projected world which he was able to maintain (though, to judge by his diaries taken at face value, able just barely at times) in his day-to-day life is abandoned completely in his art, where the world typically experienced by the paranoiac is evoked with vividness and intensity.

It might be objected, fairly, at this point that such an approach reduces Kafka's art to the ravings of a borderline psychotic, of more interest to the clinician that to the literary critic or the general reader. But paranoia is not an abnormality or disease in itself, but a way of seeing that forms a part of virtually everyone's psychic make-up, and which becomes an aberration only at the far end of its range.

In Schatz's view, this continuum includes a great many, perhaps most, people, since it reflects an outlook on life, not merely clinical paranoid or depressive illness. An individual may oscillate closer to one end or the other at various times, depending on his relative use of externalizing or internalizing defenses. All persons express the potential for both self-reference and object-reference of responsibility. . . . Both conditions are partially attempts to deal with feelings of aggression and power. The paranoid is unable to assign responsibility for events, either good or bad, to himself. He thus feels very insignificant and powerless. He tries to protect his vulnerable self from real or imagined hostilities and adopts a cautious or antagonistic attitude.

(Swanson, p. 287)

The Paranoid cities an obvious example in which paranoia becomes a dominant force in the world-view of the ordinary person. A man is leaving his office after a bad day, frustrated and late for a dinner appointment. He becomes hopelessly trapped in a massive traffic jam. Suddenly, as far as his emotions are concerned, the other drivers become not merely people caught in the same predicament he is in, but nincompoops and antagonists deliberately placed as obstacles in his path. The jam itself is an infuriating impediment put there by some nameless power just to frustrate him. Who has not, in such a situation, seen an otherwise normal-looking person leaning on his horn with all the red-faced rage of a furious infant? And what adult, in dealing with government or academic bureaucracies, has not had to remind himself that their maddening circularity and absurd impasses are the result of divided responsibility and individual indifference rather than some self-perpetuating organism designed specifically to prevent him from getting what he wants? The balanced individual will get over it once the source of irritation has been removed, may, indeed, be amused in retrospect by the irrationality of his feelings. Such readjustment is not possible for the paranoiac; the world we experience in our worst moments of fear, anger, or frustration is the world he lives in all the time. Some versions of it are the worlds of Kafka's fiction.

If recognition of paranoid projective thinking as the perceptual basis of Kafka's work can help account for the power and familiarity of his fictive world, it can also explain much about the source of the grotesque in his works. In 1912, Kafka achieved an artisitc breakthrough by writing in a single allnight session the short story, 'The Judgment'.[9] In its opening pages, the piece seems to be a completely ordinary, realistic story of European bourgeois life. Georg Bendeman, a prosperous young businessman, is preparing to get married. He is slightly concerned about an old friend of his now living in Russia, a man whose personal and professional life has been a series of failures. Bendeman is also worried about his own ageing father, who seems to be growing more and more remote from life. The first wrinkle in the surface of this mundane world appears as the protagonist recalls his fiance's reaction to the problems of his friend: '"So he won't be coming to our wedding," said she, "and yet I have a right to get to know all your friends. . . . Since your friends are like that, Georg, you shouldn't ever have got engaged at all."'[10]

At this point, there is no reason to think that Kafka is doing more than portraying a somewhat eccentric and irritable young woman. But when Georg visits his ailing father's room, there is a sudden change in the technique of the story. The morbid, threatening, bizarre world of the paranoid vision emerges – erupts – as the father metamorphoses from a melancholy and feeble old man into a figure of implacable and irrational accusation:

'No!' cried his father, cutting short the answer, threw the blankets off with a strength that sent them flying in a moment and sprang erect in bed. Only one hand lightly touched the ceiling to steady him.

'You wanted to cover me up, I know, my young sprig, but I'm far from being covered up yet. And even if this is the last strength I have, it's enough for you, too much for you. Of course, I know your friend. He would have been a son after my own heart. That's why you've been playing him false all these years.'

(pp. 84–5)

From this point on, the departure from a rationally explicable world becomes ever more radical. What we have here is not the raving of a deranged old man, but rather a world that operates by a logic of its own, or more exactly, by a peculiar anti-logic that Georg himself recognises. The father has been serving as an agent for the friend whom Gregor has in some nameless way betrayed. In fact, all guilt has become generic rather than specific and can coexist with innocence. '"An innocent child, yes, that you were truly, but still more truly you have been a devilish human being!"' (p. 87).

At the same time, the action veers towards the grotesque, becomes ludicrous but threatening and physically repulsive. Still standing up in the bed, the father begins to taunt his son about the impending marriage. '"Because she lifted up her skirts," his father began to flute, "Because she lifted her skirts like this, the nasty creature," and mimicking her he lifted his shirt so high that one could see the scar on his thigh from his war wound. . . . And he stood up quite unsupported and kicked his legs out. His insight made him radiant' (p. 85). Finally, there is a willing, even obsessive, acquiescence by the son to the father's indictment and the sentence to death by drowning. Georg rushes from the house crying, 'Dear parents, I have always loved you all the same', and throws himself into the river.

In interpreting this strange and powerful story, there is no need to resort to allegories of Kafka the artist versus Kafka the son.[11] We have, rather, a rift between inner and outer man, the outer being calm, competent and thoroughly ordinary, but the inner quailing before nameless guilts and terrors which declare themselves in the form of the grotesque, holding a view of the world which is irrational, even maniacal, and burning with a thirst for self-destruction. The source of Georg's guilt, and hence, his desire for punishment, is the very competence, ambition, and maturity which are his outer self. The father's emphatic preference is for the unseen 'friend', i.e. the failed bachelor who cannot replace him as head of the business and family. When he accuses the son of trying to 'cover him up', Georg at once accepts the verdict that he is a 'devilish human being', who must be destroyed. Years after writing this story, when Kafka composed the letter to his father to clarify his feelings about their relationship, he described a similar problem, attributing his failure to marry to his inability to see himself in the same role as his father (*Dearest Father*, p. 190). Insofar as he was writing about his own experience at all in 'The Judgment', he was writing about this situation. But what makes the story much more than a psychological portrayal of parent-child conflict is that the son's irrational fear and guilt over being more than a submissive child are not treated as symptoms in the mind of the character, but are given physical reality as the external facts of the story. This epitomises the technique of projective thinking applied to artistic creation; the outer world is grotesquely distorted to conform to the protagonist's inner view of it. Moreover, at precisely the point where projection replaces realistic depiction of the world's surfaces, the grotesque comes into play. Kafka himself at once recognised this short story as the discovery of what was to become his most charactertistic kind of fiction.

In the opinion of Schatz cited above, the projective thinking of paranoia is often associated with attempts to deal with aggression and power. This brings us to the second constituent category of the paranoid viewpoint, hostility, the feeling of living in an overwhelmingly hostile world. 'I have come to believe', states H. F. Searls, 'that [the paranoiac] experiences instead [of anxiety] an awareness of various ingredients of his surroundings – or, less often – of things within his body as being charged with sinister meaning, charged with malevolence toward himself' (Swanson, pp. 12–13). That Kafka's characters have such feelings scarcely needs demonstration, and their intimations are always right. What is of particular interest here, however, is the special kind of hostility that the Kafka-world directs toward his protagonists, and here again, 'The Judgment' illustrates the basic pattern which will be repeated with dozens of variations in Kafka's subsequent fiction: accusation, offered in a particularly spiteful manner, is followed by annihilation, an annihilation in which the protagonist is both complaining victim and willing accomplice.

In Kafka's fiction, accusations and reproaches form a mechanism of hostility turned against characters deliberately, though not necessarily rationally. Accusations have to do not so much with guilt or innocence as with a pervasive enmity in the environment; they are instruments through which the accuser exercises inexorable power over the accused. It is the act of accusation itself that the individual finds overwhelming, and the more patently untrue the accusation, the more overwhelming it is. It is usually accompanied, as in 'The Judgment', by an assertion that the individual's previous appearance of virtue and good intentions was a pernicious façade – that is, the accusation is an attack upon identity itself. 'You amaze me, you amaze me', blusters the chief clerk at Gregor Samsa. 'I thought you were a quiet, dependable person, and now all at once you seem bent on making a disgraceful exhibition of yourself. The chief did hint to me early this morning a possible explanation for your disappearance – with reference to the cash payments that were entrusted to you recently – but I almost pledged my solemn word of honour that this could not be so. But now I see how incredibly obstinate you are, I no longer have the slightest desire to take your part at all.'[12]

For the accused, the problem is not merely to establish his innocence, but to attempt, futilely, to reclaim the reputation for virtue and innocence that before had been the core of his whole conception of himself. Samsa pleads with the clerk not to destroy the image of him as dutiful son and provider. The patent falseness of such accusations sets the reader himself on edge, and that edginess plays a major part in our disquieting response to some of Kafka's most effective scenes.

Accusations do not stop even at the denial of 'good' identity. The character is called upon to deliver a full account of himself – not merely of his behaviour in a particular instance, but of himself – an account which, due to the malice and prejudgement of the accuser, is bound from the first to fail. Hence, the pervasive air of moral frustration in Kafka's works. 'I am speaking here in the name of your parents and your chief, and I beg you quite seriously to give me an immediate and precise explanation', demands the chief clerk imperiously (p. 97). It is the archetypal challenge in

Kafka; his fiction abounds with characters whose minds are already convinced of the worst, but who demand that someone give 'an immediate and precise' account of himself. Taken literally, and Kafka never means it any other way, it is the most unnerving demand that a person in authority can make of another. Faced with helping to prepare his defence brief for the Court, Joseph K. can think of nothing else to do except sit down and write a comprehensive autobiography, explaining every action of his life in minute detail. In real life, too, Kafka's letter to his father is certainly an astonishing attempt to go over *everything* in their relationship from his earliest memories, and a fragment of the journals reads: 'Creative! Stride forward! Come along the road! Render me account! Call me to account! Judge! Kill!' (*Dearest Father*, p. 268).

The hand-in-hand companion of the accusation in Kafka is the reproach. Scarcely a relationship can be conducted without them in abundance. A long section in the early diaries contains a veritable dissertation on the subject, culminating in a bitter retrospective: 'There were times when I had nothing else inside me except reproaches driven by rage, so that although physically well, I would hold on to strangers on the street because the reproaches inside me tossed from side to side like water in a basin that was being carried rapidly. Those times are past. The reproaches lie around inside me like strange tools that I hardly have the courage to seize and lift any longer' (*Diaries 1910–1913*, p. 20). What these 'strange tools' can be most effectively used to build or demolish in Kafka's fiction are positions of superiority. Behind a reproach lie two tacit assumptions: first, that the receiver of a reproach is guilty of some offence or shortcoming while the giver is not; and second, that the giver assumes a certain degree of power over the receiver. Such power may be merely that of correcting a person to his face and more or less humiliating him; but in Kafka's fiction a morbid sensitivity to reproaches, a constant fear that one is about to be delivered, make of reproaches a powerful weapon: 'a man simply cannot endure being a continual target for someone's spite, even when he knows well enough that the spite is gratuitous', complains the anonymous narrator of 'A Little Woman' (*Complete Stories*, p. 323). In that story, the little woman, who finds the narrator totally objectionable for no specific reason, has become a walking reproach to him by her barely restrained rage and the toll that her irritation is taking on her health. So powerful is the effect on him that he must actively resist the temptation to throw over his life and move somewhere else. In Kafka's nonfiction writing, reproaches are weapons, and never more so than in the letter, that medley, that orchestration – of reproaches, counter-reproaches, and counter-counter-reproaches.

If the accusation and the reproach are the instruments of moral terrorism by which the hostile world assaults the dignity and worth of the individual, that hostility usually leads to some very physical results, and it is here that the magic and monstrosity of the grotesque most characteristically emerge. 'Always the image of a pork butcher's broad knife that quickly and with mechanical regularity chops into me from the side and cuts off very thin slices which fly off almost like shavings because of the speed of the action.' That passage is not from the fiction but from the diaries, and it is but one of many horrible vignettes which are perhaps sketches for fiction, or perhaps nightmare wish fantasies.[13] 'To be pulled in through the ground floor window of a house by a rope tied around one's neck and to be yanked up, bloody and ragged, through all the ceilings, furniture, walls and attics, without consideration, as if by a person who is paying no attention, until the empty noose, dropping the last fragments of me when it breaks through the roof tiles, is seen on the roof' (*Diaries 1910–1919*, p. 291).

What is involved in these and dozens of images of gross physical mutilation or mutation in the fiction is not murder but annihilation by brutal and inexplicable forces, and the result is not just death but total oblivion – nothing discernibly human remaining, the subject never being heard of again. In both *The Trial* and *The Castle* and in story after story, the assault is bitterly resented, but the oblivion, though dreaded, is also desired, and ultimately the victim loves his tormentor.

The next quality by which clinicians describe paranoid thinking is suspicion, by which is meant not merely an inkling of evil in others, but an active seeking out of such evil, even when there is no reason to suppose that it exists. The paranoiacally suspicious person is hyper-alert, actively searching for clues, often reading more from between the lines than from the lines themselves. About this quality in Kafka's world, little need be said; one could open virtually any of his works at random and find examples of characters scrutinising each other in full expectation of finding sinister motives behind every seemingly trivial action. From this scrutiny comes the endless long division of possible motives and likely outcomes, as one calamitous possibility is weighed against another. 'The Burrow' consists almost entirely of such considerations as they pour through the mind of the single rodent character, whose suspicions, as usual in Kafka, are completely borne out in the end. Moreover, this pervasive air of scrutiny in expectation of finding the worst becomes more intense as we move from early works to late. While Bendeman, Rossman, and Samsa are the objects of groundless suspicion, they themselves are exceptionally naive, seldom suspecting other peoples' motives even when they have good reason to. But some of the later anti-heroes, especially K. in *The Castle*, are capable of giving as good as they get. Indeed, in *The Castle*, perpetual suspicion has become a universal way of life, and is even extolled as a positive virtue to be cultivated. Describing the Castle official, Sordini, the mayor tells K., 'I admire the man, though he is a plague to me. He literally distrusts everyone: even if, for instance, he has come to know somebody, through countless circumstances, as the most reliable man in the world, he distrusts him as soon as fresh circumstances arise, as if he didn't want to know him, or rather, as if he wanted to know that he was a scoundrel. I consider that right and proper, an official must behave like that.'[14]

Some of Kafka's most characteristic and unsettling effects rest upon the next category in the clinical description of paranoia, centrality, the paranoid's conviction that he is the constant centre of interest to the outside world, that he is always being observed and discussed, sometimes with approval but more often censoriously. When Joseph K. is arrested in his room, he glances out the window and notices an old man and an old woman whom he apparently does not recognise staring at him openly from the building across the street. When he and the officers move into the next room for an examination by the magistrate, the two onlookers shift to another window to get a better view, and are joined by a man with a red beard. Two assistants from the bank are present in the room with the examining magistrate, and follow the proceedings with unabashed interest. It subsequently develops that virtually everyone Joseph K. knows is aware that he is in the hands of the Court, and no one seems particularly surprised.

Most of Kafka's protagonists find themselves the objects of unwanted and often hostile attention, and none of them more so than K. in *The Castle*. Wherever he turns, he encounters the same response: 'Oh, I know all about you, you're the Land-Surveyor', and he himself is painfully aware that 'there was no lack of people who knew him, this was indeed one of the main obstacles in his way' (p. 328). In the nightmarish school scene, K. and Frieda wake up to find themselves surrounded by a group of staring children who are more amused than surprised to find them sleeping at school. As K. is abused, humiliated, and even struck by the schoolmaster and Fräulein Gise, the children provide a nerve-wracking chorus of shouts and laughter.

Though most of such unwanted attention is directed at the protagonists, other characters suffer from it too. In *The Castle*, when Olga describes the problems of her persecuted family, she gives an exact summary of the way centrality operates in a great deal of Kafka's fiction: 'Everyone knows something about us, either the truth, so far as it is accessible, or at least some exaggerated rumour, mostly invention, and everybody thinks about us more than need be, but nobody will actually speak about it, people avoid putting these things into words. And they're quite right in that' (p. 239).

The next categories, grandiosity and fear of loss of autonomy are the opposite sides of the same coin. According to Swanson, grandiosity, the tendency to see oneself as celebrated and powerful, is less frequent in paranoia than its opposite is, and so too, it is less frequent in the fiction of Kafka, though it is present. Usually it takes the form of the character's fondness for theatricality and for casting himself temporarily in a romantic or heroic role – champion of truth, defender of the weak – as in Joseph K.'s first appearance before the Court. Occasionally, however, episodes in Kafka remind us of the elaborate, self-aggrandising fantasies of underground man. A clear example is the story variously titled 'The Village Schoolmaster' and 'The Giant Mole'. A six-foot mole had been sited some time before in the vicinity of a village, and the elderly local schoolmaster had written a pamphlet about it. After brief notoriety, the pamphlet had sunk into obscurity and the schoolmaster had complained in a brochure about the condescending treatment he had received from the academic establishment. A sympathetic businessman, the narrator of the story, has come to the aid of the schoolmaster, and the old man speculates about what the results of this intervention might be. Because of the businessman's prestige, everyone will admit that something can be learned from an old village schoolmaster. Pretty soon everyone in the city will be talking about him. A collection will be taken up on his behalf; a large group of citizens will come to the village to present the schoolmaster with the money and bring him to the city. They will all drive back toward the city in a long procession of carriages, and other citizens will drive out to meet them. '"All the people who haven't managed to drive out and meet us in carriages are waiting in front of the hotel; others could have driven out but they were too selfconscious. They're waiting too. It's extraordinary, the way the gentleman who collected the money keeps an eye on everything and directs everything"' (*Complete Stories*, p. 178).

Such a detailed panorama of hypothetical glories is more than a delusion of grandeur; it is the progressive exaggeration of fantasy feeding on itself, the obverse of the endless exposition of potential disasters that forms such a conspicuous part of Kafka's fiction. By such techniques, Kafka pushes us further and further from our own sense of reality while inducting us into his. As a character contemplates a situation or future event, he seems to become obsessed with it, going into minute detail and becoming steadily more outlandish the longer he focuses his attention. And it is not just the schoolmaster who does so, for Kafka is not merely characterising paranoid behaviour but delineating a world experienced from the paranoid perspective. The supposedly level-headed businessman can see that the schoolmaster expects too much, but when he offers what he considers a more likely prediction, he too gets caught up in the process of his own elaboration. The pamphlet defending the schoolmaster's pamphlet will come to the attention of a professor, and the professor will delegate a student to come out and make investigations. The student will publish a further pamphlet which may be derided, but then again, may achieve some acceptance, in which case people will say, 'Our village schoolmasters have sharp eyes', and the journal that scorned the original pamphlet will have to make a public apology, and a group of professors will invite the old schoolmaster to come to the city and will commend his efforts, and perhaps they will secure him a scholarship, but on the other hand . . . and so on for two obsessive pages (pp. 179–80). In such passages, once an event has been envisioned, it assumes for the character all the concreteness and persuasiveness of an actual occurrence. The same thing can be seen in 'In the Penal Colony', when the grandiose officer imagines with exaltation the scene in which the explorer will vindicate the Old

Commandant's methods. The frantic speech goes on for pages, weighing contingencies against counter-contingencies, concluding, '"if my indictment doesn't drive him out of the conference hall, it will force him to his knees to make acknowledgement: Old Commandant, I humble myself before you"' (*Complete Stories*, p. 159).

Grandiosity, however, is much less typical of Kafka's world than the fear of loss of autonomy, which is, indeed, its pervasive, overwhelming concern. Moreover, in Kafka's fiction, this fear is closely conjoined – almost identical with – the Swanson–Bohnert–Smith category that I have postponed considering, the delusional aspect of paranoia. The fusion of the two gives rise to the grotesque as it is most often encountered in Kafka, and for a particularly clear example, I want to consider a short and relatively obscure story or sketch entitled 'An Old Manuscript'.[15] The narrator is a cobbler living in the capital of an unnamed country which has been invaded by nomads from the north. The nomads camp all over town in great filth and take whatever they want. The people who fare worst are the butchers, because the invaders eat huge quantities of raw meat. 'Even their horses devour flesh; often enough a horseman and his horse are lying side by side, both of them gnawling at the same joint, one at either end. . . . If the nomads got no meat, who knows what they might think of doing; who knows anyhow what they may think of, even though they get meat every day' (*Complete Stories*, p. 417). In order to keep up with the demand, a butcher procures a live ox, but this turns out to be a terrible mistake, because the barbarians fall upon it and devour it alive, and the animal's bellowing horrifies the town for an hour. The country is utterly incapable of defending itself and the Emperor has withdrawn into his palace. 'The Emperor's palace has drawn the nomals here but does not know how to drive them away again. . . . It is left to us artisans and tradesmen to save our country; but we are not equal to such a task; nor have we ever claimed to be capable of it. This is a misunderstanding of some kind; and it will be the ruin of us' (p. 417).

The invasion and subjugation of a country can never be anything but terrible, but when the invaders communicate by screeching at each other like birds, when they periodically roll their eyes and froth at the mouth because it is their nature to do so, when they gnaw joints of raw meat with their horses and devour oxen alive, we are in the mainstream of the modern grotesque. The grotesque in Kafka emerges at that point where the general threat of existence assumes animated, magical, physical form. There are other kinds of threats (in the world of Kafka, where are there not threats?), but the grotesque threats are those which are alive and monstrous, which threaten the individual with particularly gruesome or debasing forms of physical subjugation and ultimate annihilation. They arise in and from the paranoid vision, and are its most powerful manifestations, just as in clinical practice, delusions of control or persecution through magical means mark the most acute cases of paranoia. But since Kafka has made projective thinking the basic principle of his art, paranoid delusion becomes artistic illusion; in the world of his fiction, it all *really happens*.

One result of animating the threats of a hostile and domineering external world in the form of grotesque embodiments is to radicalise the rift between self and other. The threats against individual autonomy, like the invaders in 'An Old Manuscript', have issued from an alien outer world, have usurped the autonomy of civilised men, and nothing can be done about them. The forces they present are magical and inexplicable, yet at the same time immediate and appalling; their source is incomprehensible but not their capacity for destruction. What one senses more often than not behind the grotesque in Kafka is not Kayser's 'ghostly it', but the paranoid's ubiquitous *them*. The simplest vicissitudes of life become traps and quagmires whose potential dangers must be inventoried and played out in the imagination. Even so mundane a pleasure as acquiring a pet dog is so fraught with difficulties, so rich in potential for disaster, the Blumfeld, the elderly bachelor, frets over them for pages before deciding that he is better off without one.

But the radical breach between self and other is not entirely due to the mysteriousness and malevolence of the external world. As I have said, the essential situation in Kafka is a paranoiac living in a world in which the paranoid interpretation of reality is entirely correct. There is an elusiveness but unmistakable *fittingness* to the things that happen to Kafka's anti-heroes, just as the delusions of the paranoiac often have a kind of screwy logic of their own. 'Since the paranoid often senses the unconscious processes of others his distorted thinking often has sufficient pertinence to the uncomfortable' (Swanson, p. 167). In Kafka, part of this fittingness is, of course, metaphorical; a man whose life has already been drained of almost all human content is deprived of his human form as well.

But beyond metaphor, characters in Kafka are often swept up

by the anti-logic of their own persecution. 'The suicide is the prisoner who sees a gallows being erected in the prison yard, mistakenly thinks it is the one intended for him, breaks out of his cell in the night, and goes down and hangs himself' (*Dearest Father*, p. 87). This strange alliance between persecutor and victim, this combination of methodical procedure and the preposterous verging on insanity, expresses the ambivalence of Kafka's characters about what they want from the world – on one hand, vindication, acceptance, acknowledgement of their right to enjoy life and love, and on the other hand, judgement, punishment, annihilation. Kafka's fiction consistently presents the protagonist with a world he has not created but has been forced into or has simply blundered into. But finding himself in it, he tries to normalise his situation not by rejecting it, but by carrying it to the conclusion of its own demented thinking, even if this requires a series of self-destructive acts. '"I can't go away," replied K. "I come here to stay." And giving utterance to a self-contradiction which he made no effort to explain, he added as if to himself: "What could have enticed me to this desolate country except the wish to stay here?"' (*The Castle*, p. 177). Victim and victimiser have a natural affinity for each other, the exact counterpart of their implacable enmity. The aim of existence is to withhold from the individual precisely that thing, however modest it might be, that would give meaning or fulfillment to life. The peasant waits in vain before the portal of the Law. At the end of his life, as the door is about to be shut in his face, he is told that no one else tried to enter because that door was meant especially for him. Each man's life-frustation is uniquely suited to his aspirations and is designed just for him by an inexplicable order for whom frustrating him is a desirable goal in itself, indeed, a reason for existence.

It seems to me that the worst way to read Kafka is to try to demystify him by reducing him for some scheme that makes moral sense – just as Joseph K. becomes hopelessly entangled when he tries to explain the parable of the Law in terms of rational behaviour. Kafka's art arises from and is directed to a more remote and sinister area of consciousness, and gives shape to our vague and disturbing intuitions about the way reality might be, intuitions which all of us have experienced at various times and in varying degrees. The kind of translation into allegory or parable which Kafka's work seems to invite and has so generously received draws attention away from the dark splendour of his achievement, the realisation in the full power of its unmitigated state of a world familiar to us all but not ordinarily predominant for most of us.

II

I have argued that the grotesque is a continuum; it can be present in varying degrees of intensity and seriousness, and the boundaries of where it begins and ends are necessarily vague. The line between the grotesque and the non-grotesque in Kafka is particularly indistinct, but a specific example might indicate where I, for one, would draw it. The execution of Joseph K. is grisly and weird. It is depicted with a merciless touch of anatomical detail that one can almost feel as a physical sensation in the chest. 'But the hands of one of the partners were already at K.'s throat, while the other thrust the knife into his heart and turned it there twice.'[16] If one were to accept a comic-combined-with-the-fearsome theory of the grotesque, it might include this scene, since the Alphonse and Gaston routine of the killers is certainly ludicrous. But ultimately a man being stabbed is a man being stabbed, and not even the strange events leading up to it can transform the event into a thing of animalism and magic. But a man being engraved to death by a mechanical contraption that turns out to have a psychic life of its own, or an insouciant victim being sliced like so much salami by an equally insouciant butcher – that is another matter entirely. Here the world has been transformed into a magical place, the threat is more monstrous than anything that could actually happen, the fate more uncanny, the fear more mysterious, more primitive or child-like. The denizen of the burrow, who has heard and believes tales of monsters tunnelling through the earth, describes his anxieties in terms that define very well the difference between dangers posed by the familiar in Kafka and those that arise in connection with the grotesque: 'These anxieties are different from ordinary ones, prouder, richer in content, often long repressed, but in their destructive effects they are perhaps much the same as the anxieties that existence in the outer world gives rise to.'[17]

In proportion to their length, the novels make less use of the grotesque than do the short stories in which the entire piece can be organised around a single grotesque image.[18] The most famous of these, of course, is the *Ungeziefer* that Gregor Samsa finds himself metamorphosed into one morning. There are some individual strokes of creation that stand in a class by themselves, that are significant in ways that seem to invite analysis and then mock its inadequacy, and which go on exerting their disturbing power whether they are explained or not.[19] Such works, whether in literature or other art forms, owe much of their power to their ability to operate with equal effectiveness on several levels at once, to express contradictory views or elicit irreconcilable feelings simultaneously; and so of 'The Metamorphosis'.

First of all, Kafka is exploiting one of the most pervasive of all myths, a man turned into an animal. The inexhaustible fascination of this topic in myth, fantasy, and folk tale has never, I think, been satisfactorily explained.[20] No doubt it draws upon a special, essentially primitive sense of the relationship between men and animals, upon the recognition of similarities and parallels between human and animal realms, on the ease with which we imagine animals as having thoughts, feelings, and self-consciousness like our own, and on the frequently paradoxical sense we have of our abstract, self-aware intellects inhabiting animal bodies. In Gregor's case, the mythic association is reenforced by the *kind* of animal he is turned into. As I noted in the opening chapter, there are certain kinds of creatures that, often without explicable reason, induce revulsion in most people, and large insects are certainly among them. But when the insect is approximately the size of an adult human, the situation has been charged with the powerful energies of the grotesque – the intuition of a monstrous world bent upon irresistible, magical assaults. The opening paragraphs stress not only the uncanny nature of Gregor's transformation but his complete powerlessness before it; his first reaction is horror at having been acted upon. 'What has happened to me? he thought' (*Complete Stories*, p. 89). It is a question that is never fully answered, because its most obvious corollary, 'Who or what could have done this to me', is never even asked. Most of his struggles throughout the story will be to regain his shattered autonomy.

Kafka habitually used humanised animals and animalised humans to reduce human relationships to an elemental state by stripping them of the rationalisations and illusions which are often the only things allowing them to exist. The unmasking function of the grotesque is paramount. The illusion most frequently destroyed is that there exist some compensating values that make a really intolerable situation seem tolerable. In his new shape, Gregor not only discovers the true nature of those around him and their feelings toward him; he also discovers his true feelings toward them, emotions which had to be denied or smothered under the exigencies of family obligations. Magical transformation becomes the tool for stripping away apparently real but actually false arrangements to reveal beneath them the paranoid vision, the strata of threat, fear, resentment, domination, and deprivation where, for Kafka, life is really lived.

'The Metamorphosis' is, among other things, about the duality of human feeling and behaviour. Gregor had always felt loathed by his family, especially his father, and so had tried to ingratiate himself by being what they expected of him. In one way, this earned him a surface gratitude, but in another way it brought him more under their loathing, for all docile, willing victims are loathed by those who exploit them. The victim, meanwhile, gains a certain pleasure from his victimisation, but at the same time loathes himself and hates his tormentors. Thus the metamorphosis gives actual shape to the inner feelings of the Samsa household. The family now has a palpable reason for loathing Gregor, yet also feelings of guilt for doing so, since they know his loathsomeness is not his fault, and also feelings of pity because, in a sickly way, they love him. Gregor can at last feel open resentment for the way they treat him, yet at the same time satisfaction that the world has openly borne out his worst suspicions that everything is designed to be against him. Yet still, he feels that because of it is his fault, he should still be cherished as 'good'.

No doubt, there is something masochistic in the pride that Gregor takes in having been so docilely exploited for years, but his self-abnegation is basically a plea for love. In an interesting article, Douglas Angus has related 'The Metamorphosis' to a long tradition of beauty and the beast tales in which the deformed creature asks for love despite his loathsome appearance, and when the plea is granted he is transformed from ugliness to beauty.[21] 'The Metamorphosis' is an inversion of this pattern; repeated pleas for love are repeatedly refused, thereby substantiating Gregor's feeling that he is unloved because he is repulsive, and not even all his 'goodness' will defuse the hatred people have of him. An intriguing clinical parallel of such a reading is given by the psychiatrist, Peter A. Martin, who treated two patients who, in dreams which were probably influenced by Kafka's story, identified themselves with cockroaches. Two factors were central in each case: a feeling of being unloved and criticised by the dominant parent; and the inability to conceive of a self-evaluation except on the basis of others' opinions: 'every fibre of this type of patient is directed toward another person, placing the decision of life or death in the other person's hands, and thus making of rejection a deadly weapon. These patients as a somebody or a something do not exist on their own. They exist only if they win favour in the eyes of another person'.[22] Striving to win such favour has been and continues to be Gregor's most characteristic activity. His transformation not only denies him possibility of success, it also shows him that he never really had that possibility to begin with.

Gregor's emotional life undergoes not so much a transformation as a clarification through the instrument of his metamorphosis. For the most part, his secret inner life has consisted of keenly felt but never articulated grievances. Such thoughts and feelings are our first introduction to him after he has fully awakened. Outwardly a born victim, he is inwardly a born complainer. Like so many of Kafka's characters (and like Kafka himself in so many of the letters and diary entries), he never tires of enumerating privately the ways he has been misunderstood and abused. As long as Gregor was in the role of dutiful son and provider, such complaints had to be repressed or rationalised away. After the metamorphosis, however, his resentment becomes more accessible, his hire more permissible to himself, and each of his forays from his room into the family parlour constitutes a progressively stronger attempt to assert his own individuality.

One of the special achievements of 'The Metamorphosis' is that Kafka, like Tolstoy and O'Neill in completely different contexts, has given us a powerful depiction of a family who love each other but whose love, under the pressure of hopeless circumstances, has become a source of conflict, guilt, recrimination, resentment, wounded feelings, and mutual torment. Every positive affection immediately confronts an even stronger negative reaction. Along with gratitude there is resentment at being placed under an obligation. Self-sacrifice is abundant, but with it anger that a sacrifice should be necessary and expected. There are protectiveness and generosity, and with them the ego inflation and condescension that come with having assumed the upper hand. Solicitude and compassion are not lacking, but neither is annoyance at the imposition caused by another person's needs or suffering. As the story unfolds, life in the Samsa flat comes increasingly to be dominated by a particularly vicious cycle. A feeling of guilt gives rise to a feeling of bitter resentment (since no one enjoys being made to feel guilty). Sooner or later the resentment is vented in an act of open hostility, which subsequently gives way to anguished regret, which produces a feeling of guilt – and the cycle is all primed for another revolution.

After many ever-tightening repetitions of the cycle, the four Samsas are transformed into what they were potentially all along: the family paranoiacally conceived, the family as death-trap.

> Hardly had his sister noticed the changed aspect of his room that evening than she rushed in high dudgeon into the living room and, despite the imploringly raised hands of her mother, burst into a storm of weeping, while her parents – her father had of course been startled out of his chair – looked on at first in helpless amazement; then they too began to go into action; the father reproached the mother on his right for not having left the cleaning of Gregor's room to his sister; shrieked at the sister on his left that never again was she to be allowed to clean Gregor's room; while the mother tried to pull the father into his bedroom, since he was beyond himself with agitation; the sister, shaken with sobs, then beat upon the table with her small fists; and Gregor hissed loudly with rage because not one of them thought of shutting the door to spare him such a spectacle and so much noise.
>
> (p. 126)

Finally, when the meagre resources of forebearance and sacrifice have been utterly exhausted, comes the inevitable, 'We must try to get rid of it' (p. 133).

The cycle of guilt followed by hostility followed by more guilt provides the basic rhythm of the final section. Having maimed him, the family now concedes that Gregor is still one of them, and 'family duty required the suppression of disgust and the exercise of patience, nothing but patience' (p. 122). But against patience are arrayed not only disgust but the pressures of the outside world. The three Samsas are now preoccupied with the business of earning a living, exhausted at night, demoralised by 'the belief that they had been singled out for a misfortune such as had never happened to any of their relations or acquaintances' (p. 124). As Gregor's room fills with filth and debris and the apple rots in his back, his mood alternates between bitter retrospection – especially regret at not having established any emotional ties of his own in his former life – and rage at being denied the care, the human acknowledgement he feels he deserves: 'he was filled only with rage at the way they were neglecting him, and although he had no clear idea of what he might care to eat he would make plans for getting into the larder to take the food that was after all his due, even if he were not hungry' (p. 125).

It is a similar impulse to forget all consideration and grab what he wants that lies behind the most elaborate plan for an excursion from his room, and this time what he wants is his sister. Aggression, strongly laced with sexual energy, is completely unrepressed: 'He would never let her out of his room, at least not so long as he lived; his frightful appearance would become, for the first time, useful to him; he would watch all the doors of his room at once and spit at intruders' (p. 131). Yet Gregor's nature is such that the desire to be loved always defeats his self-assertive impulses. The sister will stay of her own free will. And why? Because he will tell her of how he had intended to sacrifice himself to send her to the music academy. In this sentimental revery, the story makes its closest contact with the fable of beauty and the beast: 'his sister would be so touched that she would burst into tears, and Gregor would then raise himself to her shoulder and kiss her on the neck . . .' (p. 131).

As always, Gregor finds the truth of his life and relationships waiting for him out in the family parlour. This time it comes in the form of a death sentence from the lips of his sister, and final defeat in his battle to preserve his human identity. The bug, Grete asserts, cannot possibly be Gregor, and is, in fact, an insult to his memory, for it lacks completely the defining quality of Gregor's character, a willingness to sacrifice himself to make them happy. The statement hits Gregor with all the force of a simple, elemental truth that had somehow been lost sight of but now has snapped back into focus. His final thoughts show, as so often in Kafka, the victim's concurrence in his being victimised, his alignment of sympathy with his tormentors. As with underground man, his resentment of the low opinion the world holds of him is exceeded by the strength with which he agrees with it. 'He thought of his family with tenderness and love. The decision that he must disappear was one that he held to even more strongly than his sister, if that were possible' (p. 135).

The ending of 'The Metamorphosis', like that of 'A Hunger

Artist', leaves the reader with uncertain feelings. Prolonged morbidity is replaced by good health and an excursion outside the flat for the first time in the story into the fresh air and sunshine. The reader cannot help but share in the lightening of oppression, the sense of relief that follows the termination of a long and hopeless illness. Gregor in his agony commands our sympathy as a finer, more amiable person that any other member of his family, but we share their relief in finally being rid of him.

Yet we sense in the family's healthy recovery and cautious optimism a failure to grasp the real depth of the tragedy; they never fully comprehend that it was Gregor imprisoned in the carapace. Moreover, the question is left open exactly who was parasitic off whom. Surely Gregor was routinely exploited by his family, but the troika of senile old man, dependent old woman, and aimless adolescent was, after all, his creation. It could not have existed had he not provided a willing host. As soon as his services were no longer available, the family quickly took hold of itself and managed to cope with reduced circumstances. It turns out that the too-large apartment for which Gregor drudged away his nights and days had been Gregor's idea to begin with. The central irony of this story is that the victim creates his own parasites who then proceed to destroy him.

No one approach can satisfactorily account for 'The Metamorphosis'. Myth of an uncanny universe, parable of the animal in man, story of suffering and slow death, battle for human identity in a dehumanising world, depiction of the family as death-trap, exploration of the relationship between love and loathing, paranoid nightmare of persecution, Kafka's attempt to find a metaphor for his own everlasting sonship – the story is all these things and more, the many strains synthesised by the central precipitating event, the metamorphosis. The common denominator is the overwhelming of a helpless, humiliated man by forces within himself, in the outer world around him, and in a magical universe, implacable and inexplicable, forces that manifest themselves in the grotesque.

Claude Magny has asserted that the central concern of all Kafka's fiction is the thinness of the crust of civilisation and reasonableness which separates modern man from the atrocious, the barbarous, the unthinkable. 'Kafka has strongly the sense that human life is entirely bordered by the inhuman. . . . We are surrounded on every hand by what is horrible, monstrous; here it is, at our side in the frame and structure of our life. Its intrusion is not exceptional, it is the rule, and it is enough for the crust to crack in any place to make us aware of it.'[23] This statement, so true of Kafka's work in general, seems to apply with special accuracy to 'In the Penal Colony' – but with a difference; in this story, in contrast to 'An Old Manuscript', the source of the monstrous is not some untamed outside horde that inundates civilisation, nor is it, in contrast to *The Trial*, some bizarre dream-culture that runs parallel to the official establishment. In 'In the Penal Colony', the source of barbarism arises from civilisation itself; brutality is perpetrated in the name of an exalted, even mystical concept of justice which enlists in its service science, aesthetics, and altruistic sentiments. The machine, the acolyte who attends it, and the system of justice they administer are meticulous, fervent, philosophically defended, and monstrous.

In this story, as in so many others, the core of Kafka's effect is his skill at finding a central image or situation that combines persecution with fascinated attraction, by which immediately to entrap his readers and, without their realising it, to disarm their rational defences and induct them into the world of the paranoid vision. In this case, the subject is not some beast with human qualities but an execution. However, unlike Camus, whose well-known essay against capital punishment seems to ring with many sentiments from this story, Kafka was not writing a polemic against the death penalty, though 'In the Penal Colony' has often been read as one. On the contrary, Kafka exploits a pre-existing morbid interest in his audience upon which to play his own very individual variations.

The deliberate act of taking a healthy man out and putting him to death at a specific time and place by a prescribed and often quite ingenious method has always aroused macabre public interest, not only in the times when executions were public occasions, but hardly less so in modern-day countries where they are minutely reported in the press or recreated in dozens of 'last mile' films. In part, this interest may stem from the private citizen's sense, gratified or appalled, of inclusion in an act of officially permitted, collective blood-lust, an aspect of execution dramatised most clearly in the unmistakably ceremonial nature of the process even in modern times. More often than not, the sentence is carried out by some device built especially for the purpose. In former times, as in Kafka's story, such machines were designed to prolong and intensify the death agony; now they are designed to shorten and mitigate it as much as possible. But in either case, the result is some sort of gruesome contraption that combines the inventiveness and technological skill of man with an act of ritual killing.

Now Kafka has incorporated all these aspects of an execution into his story, with his own characteristic intensifications. The setting is a tropical compound rather like Devil's Island (though the point is specifically made that the native language is not French), the outpost of a sophisticated, temperate country; the upper echelons of the garrison even try to maintain some vestiges of civilised living. Just as in many countries of the world an elaborate ethical and legal defence of capital punishment and its benefits to society has been argued, so an almost metaphysical apologia for the punishment devised by the Old Commandant constitues a large part of this story. The officer, as we might expect in Kafka, is a paranoid obsessive whose life has long been centred around one fixation: the execution of offenders by the Old Commandant's method.

But the immediate centre of attention is the machine. '"It's a remarkable piece of apparatus",' the officer tells us in the opening words of the story, and it grows more and more remarkable as its history and principles of operation are revealed (*Complete Stories*, p. 140).[24] As I argued in the preceding chapter, purely mechanical grotesques are rare; machines can move toward the grotesque only as they combine with human or animal qualities, and there has to be something of the magical and monstrous about the combination. Computers can seem uncannily human but they are not grotesque, nor are most robots of science fiction. But Kafka's machine is a rare example of the mechanical grotesque for several reasons. First of all, it is invested from the first with magical properties; its operation as described is physically impossible. If the Bed is solid and completely covered with cotton wool, and the condemned man is securely strapped to it, then rotating the layer of cotton to bare fresh surfaces of the victim's body would be impossible. Kafka, a lawyer for a workmen's insurance bureau, spent much of his professional life examining detailed accounts of industrial accidents. He could not, I think, have been unaware that the mechanical operation he was describing is a physical impossibility. Rather, the delusional element of the paranoid vision is deliberately introduced as actual reality.

Moreover, as the officer describes it, the ultimate effect of the torture is magical and mystical rather than merely physical, and at the end of the story the machine takes on a life of its own, wilfully destroying the officer and itself. But most of all, the machine is grotesque because of its symbiosis with human beings. As the story progresses, the instrument becomes an extension of the Old Commandant, the symbol of his rule, almost a surrogate of his presence itself.

Were the officer no more than the cynical enforcer of an authoritarian system, we would have the well-known banality of evil. But he is depicted initially as a man of intelligence and education, with fluency – even eloquence – in more than one language. He is a man of sentiment who feels that the system he represents and, above all, its method of execution, is '"most humane and most in consonance with human dignity"' (p. 156). So convinced is he of the rightness of his position that he is certain that a man of experience and right-mindedness like the explorer cannot possibly fail to see its self-evident worth. In this characterisation, what would ordinarily be virtues and accomplishments are perverted by his single-minded devotion to an instrument of torture and mutilation. He is an adherent of science, but the only scientist he knows or admires is the Old Commandant who designed the machine as '"soldier, judge, mechanic, chemist, and draughtsman"' (p. 144). Even more than a devotee of science, he is a connoisseur of art, but the only art he loves is the operation of the machine. The movement of the engraving arm is likened to that of a harrow, '"but contrived with much more artistic skill"' (p. 142). He apologises that because of a broken strap, '"the delicacy of the vibrations for the right arm will of course be a little impaired"' (p. 151). At the completion of an execution, as he describes it, the machine discards the mutilated corpse '"with an incomprehensibly gentle wafting motion"' (p. 154). 'In the Penal Colony', like 'A Hunger Artist', achieves much of its effect by asserting that a hideous process which slowly debases and destroys a human being is actually a thing of beauty and value, was until recently admired by the community, especially by ladies, and was thought to be suitable for witnessing by children. Aesthetics, science, and ethics are juxtaposed against cruelty, barbarism, and blood-lust, not to draw attention to the oppositions between them, but to dramatise the ease with which they shade into each other.

The epitome of that coexistence is the officer's feverish assertion that the main function of the machine is not punitive but educational;

the pain is a mere preliminary, a crude means to an exalted end, and that end is enlightenment, transcendence, understanding. The beauty and majesty of justice are revealed in the individual's recognition of the law and acquiescence to it. The law, as usual in Kafka, is absolute but inscrutable; the ordinary individual cannot grasp its meaning, but the smallest infraction will, nonetheless, be punished. The precepts of the Old Commandant, which the officer treats as sacred documents, are quite indecipherable, but their fundamental simplicity is understood and justice is achieved when, after six hours of agony, the condemned begins to read through his wounds the text which, with lavish embellishments, has been inscribed on his body. '"Enlightenment comes to the most dull witted. It begins around the eyes. From there it radiates"' (p. 150). '"Often enough I would be squatting there with a small child in either arm. How we all absorbed the look of transfiguration on the face of the sufferer, how we bathed our cheeks in the radiance of that justice, achieved at last and fading so quickly! What times these were, my comrade!"' (p. 154). According to the officer, the aesthetic beauty of the moment, its transcendence of the dog-like incomprehension of the prisoner, its judicial perfection, its ethical completeness are such that they '"might tempt one to get under the Harrow oneself"' – which ultimately he does.

'Be Just', the text the officer selects to have inscribed upon himself, is quite different from the arbitrary command, 'Honor Thy Superiors', that was to be inscribed upon the prisoner; its two monosyllables contain the most complex and endlessly debated problem in ethics. The story places two contrary ideas of justice in opposition to each other. The explorer advocates the enlightened, humanistic, procedural justice which acknowledges that the individual has rights which must be protected even as he is made to answer to authority, and which asserts that mitigating factors such as intention and premeditation must be considered in judging guilt and assigning punishment. The officer speaks with an older, harsher, more primitive voice, the voice of the patriarchal Old Commandant: the law is absolute as is the authority that validates it, even though both law and authority are invisible and unknowable. Since the intentions of the transgressor have no moral significance there is no point in inquiring into them. It is the fact of transgression that has weight. Thus the story is concerned not with the confrontation of democracy and totalitarianism in our times, but with one of the fundamental disputes of all time, a battle fought over and

over again in many religions, in philosophy, and in ethics, not to
mention in myth and literature, especially Greek tragedy. Kafka is
certainly not treating the problem tragically; rather he is recasting
the dispute in terms of the paranoid vision in which 'Guilt is never
to be doubted', and the terrible patriarchal retribution is desired
even more than it is dreaded.

The officer fervently insists that he has been serving justice all
along; if that is true, he should deserve no punishment, and it is
not punishment he seeks beneath the Harrow. He wishes to follow
what is for him the only path to true understanding, to achieve
the exalted enlightenment that he had seen in others, a realisation
of the absolute meaning of the utterly simple, utterly inscrutable
precept, 'Be Just'. The moment of enlightenment will not only
enrapture him, it will vindicate the Old Commandant's concept of
justice (something which the explorer has just refused to do) by
demonstrating that some truths are so simple they can only be
deciphered by pain. The new commandant and his liberal reforms
will be confounded.

The result is carnage. The machine does not merely go haywire;
it assumes a life of its own, spewing out cogwheels while stabbing
the officer randomly until he is fully impaled. The machine treats
the officer exactly as the gatekeeper treats the peasant in the
parable of the law; the monster waits until the suppliant has
sacrificed everything to gain admittance to the radiance of the Law,
and then denies it, for no other reason than denial itself.

'In the Penal Colony' is Kafka's most cunningly told story.[25] The
sympathy we might naturally feel for the condemned prisoner is
short-circuited at once by treating him as a low comic character
straight out of a puppet show. Moreover, between the objective,
very unobtrusive narrative voice and the obsessed, loquacious
officer stands a mediating character, one of the very few in Kafka's
fiction. The explorer is – or, more exactly, seems at first to be – a
perfectly sane man of the period whose reactions are about what
we would expect. Humane, self-confident, a staunch middle-of-
the-roader, he has vast experience and not much imagination. He
does not want to witness an execution, but he is a foreign guest
and does not want to offend his host. As he learns precisely what
is done in a Penal Colony execution, he is appalled but feels
powerless to interfere because it is none of his or his country's
business. Finally, when he discovers that the new commandant is
opposed to the old methods, the explorer knows exactly what he

must do, protest against executions of this kind, not in the grandiose kind of scene envisioned by the officer, but discreetly, man-to-man, in the privacy of the commandant's office. Since all the officer's speeches are addressed to the explorer, we have the impression of seeing the obsessed idealogue through the eyes of the reserved pragmatist.

It is all a hoax. For three-quarters of the story, Kafka fools his reader completely. After twenty pages of all that reasonable circumspection, the explorer suddenly begins to think and act more like a character in Kafka. He begins, in short, getting drawn into the patent insanity of the officer's fantasies, conceding that there may be something to the Old Commandant's methods after all. The first hint comes when, before refusing the officer's frantic plea for support, the explorer hestitates for just a moment. 'From the very beginning the explorer had no doubt about what answer he must give; in his lifetime he had experienced too much to have any uncertainty here; he was fundamentally honourable and unafraid. And yet now, facing the soldier and the condemned man, he did hesitate, for as long as it took to draw one breath. At last, however, he said, as he had to: "No"' (p. 159). The hesitation is significant; its briefness, only the duration of a breath, is expanded by the 'at last' which follows.[26] His refusal is punctuated with conventional assurances that under the circumstances are bizarrely inappropriate: '"of course I shall never in any circum- stances betray your confidence,"' and '"your sincere conviction has touched me, even though it cannot influence my judgment"' (p. 160). Then, as he watches the officer place himself beneath the Harrow, he refuses to interfere, not because he is a foreign visitor, but because he thinks the officer might be right. 'If the judicial procedure which the officer cherished were really so near its end – possibly as a result of his own intervention, as to which he felt himself pledged – then the officer was doing the right thing; in his place the explorer would not have acted otherwise' (p. 163). The last phrase is, of course, the perfect touch, the little gem of pure insanity smuggled in as if it it were the most licit thing in the world.

The officer's fervent devotion to the majesty of the law is in some perverse way *compelling*, and the explorer, like so many characters in Kafka, finds himself swept up in the vehement flow of anti-logic. 'And here, almost against his will, he had to look at the face of the corpse. It was as it had been in life; no sign was visible of the promised redemption; what the others had found in the machine, the officer had not found; the lips were primly pressed together, the eyes were open, with the same expression as in life, the look was calm and convinced, through the forehead went the point of the great iron spike' (p. 166). Overcoming his repugnance, the explorer has to look in the officer's face, as if he were willing to concede that the enlightenment might actually be there. In the final paragraphs of the story, he sees the epitaph on the Old Commandant's grave and, beating off the reprieved prisoner and his guard, flees from the colony without even taking leave of his host. Just as Kurtz shows Marlow a human horror that Marlow deplores but recognises as his own, so the officer shows the explorer the love of implacable, patriarchal justice that sends the explorer scurrying, not only because he abhors it, but because he felt for an instant the flicker of its allure, the momentary concession that there might be some truth to be learned beneath the Harrow after all. After such an exploration, the explorer wants only one thing – out!

The Old Commandant's system is defeated, but the defeat is provisional and perhaps only temporary. The qualities of civilised man which the officer embodied – the equation of justice with absolute, archaic law; the committing of barbarous acts in the name of lofty values; the enlistment of science in the service of death; the easy coexistence of exquisite aesthetic sensibilities and blood-lust; the affinity between ingenuity and cruelty; the pairing of rarefied questions of ethics with ritual killing – these are too much a part of human nature and human history to be put finally to rout. The officer has not achieved his exalted confirmation, but in death his face is 'calm and confident', and the epitaph on the Old Commandant's grave cites a prophecy that the patriarch will rise again and lead his followers back to power.

In the final years of his life, Kafka experimented several times with the form of the bestiary, stories which give us thinking, talking, even singing animals, but in settings that are fundamentally different from 'The Metamorphosis' or 'A Report to an Academy' in that the creatures have undergone no transformation from human to animal or vice versa, nor are they conscious of any incongruity between their human intellects and their animal forms. Rather, by the convention of an ancient kind of story telling, human affairs are transposed into the animal world, in the same way the world of sophisticated courtly matters could be translated into the bucolic world of the pastoral. The transformation is conventional rather than magical because literary play has supplanted the element of magic.

A bestiary is not necessarily grotesque; whether it is or not depends upon the kind of animal involved and what goes on in the story. Casting a singing mouse in the role of a temperamental prima donna is a stroke of pure whimsy, more akin to animal cartoons than to 'The Metamorphosis'. In grotesque bestiaries, a repugnant animal may be used to depict the repugnant side of human nature, while the non-grotesque bestiary may use animals to depict a sympathetic, even noble, version of humanity. It is difficult to formulate a distinction that would hold up in all cases, but the basic difference is between Houyhnhnms and yahoos.

In 'The Burrow', Kafka effects the grotesque by placing a morbidly sensitive human consciousness into the predatory world of animals where life is 'one indiscriminate succession of perils'. In contrast to the other two bestiaries of his later years, 'Josephine the Singer', and 'Investigations of a Dog', there is no large infusion of human culture – no music or science, no metaphysics – into the animal world. The denizen of the burrow lives an animal's life, his architecture is an animal's digging, he has an animal's concerns and an animal's fears. His only human qualities are his self-consciousness, his full awareness of his fears and his power to articulate them.

Though the narrator/protagonist of this story is never fully described or named by species (and attempts to identify him as, say, a badger defeat Kafka's design rather than elucidating it), he is obviously a large, burrowing carnivore who seems to combine the most unattractive qualities of a rat, Kafka's giant mole, and Dostoyevsky's underground man. The animal lives in a vast and intricate burrow which he has spent his lifetime constructing, and when he is not scurrying about to secure himself in a world in which 'my enemies are countless', he delights in the intricacies of his underground architecture. 'You belong to me, I to you, we are united', says the builder to his construction, and they *are* very much like one another, the burrow being the perfect physical equivalent of its creator's rambling, involuted mind (*Complete Stories*, p. 342).

Like underground man, underground animal has only to assert something for its opposite to appear at least equally convincing. The burrow shares this complementarity: it is his proudest possession but his most tormenting worry; it is his castle and his prison, his secure fortress and his death-trap; the product of his greatest ingenuity and industriousness, but after all, only a fetid hole. It is the expression of his inmost dreams, but also something forced upon him by the merciless conditions of the world. Though its completion is announced in the opening sentence, it can never be really complete since it can never be perfectly secure. In the last pages of the story, as the sounds of some nameless beast are heard approaching, the burrow, like its owner, is reduced to a shambles in the ensuing panic. 'But simply by virtue of being owner of this great vulnerable edifice I am obviously defenseless against any serious attack. The joy of possessing it has spoiled me, the vunerability of the burrow has made me vulnerable; any wound to it hurts me as if I myself were hit' (p. 355).

'The Burrow' is a perfect, undiluted example of the paranoid vision. In this respect it is comparable to 'An Old Manuscript', except that the protagonist is not a sympathetic artisan overwhelmed by monstrous nomads, but a cruel, cunning, repulsive, and very worried animal which is threatened by forces even more monstrous than itself. The characteristics of paranoia – obsessive suspicion, hostility, centrality, the fear of loss of autonomy – are the prime matter of the creature's view of the world. Though he lives in constant dread of predators, he takes delight in his own capacity for preying upon rats and 'small fry'. He would like to have a confederate to help guard the entrance, but he can trust absolutely no one. 'I can only trust myself and my burrow' (p. 388), and much of the time he cannot even trust the burrow. His thought carries to an extreme the visualising and itemising of potential disasters common in Kafka, and he is certain that the entire world would find his burrow the centre of overwhelming and hostile interest were its existence discovered. He would like to appreciate his construction as a thing of beauty, a genuine home in which he could meet even death with equanimity, but in panic, his most characteristic emotional state, such value evaporates entirely; the burrow's sole function upon which its success or failure depends exclusively is to be a refuge from 'the destroyers'. He sums up his life perfectly in a single image: 'I find myself sensing an atmosphere of great dangers, actually as if my hair were growing thin and in a moment might fly off and leave me bare and shivering, exposed to the howls of my enemies' (p. 332).

The animal's frenetic energy, his visions and revisions of terror, are due to his pursuing what he himself recognises as an unattainable goal, a 'completely perfect burrow'. He dreams of it in his sleep and wakes with tears of joy in his beard. But it is not simply an impregnable fortress he wants, nor even just a feeling of complete safety and peace. What he desires is to enjoy perfect security, and to enjoy his enjoyment of it, to apprehend his security from a point outside himself.[27] At the end of one of his periodic hunting forays, he crouches at the entrance of his burrow and imagines himself as a separate being inside. 'At such times it is as if I were not so much looking at my house as at myself, sleeping, and had the joy of being in a profound slumber and of keeping vigilant guard over myself. I am privileged, as it were, not only to dream about the specters of the night in all the helplessness and blind trust of sleep, but also at the same time to confront them in actuality with the calm and judgment of the fully awake. And strangely enough I discover that my situation is not so bad as I had often thought, and will probably think again when I return to my house' (p. 334).

This strange desire to exist outside himself, both to guard his existence and to contemplate its security, he would like to incorporate into the architectural design of his masterpiece, the Castle Keep, the chamber at the heart of his burrow. He wishes he could completely surround it with empty space that would detach it from the walls, so that it would be within the burrow but at the same time separate from it. He would love to live all the time in that empty space.

> What joy to be pressed against the rounded outer wall, pull oneself up, let oneself slide down again, miss one's footing and find oneself on firm earth, and play all those games literally upon the Castle Keep and not inside it; to avoid the Castle Keep, to rest one's eyes from it whenever one wanted to, to postpone the joy of seeing it until later and yet not have to do without it, but literally hold it safe between one's claws, a thing that is impossible if you have only an ordinary open entrance to it; but above all to be able to stand guard over it, and in that way to be so completely compensated for renouncing the actual sight of it that, if one had to choose between staying all one's life in the Castle Keep or in the free space outside it, one would choose the latter, content to wander up and down there all one's days and keep guard over the Castle Keep.
>
> (p. 346)

To express this dream of two simultaneous modes of existence with one providing security for the other, Kafka has made ingenious modifications of first person narration. The format of the story appears to be an unbroken discourse in which the burrower addresses the reader directly. The writing is mostly in the present tense, and the 'present' of the story is the time of narration. The place from which the narrator/protagonist is speaking is obviously the burrow. In other words, Kafka seems to be using exactly the same technique Dostoyevsky used in part one of *Notes from Underground*. But a second time scheme has been superimposed upon the narrative present, a scheme which exists simultaneously with it, though the two are not congruent with each other. Several times the action reverts to the past, but there is no shift in tense to indicate a retrospective point of view.[28] The narration continues to use the present, and though several days of action elapse, only a few minutes of narrative time are required to describe them, even though the actions are described as taking place while they are being narrated. For instance, in the passage in which the creature describes his past hunting foray when he lurked at the burrow entrance imagining a dual existence and agonising about the risk of revealing the location of the entrance by going home, the point of view is from his eyes as he engages in those actions, and the tense is present. Several days pass, but the action remains in the present, even though the narration itself covers only a few minutes. The narrator speaking from inside the burrow at a time after the hunting foray has been allowed simply to lapse out of existence for the time being.

An even more unusual dual time effect is achieved in the second half of the story. The animal has regained the security of his burrow. 'I have no intention of sleeping here, I have merely yielded to the temptation of making myself comfortable and pretending I want to sleep. I merely wish to find out if this is a good a place for sleeping as it used to be. It is, but it is a better place for sleep than for waking, and I remain lying where I am in a deep slumber' (p. 343). A first person narrator describing himself in the present tense as sleeping is unusual enough, but even stranger things are in store.

As the animal awakes, the story makes one of its very few shifts into past tense: 'I must have slept for a long time. I was only awakened when I had reached the last light sleep which dissolves itself, and it must have been very light, for it was an almost inaudible whistling noise that awakened me' (p. 343). It would seem that the story has switched to the usual mode of first person narration, with the past tense clearly implying that the narrator is describing actions in retrospect. This conventional technique lasts, however, for only one more sentence, and then Kafka shifts us back into the present tense: 'What an indefatigably busy lot these small fry are, and what a nuisance their diligence can be! First I shall have to . . .'.[29] For the remainder of the story the animal seems to be describing actions as they occur in the present, but the actions described and the act of describing them are not congruent with each other. The animal furiously digs up his burrow searching for the source of the dreaded approaching sound. While the digging goes on for hours, its present tense narration lasts only for seconds: 'at many places already there are heaps of earth which block my way and my view. Still that is only a secondary worry; for now I can neither wander about my house nor review it nor rest; often already I have fallen asleep at my work in some hole or other, with one paw clutching the soil above me, from which in a semistupor I have been trying to tear a lump' (p. 348). Not for a moment have we left the animal's present consciousness, yet we have seen none of the action which he now says has been taking place. Indeed, having a character whose mind is disintegrating from panic and exhaustion narrate his experience in the first person present is itself taking a long chance. The upshot of all this finagling with time and tense is that the burrower *does* seem to have the sort of dual existence he aspired to, at once inside and outside the action he is engaged in. But the effect is the opposite of the comfort and secure self-contemplation he had imagined; rather it is as if an individual could lucidly relate a nightmare while in the process of having it.

We must remember that in the ficiton of Kafka, the paranoiac is not a mental case, but has made a correct assessment of the world. Quite early in the story we are told: 'There are also enemies in the bowels of the earth. I have never seen them, but legend tells of them and I firmly believe in them. They are creatures of the inner earth, not even legend can describe them. Their victims can scarcely have seen them; they come, you hear them scratching their claws just under you in the ground, which is their element, and already you are lost. Here it is no avail to console yourself with the thought that you are in your own house; far rather, you are in theirs' (p. 326).

Any sound reading of 'The Burrow' must, I believe, postulate that the noise is real, not imagined by the narrator, and that some unknown beast actually is approaching. This interpretation has been rejected by some critics, most notably Hermann Weigand who sees the story as presenting its narrator's passage from neurosis to psychosis with auditory hallucinations.[30] This argument rests primarily on the fact that the animal hears the approaching sound at equal intensity from all parts of his burrow, and when he considers tunnelling to its source its source seems to be everywhere. Since such a situation is physically impossible, so the argument goes, Kafka clearly intends us to understand that the speaker is hallucinating.[31]

But here, as in practically every story Kafka wrote, we are in a world where the laws of possibility may be suspended whenever the author pleases. Moreover, the burrower himself speculates at great length about the omnidirectional sound, and reaches precisely the conclusion Kafka intends the reader to: 'it only remains for me to assume the existence of a great beast, especially as the things that seem to contradict the hypothesis are merely things which make the beast, not so much impossible, as merely dangerous beyond all one's powers of conception' (p. 353). The beast approaches from all directions at once, just as in *The Trial* the Court conducts proceedings in many attics, perhaps in *all* the attics, not to mention the lumber room of Joseph K.'s bank. Obviously, if we are going to be literal-minded about what is and is not physically possible, we had better choose some other writer.

The strongest evidence that the beast is not to be understood as a hallucination but as real is provided by Max Brod in a note in the collection in which 'Der Bau' first appeared.[32] Citing as his authority Dora Dymant, Kafka's companion when 'Der Bau' was written, he asserts that the story was completed in a few more pages; in them, the narrator fought the beast and was overcome. Weigand rejects this as an error since a story is not likely to present a character narrating his own death. But there is nothing in Brod's note to indicate that the narrator is dead at the end of the story, merely overcome (*unterliegen*); perhaps we may assume he is dying. John Gardner brings off a similar effect at the end of *Grendel* and it works quite well, considerably better than the hypothetical ending Weigand suggests for 'The Burrow'.[33] As we have seen, Kafka has already gotten away with doing things to first person narration in this story, achieving sleight of hand effects that one would think impossible if they were merely described.

But the most convincing reason for rejecting a reading in which the beast is a hallucination is that it goes against Kafka's basic technique in almost all his fiction. Time and again he presents us with events that can only be explained as dreams or madness, and then insists relentlessly that it is all really happening. The relationalistic reader encountering 'The Metamorphosis' or *The Trial* for the first time keeps expecting Gregor to wake up or Joseph K. to be hauled off to a madhouse, but that is precisely what does *not* happen in Kafka. Kafka would not be Kafka if it did. He does not write about characters who engage in projective thinking; he makes projective thinking the premise of his fictive world. I am very skeptical that he would abandon a fundamental method of his art for one so much less daring and effective, one that gives the reader a way out of the artist's haunted and haunting world – and my skepticism is only increased by the existence of the perfectly acceptable external evidence that he did no such thing. 'And the danger is by no means a fanciful one, but very real', the burrower insists about his whole life-situation, and within the world of the story he is right (p. 337). The beast is a mysterious, as yet invisible, inexorably approaching power over which the burrower has no control, with which he can reach no 'understanding', against which he has no adequate defence. 'Compared with this, what are all the petty dangers in brooding over which I have spent my life!' (p. 355). It is a paranoid nightmare come to life.

Yet, for all the desperate pessimism of his vision, Kafka is often spoken of as a comic writer. It is easy to misjudge that aspect of his work. We do not find in him anything like the comic appreciation of the human predicament we encounter in Joyce or Márquez. Rather, the grotesque world itself becomes an object of heightened play for the author and, by extension, for the reader as well. The macabre humour which surfaces unexpectedly at some of the grimmest moments of his fiction (such as the antics of the prisoner and the guard in 'In the Penal Colony') is really a function of this wider play.

A diary entry provides a useful clue to the author's own attitude toward the horrors his fiction invents:

I forgot – and later purposely omitted [from a conversation with Max Brod] – to add that the best things I have written have their basis in this capacity of mine to meet death with contentment.

All these fine and very convincing passages always deal with the fact that someone is dying, that it is hard for him to do, that it seems unjust to him, or at least harsh, and the reader is moved by this, or at least should be. But for me, who believe that I shall be able to lie contentedly on my deathbed, such scenes are secretly a game, indeed, in the death enacted I rejoice in my own death, hence calculatingly exploit the attention that the reader concentrates on death, have a much clearer understanding of it than he, of whom I suppose that he will loudly lament on his deathbed, and for those reasons my lament is as perfect as can be, nor does it suddenly break off as is likely to be the case with a real lament, but dies beautifully and purely away. It is the same thing as my perpetual lamenting to my mother over pains that were not nearly so great as my laments would lead one to believe. With my mother, of course, I do not need to make so great a display of art as with the reader.[34]

Though life and death are usually what is at stake in Kafka's fiction, the emphasis is on the process by which the individual is dragged or pushed toward death, outwardly resisting and complaining, but inwardly acquiescing, even cooperating with the implacable and irrational forces that have seized control of him. It was the transformation of such deep and irrational fears into the mad structure of art that perhaps allowed Kafka to assert control over them when they threatened to take control of him.[35] One is reminded of underground man's contention that, to a certain kind of sensibility, even a toothache can be a source of pleasure. The sufferer's moans are transformed into a kind of embellished art work, and then into a cruel game with his hearers, played consciously for its own sake. Kafka's mastery through art of the most obsessive, even psychotic, fears allows us as readers to regard his nightmarish creations with recognition and fascination because the paranoid intuition of the world is one that we all share to varying degrees at various times. The paranoid vision itself becomes the subject of a shared game, even, at times, of laughter.

3

Bloomsbody

Taken as a whole, *Ulysses* cannot be called a novel of the grotesque in the same way that, say, Günter Grass's *The Tin Drum* can. That is, the presentation of a grotesque world is not dominant from beginning to end. But there are many passages that employ the grotesque, and standing at the novel's centre is a 180-page psychodrama that is one of the most elaborate grotesques in modern literature.[1] However, the grotesque in Joyce does not arise from or in a paranoid reading of the world, even though fantasies of persecution abound in certain chapters of *Ulysses*. The whole sense of the grotesque that the novel embodies is different from the haunted claustrophobia of the paranoid vision.

Joyce described his novel as, among other things, an epic of the human body, and in his elaborate scheme of multiple correspondences, he assigned many of the individual chapters an organ of the body as an emblem.[2] Less attention has been paid to this aspect of the book's organisation than to the mythological, literary, ethnic, and geographical cross-references, a neglect which is strange when once considers that the scandal that surrounded the publication of *Ulysses* arose mainly because of Joyce's depiction of the body and its functions.

The relationship between the grotesque and an awareness of the gross physicality of the human body, its participation in the animal world, is well established. The most extensive discussion is in Mikhail Bakhtin's superb study, *Rabelais and His World*.[3]

> The grotesque body . . . is a body in the act of becoming. It is never finished, never completed; it is continually built, created, and builds and creates another body. Moreover, the body swallows the world and is itself swallowed by the world. . . . This is why the essential role belongs to those parts of the grotesque body, in which it conceives a new body: the bowels and the phallus. These two areas play the leading role in the grotesque image and it is precisely for this reason that they are predominantly subject to positive exaggeration, to hyperboliz-

70

ation; they can even detach themselves from the body and lead an independent life. . . . Eating, drinking, defecation and other elimination (sweating, blowing of the nose, sneezing), as well as copulation, pregnancy, dismemberment, swallowing up by another body – all these acts are performed on the confines of the body and the outer world, or on the old and new body. In all these events the beginning and end of life are closely linked and interwoven.

(p. 317)

Rabelais is a writer to whom Joyce has often been compared, and perhaps their depiction of the grotesque body is the closest link between them, for it seems to me that they have little else in common. The celebration of copulation, birth, devouring, and elimination that Bakhtin finds in Rabelais is everywhere in Joyce, culminating in Molly's ruminations in the final chapter. In fact, I would say that the four great themes that tie together the diversity of *Ulysses* are the four irreducibles of human life (and, indeed, all the more complex forms of animal life): birth, food, sex, and death. Each occupies the centre of at least one chapter, and the four together are interwoven elaborately throughout the novel. Sex, both explicit and implicit, dominates the book, and many of the other major themes – the relation of parents and children, of husbands and wives, of lovers and cuckolds – proceed directly from the larger issues of sex and birth. Food is almost as central. No fewer than seven chapters – 'Telemachus', 'Calypso', 'Lestrygonians', 'Sirens', 'Circe', 'Eumaus', and 'Ithaca' – take place while a meal is being eaten or food is being offered, not to mention the drinking and snacking that go on in 'Aeolus', 'Cyclops', and 'Oxen of the Sun'.[4] Who gets breakfast for whom becomes a matter of more than culinary importance in the Bloom household, and a home without Plumtree's Potted Meat is incomplete. That running joke is also linked to sex by more than the obvious double entendre; Molly and Boylan refresh themselves with Plumtree's during their tryst, and Bloom discovers the crumbs from their snack when he gets into bed. 'Potted meat' is also given a momentary association with death when Bloom recalls the slogan while Paddy Dignam is lowered into his grave. The presence of the dead as disconcertingly live memories is central to the characterisations of both Bloom and Stephen, and in 'Circe' numerous of the living dead put in appearances.

Joyce's depiction of the grotesque body, however, is not always as celebrative as Bakhtin finds Rabelais' to be. Taking issue with Kayser, Bakhtin assigns little importance to fear in his model of the grotesque.[5] Joyce, however, frequently uses the grotesque to depict the fear, revulsion, guilt, and shame which various characters, especially Bloom and Stephen, feel about their own bodies.

As early as *Portrait of the Artist as a Young Man*, Joyce used images of the grotesque to dramatise Stephen's mingled curiosity and guilt about his own adolescent body. 'It shocked him to find in the outer world a trace of what he had dreamed till then a brutish and individual malady of his own mind. His recent monstrous reveries came thronging into his memory. They too had sprung up before him, suddenly and furiously, out of mere words. He had soon given in to them, and allowed them to sweep across and abase his intellect, wondering always where they came from, from what den of monstrous images, and always weak and humble towards others, restless and sickened of himself when they swept over him.'[6] In 'Circe', mere words will time and again trigger monstrous images which will spring suddenly and furiously not only to the minds of Stephen and Bloom, but to the stage of the action itself. In *Portrait*, however, such monstrous fantasies of debasement are restricted to Stephen's dreams, 'peopled by apelike creatures and by harlots with gleaming jewel eyes' (p. 115). In one of them he finds himself on a foul heath, surrounded by repulsive, satyr-like creatures. 'One was clasping about his ribs a torn flannel waistcoat, another complained monstrously as his beard stuck in the tufted weeds. . . . They moved in slow circles, circling closer and closer to enclose, to enclose, soft language issuing from their lips, their long swishing tails besmeared with stale shite, thrusting upwards their terrific faces . . . Help!' (pp. 136–8).

For someone whose adolescence was filled with precocious sexual experience, the Stephen Dedalus we meet in the opening pages of *Ulysses* seems an undersexed young man.[7] The preoccupation with the body as an animalistic source of revulsion is still with him, but the emphasis has shifted from sex to death. He objects to Mulligan's crass reference to Mrs Dedalus as being 'beastly dead', and to the assertion that death in its physical agony is 'all a mockery and beastly', but in his private reveries of his mother's death he replaces the experienced cynicism of Medical Buck with the morbidity of the self-torturing introvert.

In a dream silently, she had come to him, her wasted body within its loose graveclothes giving off an odour of wax and rosewood, her breath bent over him with mute secret words, a faint odour of wetted ashes.[8]

Her glazing eyes staring out of death, to shake and bend my soul. On me alone. The ghostlike candle to light her agony. Ghostly light on the tortured face. Her hoarse loud breath rattling in horror, while all prayed on their knees. Her eyes on me to stike me down. *Liliata rutilantium te confessorum turma circumdet: iubilantium te virginum chorus excipiat.*

Ghoul! Chewer of corpses!

(p. 10)

So too, his own Godsbody, which he had been so conscious of polluting in *Portrait*, has become by simple inversion 'This dogsbody to rid of vermin' (p. 6). The two preoccupations with decay of the body after death and the nearness of the human to the animal are fused playfully in his nonsense riddle of the fox burying his grandmother under a hollybush and more grimly in his reflections about the living and dead dogs he sees on the strand and his imaginings of the drowned corpse being searched for off shore. But as yet, these are daydreams and reflections existing in his mind only, not in the external world of the novel.

Mr. Leopold Bloom is another character who is acutely aware of his body as a physical entity. Filling it with the inner organs of beasts and fowls and emptying it in the jakes are central events of his early morning ritual, and interest in its hygiene and diet occupies his mind throughout the day. Bloom would appear to be on easier terms with his body than Stephen is with his, but in his more depressed moments he shares a similar morbid preoccupation with physicality and its four-beat cycle of birth, food, sex, and death. 'Hades' and 'Lestrygonians' particularly show a Bloom who feels imprisoned and degraded by physical acts repeated endlessly and without further purpose than to perpetuate a life without meaning, dignity, or satisfaction. His private reflections and fantasies point toward the grotesques which will materialise in 'Circe'.

As the funeral of Paddy Dignam winds through Dublin toward Glasnevin, a contrast is set up between Bloom's reflections upon death and those of his companions, Simon Dedalus, Mr. Power, and Martin Cunningham. For them, death is partly an emotional experience, in which sentimentality plays a larger role than grief, partly a social event, with funereal etiquette to be observed, and partly a religious experience, a passage into eternity presided over by the Church. For Bloom, death is physical and nothing but physical.[9] When the other mourners think of Dignam at all, it is always as the departed friend; Bloom is constantly aware of him as the present corpse. The passing mention of an accident in which a hearse had been overturned is enough to raise in Bloom's mind a vision of Paddy, agape and greyfaced, dumped out in the road, a vision which in turn prompts a series of Bloomian scientific speculations. 'Would he bleed if a nail cut him in the knocking about?' (p. 99).

Death is, in Bloom's eyes, a grim joke on the part of the living at the expense of the dead, a joke relished by many with great satisfaction. Simon thinks it is a 'fine old custom', for people to stop and watch a passing cortège bareheaded, but Bloom privately sees things quite differently. 'Thanking her stars she was passed over. Extraordinary the interest they take in a corpse. Glad to see us go we give them such trouble coming' (p. 87). As the procession passes the Childs house and the sensational fratricide trial is recalled, Bloom reflects further on the fascination that death in all its most physical particulars holds for the living. 'They love reading about it. Man's head found in a garden. Her clothing consisted of. How she met her death. Recent outrage. The weapon used. Murderer is still at large. Clues. A shoelace. The body to be exhumed' (p. 100).

For Bloom, death can never be anything but a defeat, a characteristically physical defeat, the worst part of which is the powerlessness of the individual before death. 'Who departed this life. As if they did it of their own accord. Got the shove, all of them' (p. 113). The mention of the resurrection of the dead that comforts the other mourners suggests to Bloom a grotesque tableau: 'That last day idea. Knocking them up out of their graves. . . . Then every fellow mousing around for his liver and his lights and the rest of his traps. Find damn all of himself that morning' (p. 106).

Though a relentless insistence upon death as a physical defeat sets the tone of the 'Hades' chapter, there are many direct references linking death with the other three irreducibles of bodily life – food, sex, and birth. Martin Cunningham is astonished to find crustcrumbs on the seat of the funeral coach. 'Someone seems to have been making a picnic party here lately, Mr. Power said' (p. 89). On the way to the cemetery the cortège keeps repeatedly coming on other reminders of food and eating: a hawker of plums, a public house where mourners usually stop for refreshments, and finally a peddler of cakes and fruit at the gate of the cemetery itself. 'Simnel cakes those are, stuck together: cakes for the dead. Dogbiscuits' (p. 100). At one point, the funeral is halted by a herd of cattle being driven to market: 'Dead meat trade' (p. 98). But the most startling link between food and death comes at the graveside when Bloom spies a rat and makes the same kind of observation that Hamlet does about Polonius' last supper. 'One of those chaps would make short work of a fellow. Pick the bones clean no matter who it was. Ordinary meat for them. A corpse is meat gone bad. Well and what's cheese? Corpse of milk. . . . Regular square feed for them. Flies come before he's well dead. Got wind of Dignam. They wouldn't care about the smell of it. Saltwhite, crumbling mush of corpse: smell, taste like raw white turnips' (p. 114).

Death in the 'Hades' chapter is also associated with sex as a function of the grotesque body, and even with birth. It is natural enough that a funeral should make Bloom recall the death of his son, but his memory is pushed back eleven years earlier to Rudy's conception when Molly became aroused by the sight of two dogs copulating: 'Give us a touch Poldy. God, I'm dying for it. How life begins' (p. 89). The same kind of association between death and sex occurs to him when the mourners meet Connel, the caretaker, and Bloom imagines what it must be like for the Connels making love in their house on the cemetery grounds. 'Tell her a ghost story in bed to make her sleep. . . . Still they'd kiss all right if properly keyed up. Whores in Turkish graveyards. Learn anything if taken young. You might pick up a young widow here. Men like that. Spice of pleasure. In the midst of death we are in life. Both ends meet. Tantalising for the poor dead. Smell of frilled [sic] beefsteaks to the starving gnawing their vitals. Desire to grig people. Molly wanting to do it at the window. Eight children he had anyway' (p. 108). That sense of 'both ends meet' is reinforced by the passing of an infant's funeral, and by the fact that the medical student, Dickson, who had served at the Misericord hospital for the dying (where Mrs. Riordan had died), is now at the Holles Street lying-in hospital where Bloom is going to visit Mrs. Purefoy that evening. 'From one extreme to the other' (p. 108).

It is ultimately this sense of teeming, sexual, renewable life even in the midst of death that raises Bloom's spirits after his funereal depression. As he prepares to leave the cemetery, he recalls the mistake in the letter he had received from Martha earlier that morning. 'I do not like that other world [for 'word'] she wrote. No more do I. Plenty to see and hear and feel yet. Feel live warm being near you. Let them sleep in their maggoty beds. They are not going to get me this innings. Warm beds: warm fullblooded life' (p. 115).

'Lestrygonians', a chapter primarily concerned with food, presents another version of animal man satisfying animal needs in terms that border on the grotesque. Bloom is still in a bad mood, feeling as if he had been 'eaten and spewed', convinced that 'no one is anything' (p. 164). Usually food and eating are presented more affirmatively in *Ulysses*; Bloom is a man who enjoys himself at the table. But in 'Lestrygonians', he associates hunger with degrading need, and its satisfaction with a sloppy, voracious process of the grotesque body. 'See the animals feed', he says to himself when he looks into the lunchroom of the Hotel Burton (p. 169). 'Am I like that? See ourselves as others see us.' Leaving the hotel in disgust, he equates feeding with universal human predation. 'Every fellow for his own tooth and nail. Gulp. Grub. Gulp. Gobstuff. . . . Eat or be eaten. Kill! Kill!' (p. 170). In a futurist fantasy of communal kitchens, his usual muddled Utopianism is overshadowed by the imaginary spectacle of the low and the high, even Queen Victoria in her bathchair, clamouring to satisfy their animal need: 'My plate's empty. . . . Want a soup pot as big as the Phoenix Park. Harpooning flitches and hindquarters out of it. Hate people all around you' (p. 170).

These images of revulsion and futility associated with food and feeding lead Bloom, toward the end of the chapter, to think longingly of the mythical beings of classical sculpture, who have neither the need for mortal food nor the equipment to digest it. 'Nectar, imagine it drinking electricity: gods' food. Lovely forms of woman sculped Junonian. Immortal lovely. And we stuffing food in one hole and out behind: food, chyle, blood, dung, earth, food: have to feed it like stoking an engine. They have no' (p. 176).

Bakhtin has asserted that the grotesque invariably discloses the potential of an entirely different world, of another order, another way of life. It leads man out of the confines of the apparent (and false) unity of the indisputable and stable and into a raucous, even chaotic parody of the official version of things (*Rabelais*, p. 48). Transformation is what 'Circe' is all about, and what gets transformed is not just the red lights district of Dublin, which becomes the grotesque dreamscape of night town, but all of the previous material of the novel itself. In the transformed world of 'Circe', all of the major and many of the minor characters reappear as grotesque parodies of themselves, their essential qualities caricatured by visual symbols of their eccentricities and preoccupations. *Ulysses* as a whole may be considered a kind of funnel; a great deal of Western (and a smattering of Eastern) civilisation gets run through the narrow neck of Dublin, 16 June 1904. 'Circe' stands in a similar relation to the rest of the book as the book stands to the Western world: replay, inventory, commentary, and parody.

'Circe' contains such a wide range of grotesques that it gives the impression of having exhausted the catalogue of possibilities. There are: men partially transformed into animals (Leputi Virag, Paddy Dignam), animals with human properties (Molly's camel), deformed people (dwarfs and gnomes), spirits and demons (the hobgoblin, the chorus at the Black Mass), ghosts (Mrs. Dedalus, Rudolph Virag), mutilations (Henry Flower caressing a severed head, the evisceration of the Croppy Boy), decomposition (Mrs. Dedalus, Paddy Dignam), the antics of the mentally aberrant (Denis Breen, the saluting idiot), combinations of human and inanimate forms (the Nymph who turns into a plaster statue and falls apart, Leputi Virag who unscrews his head), outlandish caricatures (Mr. Deasy covered with postage stamps and doused with soup riding a nag in a horse race, Simon Dedalus as a cardinal infested with fleas and trailing monkeys who peep under his robes), droll whimsicalities (the end of the world as a singing octopus with a Scottish accent), women partly transformed into men and men partly transformed into women (Bella Cohen, Bloom), and an adult partially transformed into a baby (Bloom). Above all, there is the perverse and disproportionate in human conduct, which, while not always grotesque in itself, becomes part of the overall rendering of life as grotesque, much like the riot of figures in Bosch's *The Hay Wain*.

In the midst of all this diversity, the intent is always consistent: to set up a correlation between the grotesque body and the half-stifled urges and guilts that attend it. Frank Budgen reports that in Zurich Joyce was a curious collector of facts about the human body, especially the borderline where mind and body meet, where thought is generated and shaped by the state of the body.[10] He quotes Joyce as saying, 'In my book the body lives in and moves through space and is the home of a full human personality. . . . If

they had no body they would have no mind. . . . It's all one'
(p. 21). In 'Circe', animal urges are the prime movers of human
conduct, but the pursuit of their gratification is what renders the
body grotesque. There are two distinct senses of the grotesque
that are constantly played off one another throughout the novel.
One, aversive and pessimistic, presents life as a merely physical,
mostly disgusting passage beginning with birth agony, proceeding
through a series of artificial and untenable relationships such as
marriage and citizenship, to end in death agony and decomposition. It is a sense captured in Stephen's phrase, 'dogsbody'. But
against this is a complementary view, humane and hilarious,
centered on the warm, moist, fleshy presence of Mr. Bloom and
his attitudes toward his own body – at times cowed by shame
and guilt, but irrepressibly eager to enjoy animal satisfactions.[11]
This alternative sense is unwaveringly comic, and I suggest we call
it 'Bloomsbody'. These two senses are placed in their sharpest
contrast through the magical transformations of 'Circe'.

In his elaborate scheme of the novel, Joyce designated magic as
the art celebrated in 'Circe', and called its technique hallucination.
This last term is more misleading than helpful because, except for
one or two instances toward the end of the chapter, no one is
hallucinating – that is, thinking that he sees or hears things that
do not exist outside his mind. But we are left with the very tangled
question of where these spectres are emanating from. In what
stratum of the novel do they exist? Clearly they cannot be fantasies
occurring in the minds of Bloom and Stephen, or, more exactly,
they cannot be only that in all instances. While some of the
transformations clearly relate to Bloom and others just as surely to
Stephen, some contain material taken from the private lives of
both. Thus, in the dance of death episode, Professor Magnini
directs the dance in French, indicating that the fantasy must be
Stephen's, while Professor Goodwin accompanies on the piano
and the women's braclets go 'Heigho! Heigho!', indicating that the
fantasy can only be Bloom's. The mixture becomes even more
confusing in the final Pandemonium sequence. Stuart Gilbert
speculated that the mixture of fantasies 'suggests a momentary
complete fusion of the personalities; of a "fatherless" son and
sonless father' (James Joyce's *Ulysses*, p. 333). Good, but how then
explain the presence in other fantasies of young Patsy Dignam
with his pork steaks, or hackney car 324 driven by James Barton,
Harmony Avenue, Donnybrook, or Mrs. Keogh the brothel's cook,

or Bella Cohen's lover, Charles Marsh? Patsy bought his steaks and Barton drove Boylan to Eccles Street in 'Wandering Rocks' vignettes at which neither Bloom nor Stephen were present, and neither Mrs. Keogh nor Marsh have appeared previously in the novel.

More persuasively than Gilbert, Hugh Kenner has suggested that the chapter is expressionist rather than psychological, and he cautions against trying to determine too definitely which fantasy belongs to whom.[12] The demonstrable rightness of that position should not obscure the fact that the fantasies *are* experienced as a psychological phenomenon by Bloom and Stephen who at various points react to them in the 'real' stratum of the novel. At the climax of the chapter, Stephen actually does hallucinate his mother's corpse rising in reproach and goes berserk. Joyce, characteristically is having it both ways. The fantasies are largely a function of character, and we finish the chapter with a more vivid sense of Bloom's and Stephen's inner lives than we have previously obtained from following their inner monologues. But at the same time, Joyce, the artificer is the creator of the fantasies as he is also creator of the fantasisers, and whenever it suits his purposes he takes direct charge of the fantasy, and, without intermediary, transforms the previous material of his novel into a grotesque rendition of itself.[13]

Now, the technique of dividing the novel into two realms – one of the actions and thoughts of the characters and the other the fantastic amplifications provided directly by the author – is not unique in the novel to 'Circe'. We encounter it elsewhere, especially in the 'gigantic' parodies of 'Cyclops'; in fact, the whole technique of 'Circe' is closer to that of 'Cyclops' than it is to the stream of consciousness typical of, say, 'Lestrygonians'.[14] Many of the long stage directions read exactly like passages from 'Cyclops', especially the procession of dignitaries at Bloom's coronation (pp. 479–80), and the hue and cry as Bloom leaves the brothel (pp. 586–7). One of the spectres of night town is Black Liz, a bisexual chicken which appears only in a parody section of 'Cyclops' and not in the 'real' stratum of the novel at all. The hangman, Rumbold, who is mentioned in the 'real' stratum of 'Cyclops' but appears only in the parodies, returns several times in 'Circe', where his execution of the Croppy Boy seems to complete the interrupted parody of the execution of Emmett in 'Cyclops'. But the closest similarity between the two chapters is that in both the artificer transforms the 'real' world of the novel into a grotesque, magical one. Indeed, in 'Circe', he makes that transformation, from Mabbot Street into the Surrealist dreamscape of night town, in the first stage direction, before Stephen and Bloom have even entered the scene. In 'Cyclops' the two strata, real and fantastic, are very distinct, and the transitions between them are startling by their very abruptness. In 'Circe', on the other hand, we have not two sharply divided planes, but rather a very fluid mix of realistic dramatisation, private fantasies of the characters, and fantastic transformation by the artificer; any event can combine varying amounts of the three.

In my opening chapter I said that the anti-heroes of the modern grotesque often are trapped in a dichotomy about their own definition of themselves. They want to assert their worthiness in the face of a world which they feel regards them with contempt, so they endow themselves with extraordinary, often magical powers to triumph over their enemies and win acclaim. But at the same time, they are unable to shake off a conviction that the world has judged them right, that they are fit objects for contempt, and that the persecution that they find on every side is neither more nor less than they deserve. Such a dichotomy finally produces a central figure who is not so much alienated man as humiliated man, who alternates between rebelling against his humiliation and acquiescing in it.

Bloom's whole day has moved between these poles. In the grotesque world of 'Circe', where surfaces may be transformed to reveal essential qualities, the two extremes of Bloom's situation emerge with almost schematic clarity. The basic function of grotesque transformation here, as in 'The Metamorphosis', is revelation, a stripping away of the accommodations, rationalisations, and compromises by which day to day life is made possible, to reveal the primal conflicts between self and self, and self and other that underlie them. Throughout this process of unmasking, Joyce takes a dual attitude toward his protagonist – at once concerned and sympathetic, but also detached and ironic. Pathos and parody often coexist in a single passage, as in Bloom's complaint to Bella: 'I am exhausted, abandoned, no more young. I stand so to speak, with an unposted letter bearing the extra regulation fee before the too late box of the general post office of human life' (p. 528).

All the most elaborate and extended fantasy passages that centre on Bloom have as their common substance his public exposure as a sex deviate, his fatuous defence of himself, and his condemnation to death. In all of them, there is tension between the Bloom that Bloom would like to be in the eyes of the world, and the secret Bloom just waiting to be discovered and reviled. Thus there is a corresponding tension between our perception of Bloom as a sympathetic hero battling to assert his dignity before a monstrously hostile world, and as the grotesque body, indulging in masochistic and coprophilic lusts that render any notion of human dignity ludicrous. The extreme virulence with which Bloom's enemies attack him might lead us to believe that we are back in the world of the paranoid vision and, indeed, one critic has seen fit to call 'Circe' 'a paradise of paranoia'.[15] But the crucial difference is that here the persecutors are themselves being mocked and parodied by the author in a way they are not usually in Kafka. The transformed world of 'Circe' has something of the alienated, ominous qualities that Kayser ascribed to the grotesque, but there is also a strong element of Bakhtin's model of inversion, enlargement, and raucous laughter, and nowhere are they more evident than in the New Bloomusalem.

Like the parody passages in 'Cyclops', the New Bloomusalem sequence seems to cultivate outlandishness as an art form and to reach for some preposterous outer limit of exaggeration. Such 'gigantism' is typical not only of Bloom's grandiose programs of reform, but of the crowds that alternately idolise and revile him. The overall impression is of frenetic energy in comination with mindless, fickle enthusiasm. Stylistically Joyce has conveyed the scurrying, bustling energy of the populace not only by the rapid expansion of the setting and the outrageous lists of parading dignitaries and organisations, but even more by stage directions made up of short, rapid fire subject–predicate–object sentences describing a series of actions each more outlandish than the last. Time is so drastically compressed that it seems to have collapsed completely. The New Bloomusalem, a 40,000 room crystal palace in the shape of a pork kidney, is built by 32 workmen in a matter of seconds. Bloom gives birth to eight males, who are apparently born as adults and instantly disperse to various countries to assume positions of high responsibility and prestige. The passage abounds in high-action words, always with the focus on the extreme and outlandish, often upon the violent: '(*Many most attractive and enthusiastic women also commit suicide by stabbing, drowning, drinking prussic acid, aconite, arsenic, opening their veins, refusing food, casting themselves under steamrollers, from the top of Nelson's Pillar, into the great vat of Guinness's brewery, asphyxiating themselves by placing their heads in gas ovens, hanging themselves in stylish garters, leaping from windows of different storeys.)'* (p. 492).

This Surrealistic presentation of the crowd swept along by impulse and emotion, ready to adore or condemn with equal passion and for equally bad reasons, dramatises Stephen's view of history as nightmare – for the setting of this fantastic episode is not Dublin but a frenetic stage of history, history gone mad. The parody is not just of Bloom's desire to see himself as a loved and acclaimed benefactor of humanity; even more the parody is of the tendency of populations from time out of mind to elevate their heroes beyond all sane proportion the better to make martyrs and scapegoats of them.

The same frantic energy of the crowd is imputed to Bloom as he goes through his metamorphoses from alderman, to emperor, to womanly man, to felon with asses' ears sitting in the stocks awaiting execution. Several of the stage directions are lists of his scurrying activities, unlocalised in time or space, as he tries to curry favour with the mob.

> *(Shaking hands with a blind stripling.)* My more than Brother! *(Placing his arms round the shoulders of an old couple.)* Dear old friends! *(He plays pussy fourcorners with ragged boys and girls.)* Peep! Bopeep! *(He wheels twins in a perambulator.)* Ticktacktwo wouldyousetashoe? *(He performs juggler's tricks, draws red, orange, yellow, green, blue, indigo and violet silk handkerchiefs from his mouth.)* Roygbiv. 32 feet per second. *(He consoles a widow.)* Absence makes the heart grow younger. *(He dances the Highland fling with grotesque antics.)* Leg it, ye devils! *(He kisses the bedsores of a palsied veteran.)* Honourable wounds! *(He trips up a fat policeman.)* U.p.:up. U.p.:up. *(He whispers in the ear of a blushing waitress and laughs kindly.)* Ah, naughty, naughty! *(He eats a raw turnip offered him by Maurice Butterly, farmer.)* Fine! Splendid! *(He refuses to accept three shillings offered him by Joe Hynes, journalist.)* My dear fellow, not at all! *(He gives his coat to a beggar.)* Please accept. *(He takes part in a stomach race with elderly male and female cripples.)* Come on, boys! Wriggle it, girls!
>
> (p. 486)

All these activities, as well as the parodic transformations that Bloom undergoes, have as their central reference point the image of Bloom as we have come to know him through some 500 pages of the novel – the amiable loser who eats with relish the inner organs of beasts and fowls and is fond of ogling ladies' underwear. It is from this central reference point, present at all times, even if only subliminally, that his transformations acquire their manic humour. The figure who appears in crimson and ermine, bearing the royal regalia, astride a white palfrey is a figure we know well – Bloomsbody – and his subsequent transformations chronicle the constant re-emergence of that side of his nature. As the crowd turns against him, the issue it keeps raising is not what Bloom has done but what he *is*, and his identity, even his physical appearance is determined by virtually everyone except himself. His magical powers of transformation seldom allow him to change himself into what he would like to be; the most radical transformations always proceed from what others tell him he is.

The first of the attacks upon Leopold I comes from the man in the macintosh who asserts that Bloom is not really Bloom but 'Leopold M'Intosh, the notorious fireraiser. His real name is Higgins' (p. 485). Bloom sweeps this challenge away with magical omnipotence: '(*A cannonshot. The Man in the macintosh disappears.* . . . *The instantaneous deaths of many powerful enemies, graziers, members of parliament, members of standing committees are reported.*)' (p. 485). The next attack, by Father Farley, strikes at a more vulnerable spot, Bloom's position as an agnostic or 'anythingarian' in Catholic Ireland. But Bloom is able to defuse that charge by proving his amiable personality; he sings a song, tells a joke, and Happy Holohan declares, 'Good old Bloom! There's nobody like him after all' (p. 491). The going gets rough, however, when the subject of Bloom's sex life is brought up, first by Purefoy, then by Dowie, and finally by a team of doctors headed by Buck Mulligan, sex specialist.

It is in the treatment of sex that 'Circe' most dramatically evokes the grotesque body, just as in Homer's epic it is through erotic attraction that men are ultimately turned into swine. Joyce's intention here goes quite beyond the exploration of Bloom's individual sex life; the mysterious figure of the androgyne becomes central to the novel, emerging as a comic grotesque not only in the New Bloomusalem sequence, but even more spectacularly in Bloom's confrontation with Bella Cohen. In both instances, the concern is with the very nature of sexual identity and the antipathy between male and female in the ribald epic of the human body.

That male and female had a common, bisexual origin is, of course, a widespread myth throughout the world, appearing in one form or another in both Eastern and Western religions, in the mystery of Yang and Yin, in Plato's *Symposium*, in Ovid's *Metamorphoses*, and in Jungian psychology. But if the hermaphrodite in myth is a figure of awe and mystery, in real life the occurrence of genuine or apparent hermaphroditism arouses horror and aversion. 'Androgyny is at the two poles of sacred things. Pure concept, pure vision of the spirit, it appears adorned with the highest qualities. But once made real in a being of flesh and blood, it is a monstrosity and no more; it is proof of the wrath of the gods falling on the unfortunate group in which it is manifested, and the unhappy individuals who reveal it are gotten rid of as soon as possible.'[16] In some societies, hermaphrodites were burnt alive; Diodorus of Sicily recounts how in 90 BC in Rome, a woman thought to have turned into a man was denounced by her husband and condemned by the Senate to be burnt (Delcourt, pp. 44–5). The Athenians also burned hermaphrodites, although their usual practice was to leave apparently bisexual infants exposed to perish. Androgynes were burnt in the Middle Ages in Europe; Amaury of Chartres was also burnt for teaching the androgyny of Adam before the Fall (p. 83). Even cocks thought to have laid eggs were consigned to the flames.[17] Joyce may have been familiar with these classical and medieval examples; if not, we have a remarkable coincidence here, for in both the New Bloomusalem and the Bella Cohen sequences Bloom is turned into a woman and is publicly burnt.[18]

Too often, critics missing the comic–mythic treatment of Bloom's transformation into a woman see it as merely a dramatisation of his psychosexual problems, and more than once Joyce has been cast as either sexual psychologist or sexual apologist, roles for which he is a peculiar candidate.[19] At the time he was writing *Ulysses*, Joyce referred to Jung as the Tweedledum in Zurich to differentiate him from the Tweedledee in Vienna.[20] The reason for his scorn is not hard to imagine, for modern alienists usually regard sex as the most serious thing in the world, while for Joyce – at least the Joyce who stands behind *Ulysses* – sex and all its improbable aberrations were riotously funny. Frank Budgen bears out what is implicit on every page of the novel: 'Joyce talked rarely of perversity or crime. One saw in him none of that natural awareness of sexual perversity characteristic of Proust, none of Dostoyevsky's preoccupation with the nightmare of crime. Both these aspects of life he saw from without, and in the main they were to him comic' (*James Joyce and the Making of* Ulysses, p. 187).

In the most outlandish confounding of the sexes, the confrontation between Bloom and Bella, the two must be considered as a pair, for it is as a pair that they represent both masculinity and femininity grotesquely conceived. The most stereotyped qualities of each sex are exaggerated and then super-imposed upon the other. Bella becomes a cigar-chomping, sadistic martinet resembling the Monster Maffei in the pulp novel *Ruby Pride of the Ring*, taking possession, blustering, and threatening, while Bloom becomes the simpering soubrette, coy, submissive, done up in curls and flounces, relegated to scullery work during the day and sexual exploitation at night. Moreover, what makes the parodies work so well is that the transformations in both cases are incomplete. Bloom is referred to alternately as 'him' and 'her', he has both testes and a vulva (both of which Bella/Bello assaults), and becomes the 'charming soubrette' without ever ceasing to be the cuckolded husband. 'What else are you good for, an impotent thing like you?' (p. 541). Conversely, Bella becomes the mustachioed Bello without ever ceasing to be a parody of a femme fatale with a series of deceased husbands whom she has buried under the jakes. She is a version of the Virago who had shouted abuse at Bloom (Virag) when he first entered night town. In trying to assess the spirit in which both partial changes of sex are offered, one could do no better than to keep in mind Delcourt's description of what happened to the androgynous religious rites of antiquity once they had been drained of awe and mystery. 'To begin with, reverence and fear surround [sex] with a mysterious atmosphere of taboo. When this fear is overcome, it dissolves into laughter, leaving no place for any intermediate feeling' (*Hermaphrodite*, p. 14). In 'Circe', it is neither male sexuality nor female sexuality that is the primary butt of the joke; rather, sexuality itself is seen as a joke upon humanity in general, a sexuality that runs rampant through all phases of human thought and behaviour, stripping away pretenses of order and decorum, transforming mythical heroes and goddesses into grotesque bodies. Much of the depiction of sexuality in 'Circe' is an elaboration – or, better, 'gigantising' – of a view set forth earlier in *Portrait*:

How foolish he had been! He had tried to build a breakwater of order and elegance against the sordid tide of life without him and to dam up, by rules of conduct and active interests and new filial relations, the powerful recurrence of the tides within him. Useless. From without as from within the water had flowed over his barriers: their tides began once more to jostle fiercely above the crumbled mole. . . . Beside the savage desire within him to realize the enormities which he brooded on nothing was sacred. He bore cynically with shameful details of his secret riots in which he exulted to defile with patience whatever image had attracted his eyes. By day and night he moved among distorted images of the outer world.

(pp. 98–9)

Secret riots, the realisation of enormities, the defilement of the sacred, movement among distorted images of the outer world – these are the prime matter of 'Circe'.

In the face of the shame and humiliation at the public exposure of his sex life, Bloom is offered two opposed ways of viewing the life of the grotesque body. The first, personified by the Nymph, is the same longing toward a classical ideal of a perfect and almost ethereal body that Bloom had experienced when revolted by human voraciousness at the end of 'Lestrygonians'. But that ideal has nothing to do with the realities of Bloomsbody. Though the Nymph begins by solacing Bloom, praising him for rescuing her picture from *Photo Bits*, she soon switches to reproaching him for making her an unwilling witness to the goings-on in the Bloom household. The result for Bloom is the same as the public revilement in the trial, New Bloomusalem, and Bella sequences: 'O, I have been a perfect pig' (p. 551). But, as so often with humiliated man in the fiction of the modern grotesque, there is a part of him that resists this self-appraisal furiously. He suddenly turns upon his own fleshless ideal, whereupon she turns into the nun who invented barbed wire, then into a Templar Knight who tries to castrate him, and finally into a hollow plaster statue that falls apart.

Exactly the opposite alternative literally pops down the chimney in the figure of Lipoti Virag, Bloom's Hungarian grandfather, a 'basilicogrammate', and one of the strangest grotesques of night town. A very libidinous grandfather, he is characterised mainly as a collection of nervous tics and twitches.[21] Like virtually everyone else in the chapter, Virag knows all about Bloom's proclivities, but rather than condemning them, he encourages cynical acceptance of bizarre lusts, though still at the same time mocking Bloom with their indignity. 'That suits your book, eh? Fleshpots of Egypt to hanker after. Wellow in it. Lycopodium. (*His throat twitches*.) Slapbang! There he goes again' (p. 513). A Surrealistic figure on stilts at his entrance, he goes through a series of transformations which, more than any others in the chapter, combine animal and human parts: weasel teeth, yellow parrot beak, turkey wattles, glowworm's nose, claws, a tail (which he chases), a mooncalf muzzle, tortured forepaws, a flickering phosphorescent scorpion tongue, a coalblack throat, sloughing skins, moulting plumage, and finally a detachable head which he unscrews. He mews, cackles, yelps, gibbers like a baboon, flutters like a moth, and (detached head only) quacks like a duck. He can best be considered as mere nervous energy, sexuality as twitchings of the grotesque body. He himself equates human sexuality with that of insects, and he seems the personification of Bloom's dictum, 'Instinct rules the world'.

Birth, food, sex, and death: these, I am arguing, are the four themes that dominate *Ulysses* as an epic of the body. Now birth, in contrast to the other three, receives fairly respectful treatment in the 'real' stratum of the novel. Stephen may imagine himself being tugged bloodily into the world, but the one actual birth that takes place, in 'Oxen of the Sun', is kept discreetly off stage, and even the parody of birth in 'Circe', as Bloom is discovered to be with child, is a very brief episode. But much, much more elaborate treatment is afforded to death in the night town chapter. All of Bloom's exploits in 'Circe' lead toward his death – by hanging, burning, precipitation from a cliff, or suicide by poison. His execution at the culmination of the New Bloomusalom episode seems to parallel the public execution parodies of 'Cyclops', except that the outlandish exaggeration is now tinged with genuine bitterness and world-weariness, a death wish rendered with the same odd combination of clowning and compassion that has all along characterised Joyce's stance toward his protagonist:

BLOOM

(*In caubeen with clay pipe stuck in the band, dusty brogues, an emigrant's red handkerchief bundle in his hand, leading a black bogoak pig by a sugaun, with a smile in his eye.*) Let me be going now, woman of the house, for by all the goats in Connemara I'm after

having the father and mother of a bating. *(With a tear in his eye.)*
All insanity. Patriotism, sorrow for the dead, music, future of
the race. To be or not to be. Life's dream is o'er. End it peacefully.
They can live on. *(He gazes far away mournfully.)* I am ruined. A
few pastilles of aconite. The blinds drawn. A letter. Then lie
back to rest. *(He breathes softly.)* No more. I have lived. Fare.
Farewell. . . . *(Bitterly.)* Man and woman, love, what is it? A
cork and a bottle.

(p. 499)

When the antipathy between self and other becomes so all-
encompassing as to be beyond any hope of compromise or
reconciliation, the outcome can only be an overwhelming will
toward the destruction of one or the other. The repeated death
wishes and fantastic demises of Mr. Bloom by immolation and
suicide reflect the bitter and pervasive self-effacing side of his
nature. But in the episodes centred around Stephen, who would
insist that his country die for him, the characteristic alternative
is apocalypse, the destruction of the other which refuses to
accommodate the self.

The first apocalypse of the chapter is a drollery occasioned by
Florry's remark that she had read that the last day was scheduled
to arrive later that summer. The End of the World that appears,
however, is a parody of A. E.'s theophrastic symbols, a two-
headed singing octopus with a Scottish accent and a kilt. It is
attended by a retinue of playful grotesques: Punch Costello as a
Lipoti Virag-like Hobgoblin, 'His jaws chattering, capering to and
fro, goggling his eyes, squeeking, kangaroohopping'; Rueben J.
Dodd as antichrist, with his half-drowned son dangling from a
boatpole over his shoulder; the hucksterish Elijah of Alexander
Dowie, shouting, 'Are you a god or a doggone clod?' (p. 507).
Such drollery is quite in keeping with Stephen's ironic detachment
at this point; he is drunk but still calm and in control of himself.
But as the chapter nears it conclusion, all of Dublin, and by
implication all the world, seems to move not toward one great goal
but toward one great chaos, culminating in the hue and cry as
Bloom and Stephen leave the brothel, and the apocalyptic vision
they encounter outside. Beginning with Stephen's dance of death,
the pace of the chapter becomes almost frenetic as the world, like
the dancers, spins toward dissolution and even the style of the
writing seems to veer toward the phonetic mayhem that had closed

'Oxen of the Sun'. '(*Bang fresh barang bang of lacquey's bell, horse, nag, steer, piglings, Conmee of Christass lame crutch and leg sailor in cockboat armfolded ropepulling hitching stamp hornpipe through and through, Baraabum!)*' (p. 579).

The Pandemonium sequence which follows is an explosion of the world of the novel itself, a brilliant collage of visual images in chaotic flux. The episode, on the simplest level, corresponds to Stephen's drunken hysteria, his private view of the world as driven by violence and beyond hope of redemption. Stephen *wants* to see Dublin burning because its existence affronts him, and that is the final measure of his estrangement, disgust, and arrogance. But on a level that has little to do with Stephen's personal struggle, Pandemonium, along with the hue and cry that precedes it, is a compendium of the 'Circe' chapter in much the same way that the chapter is a compendium of the novel. It completes the movement begun as early as the parodies in 'Cyclops', toward a nightmare vision of history, animated by perverseness, by human fondness for turmoil for its own sake. Dragon teeth sprout mythical heroes who turn out to be a mixture of historical persons and nonsense figures who engage each other in combat. Tom Rochford, a Dublin hero who had saved men from death, leads a footrace toward a lemming-like leap into the void. The last judgement becomes a juxtaposition of Godsbody and dogsbody, as Malachi O'Flynn's Black Mass celebrated on the pregnant body of Mina Purefoy becomes the culminating image of the grotesque body in its endless permutations.

FATHER MALACHI O'FLYNN
(Takes from the chalice and elevates a blooddripping host.)
Corpus Meum.

THE REVEREND MR HAINES LOVE
(Raises high behind the celebrant's petticoats, revealing his grey bare hairy buttocks between which a carrot is stuck.)
My body.

THE VOICE OF ALL THE DAMNED
Htengier Tnetopinmo Dog Drol eht rof, Aiulella!
(From on high the voice of Adonai calls.)

ADONAI
Dooooooooooog!

THE VOICE OF ALL THE BLESSED
Alleluia, for the Lord God Omnipotent reigneth!
(From on high the voice of Adonai calls.)

ADONAI
Goooooooooood!

(pp. 599–600)

Throughout, the novel has utilised the mock heroic, but here we have a rarer thing, the mock demonic. This is a sham apocalypse without real god or real devil, and its culmination is not universal dissolution but Private Carr's drunken assault upon the drunken Stephen. The final comment seems to belong not to any of the characters, but, appropriately enough, to a dog:

THE RETRIEVER
(Barking furiously.) Ute ute ute ute ute ute ute ute.

(p. 601)

The odyssey through ribald and raucous nightmares ends with 'Circe', but the epic of the body does not. Two kinds of over-simplification must be avoided when we try to determine whether or not the demons conjured up in 'Circe' are exorcised. One false solution posits a kind of psychological *deus ex machina* – be it artistic self-discovery, recovered masculinity, ersatz fatherhood to surrogate sonship, or simply some kind of Bloomesque good-heartedness – by which the horrors of 'Circe' are laid to rest. Another would cast Joyce himself in the role of misanthrope and scoffer, indifferently paring his nails above a tale of mockery and nihilism. There are no easy solutions offered for the problems explored fantastically in 'Circe'. In fact, the grotesque has been evoked primarily in order to strip away solutions and everyday rationalisations, by shock tactics where necessary, and the situation does not improve in 'Ithaca'.

While 'Circe' gigantised all facets of the life of Mr. Bloom, 'Ithaca' takes exactly the opposite tack and reduces him 'by cross multiplication of reverses of fortune . . . and by elimination of all positive values to a negligible negative irrational unreal quantity' (p. 725). The result of such reduction declines from being an 'eccentric public laughing-stock seated on bench of public park under discarded perforated umbrella', to the nadir of misery, 'the aged impotent disfranchised ratesupported moribund lunatic pauper' (p. 725). Even if such a personal decline could be avoided, there would still be 'catastrophic cataclysms which make terror the basis of human mentality: seismic upheavals the epicentres of which are located in densely populated regions: the fact of vital growth through convulsions of metamorphosis from infancy through maturity to decay' (p. 697). Beyond earthly terrors there are the incertitude of the void, the chill of interstellar space, and the indifference of the stars.

These are not small problems, and the novel does not present anything I would call a solution to them. But it does present a complementary, radically altered perspective from which they can be viewed. The question is not so much whether the value of life is affirmed or denied by *Ulysses*, as upon what terms an affirmation or denial (or both simultaneously) can be made. I would suggest that the terms are those of the grotesque body itself. As Stephen and Bloom contemplate the vastness of space and the insignificance of all human life, they are not just contemplating; they are also urinating – against the garden wall of Bloom's house, and each is concerned as much with his own and the other's micturation as with the incertitude and indifference of the cosmos. In this novel, man does not just contemplate the void; he voids into it.

So too, when Bloom returns to his parlour, a lonely, sonless cuckold, bleakness is counterpoised against his pleasure at unbracing and undressing, his attention to a protruding nail on his big toe, his contemplation of the 'candour, nudity, pose, tranquility, youth, grace, sex, counsel of a statue erect in the centre of the table, an image of Narcissus . . .' (p. 710), and by 'the proximity of an occupied bed, obviating research: the anticipation of warmth (human) tempered with coolness (linen), obviating desire and rendering desirable' (p. 728). Once he has gotten into that bed, his equanimity after a day of frustration, humiliation, and defeat is prompted not alone by resignation to the apathy of the stars, but also by 'Satisfaction at the ubiquity in eastern and western hemispheres, in all habitable lands and islands explored or unexplored . . . of adipose posterior female hemispheres, redolent of milk and honey and of excretory sanguine and seminal warmth, reminiscent of secular families of curves of amplitude, insusceptible of moods of impression or of contrarieties of expression, expressive of mute immutable mature animality' (p. 734).

Such mature animality is the constant companion of the void in *Ulysses*, its antithesis, and, in a limited but very immediate way, its antidote. The brutality and banality of life are constantly confronted by the grotesque body, copulating and procreating, devouring and excreting, moving always toward death but with an onrush of animal vitality.

The most perplexing problem posed by *Ulysses* is whether it is possible not only to affirm something while mocking it but to affirm it *by* mocking it, to assent to something by exposing it as ludicrous. It would appear so, and such laughter arises from opposing the high against the low and coming out unabashedly on the side of the low, because the low is *immediate*, because it is all we can be sure we have. *Ulysses* shows us a cold universe populated by warm bodies. The laughter does not mitigate the void, but stands coequal with it, producing a duality, a complementary mirth.

The same duality runs through Molly's long soliloquy and accounts for all the contradictions it contains. She finds the male body physically disgusting but cannot keep her mind off it very long. Like Bloom, she has a classical ideal, the statue of Narcissus, desirable for its proportion, restraint, and cleanliness; but these very qualities lead her to imagine performing fellatio. She finds Bloom's personal habits repulsive, but recognises him as a better man than Boylan, and is aware of the uses that can be made of her husband's proclivities to get what she wants. She views sex as something inflicted upon women by men, but reflects on her lovemaking with Boylan, 'O thanks to the great God I got somebody to give me what I badly wanted to put some heart up into me youve no chance at all in this place' (p. 758). She considers her female body a curse with its periods and childbearing, but she is also enamoured of it and preoccupied with its beautification. The salvo of affirmation that concludes her revery is not affirmation of life in general but of physicality, especially her own physicality, erotically, even grossly conceived, as the instrument by which the self is realised and enjoyed. Bloom, Stephen, and Molly are all in their separate ways both lovers and haters of the grotesque body, and the two attitudes form important poles of the novel. To love the physical dimension of existence is to accept and affirm the basest drives and functions that are the foundation of bodily life: 'his mad crazy letters my Precious one everything connected with your glorious Body everything underlined that comes from it is a thing of beauty and of joy for ever' (p. 771). But to reject it is to reject the only existence man may be sure of – full of warmth and pleasure for which he may and will pawn his pretensions to dignity, harmony, and order.

Not all of Bakhtin's model of the grotesque is applicable to *Ulysses*, but it was Bakhtin who pointed out that one function of the raucous laughter provoked by the grotesque body was triumph over cosmic terror, terror not of the supernatural but of the immeasurable, the infinitely powerful – the starry sky, the gigantic masses of the mountains, the cosmic upheavals, the terrestrial catastrophies – the very things cited in 'Ithaca' as making terror the basis of human mentality. In *Ulysses*, the triumph is equivocal, not the universal folk laughter heard by Bakhtin in Rabelais, but hilarity in the play of contrasts between the cosmic and the mundane, the heroic and the ludicrous, the nightmarish and the erotic in fantasy. In Kafka, the play element of the grotesque was grim, self-mocking, often hard to discern. But in *Ulysses* the riotous spirit of play – play with language and form, parodic play with episode and character, the artificer's play with his own creation – seems often in danger of exploding the novel.

Bakhtin said of the grotesque in Rabelais: 'All that is sacred and exalted is rethought on the level of the material bodily stratum or else combined and mixed with its images. We spoke of the grotesque swing, which brings together heaven and earth. But the accent is placed not on the upward movement but on the descent' (p. 371). *Ulysses* is an epic of the body, and it is as Bloomsbody that its hero completes his journey, the childman weary, the manchild in the womb. And it is to that sense of physical existence, riotous and unheeding, gross and ludicrous, grotesque and indomitable that the novel addresses its final 'Yes.'

4

Insanity as a Point of View

I

In *The Tin Drum*, Oskar Matzerath says of Leo Schugger: 'I knew that one sunny day while he was still at the seminary, the world, the sacraments, the religions, heaven and earth, life and death had been so shaken up in his mind that forever after his vision of the world, though mad, had been radiant and perfect' (p. 167). The idea that the lunatic may have something to say to the supposedly sane world is not new. The figure of the prophet and poet touched with divine madness is well-known from classical antiquity, and the Renaissance was particularly aware of what possibilities lay in using a lunatic as commentator on the world, the dual peaks being *King Lear* and *Don Quixote*.[1] In real life, too, the Elizabethans and Jacobeans regarded the antics of the deranged as both amusing and intriguing, perhaps in part for reasons spelled out by Robert Burton in his *Anatomy of Melancholy*:

> But see the *Madman* rage down right
> With furious looks, a ghastly sight.
> Naked in chains bound doth he lie,
> And roars amain he knows not why!
> Observe him; for as in a glass
> Thine angry portraiture it was.
> His picture keep still in thy presence.
> 'Twixt him and thee, there's no difference.[2]

As I noted in an earlier chapter, Karl Jaspers, among other modern psychologists, was interested in certain forms of psychosis as world-views which make perfect sense to those that hold them but cannot be shared by those around them. More recently, R. D. Laing has argued that the world, at least the Western world as it is presently constituted, is itself based on schizophrenia and that certain kinds of schizophrenia, far from being aberrations, are inevitable responses to modern experience, and should be recognised as healthful and creative states of mind.[3]

94

Two features of insanity as a way of looking at the world are of immediate interest here: first, the relationship between madness and the grotesque; and second, the technique of a conspicuous number of twentieth-century writers by which the reins of a novel are delivered into the hands of a first person narrator who is insane or quite possibly insane, thereby making the world of the novel the world as he experiences it.

Insanity in its most agitated forms, as in Burton's description, deprives the individual of those qualities by which we usually describe human dignity or even define human identity: the power to reason, the power to speak intelligibly, the power to control bodily motions, the power to maintain normal postures such as sitting or standing, a correlation intelligible to others between intentions and actions, between physical surroundings and the response to them. In extreme cases, madness can produce an individual who is grotesque in the sense in which I am using the term.[4] Michel Foucault has pointed out the connection between madness and animalism in the view of the seventeenth century.

But there was a certain image of animality that haunted the hospitals of the period. Madness borrowed its face from the mask of the beast. Those chained to the cell walls were no longer men whose minds had wandered, but beasts preyed upon by a natural frenzy: as if madness, at its extreme point, freed from that moral unreason in which its most attenuated forms are enclosed, managed to rejoin, by a paroxysm of strength, the immediate violence of animality. . . . For Classicism, madness in its ultimate form is man in relation to his animality, without other reference, without any recourse.[5]

If madness can suggest to a rationalistic viewer the animal nature of man and can simulate the primitive rage below the patina of civilisation, madness can also fascinate, for it is a foreign and frightening way of life, a form of knowledge, of alien knowledge certainly, but knowledge nonetheless. It is the very *otherness* of the madman's view that can often make his observations unsettling; he can see, and can admit he sees, things that the sane man with a vested interest in the sane world must ignore, repress, or flatly deny. And when modern man confronts his primitive self in the avatar of the lunatic, such alien knowledge is essentially magical. As in the sophisticate's response to primitive magic, there is fascination-repulsion in our response to madness, together with the nervous intuition that it may embody some truth inaccessible to reason and 'reality'. Thus our response to madness is similar to our response to the grotesque, may, in some cases, be identical to it.

In the fiction of the modern grotesque, madness is often linked with physical deformity such as dwarfism (*The Tin Drum*), gigantism (*One Flew Over the Cuckoo's Nest*), or generally bizarre appearance, dress, and behaviour (*Pale Fire, Watt*). More daring, however, is the use of insanity as a point of view, a means of transforming the literal world of surfaces and possible events into a fluid, deranged, fantasy world, filled with significance and populated by grotesques.

'Granted: I am an inmate of a mental hospital.'[6] Once that has been granted of a narrator in the opening line of a novel, a great deal more may have to be granted before the story is over. Any author who ostensibly seats a lunatic at the controls of a novel necessarily undermines the 'reality' of the fictive world about to be created. Indeed, an elaborate game of hide and seek may become the whole point of the novel, as the author, standing always behind his narrator, is forever tripping him up, planting half-hidden clues by which the reader can partially separate what is actually happening from what the deranged narrator says is happening. Though Grass does not play the game quite as elaborately as Nabokov, the use of an unreliable first person narrator is a frequent device of his fiction. Oskar, Pilenz, Brauxel, Matern, Liebenau, Starusch, and the fish all give us plenty of reason to doubt them. They all have private axes to grind, and many have guilt to cover up; all are obsessed with the past they are narrating, and for many that obsession is the reason for narrating. They hedge their statements, revise previously narrated versions of events, use apparently fanciful conjecture, and sidle cautiously up to their own past misdeeds. Several are fond of referring to themselves in the third person, thus obscuring where the first person narrator leaves off and where the authorial voice takes up.

Among this bizarre gallery of deranged narrators, however, Oskar Matzerath is unique and preeminent, not only because of the brilliance of the characterisation, but because of Grass's ability to use his narrator as a perspective, a way of seeing and presenting a whole epoch of collective madness. A sizeable portion of Western civilisation went berserk, ran amok, and destroyed everything in sight including itself. Had they not had their historical reality, some of the leaders of Nazi Germany could only be conceived of as outlandish caricatures veering toward the fantastic, the delusional, the grotesque. Presenting a mad epoch through the eyes of a madman in one of those strokes, like Swift's Lilliput, the genius of which lies in its simplicity, its obviousness. Once the transformation has been made, however, the possibilities become absolutely limitless. When history becomes so bizarrely improbable, improbability becomes an instrument of the artist, an instrument which Grass uses with daring and precision.

The triumph of Grass's technique in *The Tin Drum* is a balancing act by which he keeps the novel suspended between two worlds, the historical and the fantastic, while making both seem equally improbable and equally convincing. Basically there are three kinds of events in the novel: (1) those which we know to be true because they are historical (the annexation of Danzig, the invasion of Normandy, the currency reform, etc.); (2) events that are not historical but could have occurred pretty much as Oskar describes them (Agnes Matzerath's affair with Jan Bronski, Susi Kater's feeding Oskar some of the children's brick soup, Oskar's taking a job as a stone cutter); (3) events that range from the highly improbable to the utterly impossible in the world as we know it (Oskar's deliberate refusal to grow, his singing glass to smithereens across long distances, his controlling people with his drum). It is the third category that is of most interest, because it is through such incidents that Grass transforms the historical world of Nazi Germany and the bourgeois postwar era into the grotesque private world of his narrator.[7]

Narrator, I have said. So crafty is the author's technique in this novel, so tantalising are his games, that it is not possible to say with certainty how many narrators there are. Twice the story is purportedly turned over to others, first to Bruno, Oskar's nurse, and then to Oskar's friend, Vittlar, and their testimony seems to substantiate some of Oskar's most fantastic claims about himself. His story, then, must be 'true' and the world as he sees it must be the 'real' world of the novel.[8] On the other hand, we must never forget who controls the paper supply in his madhouse; there is no reason to believe that there has been a change in narrators just because Oskar says there has. William Cunliffe notes with some perplexity that Bruno's style is exactly the same as Oskar's, 'characterised by the same elaborate hypotactical participles'.[9] This similarity is certainly not due to a limitation on Grass's part; he commands a wide range of narrative styles, and in *Dog Years* each of the three narrators has a distinct voice and set of mannerisms. Moreover, Oskar and Bruno consistently refer to the latter's writing in the present – that is, Bruno is writing while Oskar is telling him the story. That in itself would be a difficult task unless one were skilled in shorthand, and we must remember, Bruno is a nurse, not a secretary. But in addition, both also declare that while Oskar was speaking, Bruno was secretly (in his pocket? behind his back?) working on one of his string sculptures which he drops accidentally as Oskar concludes part of his tale.

At the end of the chapter, Oskar supposedly resumes his own account: 'Without bothering to read over what Bruno my keeper has written, I, Oskar, take up my pen again' (p. 424). Without bothering to read it? A few pages later we find: 'As Bruno has already said, Oskar has lovely, expressive hands, fine wavy hair, and those winning, ever so blue, Bronski eyes' (p. 437). I do not think we can attribute all this to sloppiness about detail, because Grass is elsewhere anything but careless in such matters. More likely he is playing games with us and there is no change in narrators. It is Oskar, *all* Oskar.

Similar peculiarities surround Vittlar's statement – indeed, Vittlar's very existence. Toward the end of the novel, he appears to Oskar as if out of nowhere, sitting languidly in an apple tree. 'You don't see Vittlar at first. According to his surroundings, he can make himself look like a thread, a scarecrow, a clothestree, or the limb of a tree. That indeed is why I failed to notice him when I sat on the cable drum and he lay in the apple tree. The dog didn't even bark, for dogs can neither see, smell, nor bark at an angel' (p. 563). We are never quite clear about whose idea it was that Vittlar was a serpent in the apple tree in the Garden of Eden. In Oskar's account Vittlar suggests the parallel, but in Vittlar's 'statement' the idea is described as an obsession of Oskar's which Vittlar himself could never understand. If the reader feels himself to be stumbling through a Nabokovian house of mirrors, that is because indefiniteness is endemic to a story whose narrator is not only unreliable but cunning and quite probably mad.[10]

With the outlandish in human behaviour being both the principle of characterisation and the novel's centre of interest, Grass plays deftly with the boundaries of credibility, never allowing us to be quite certain at what point behaviour becomes so outlandish that we must conclude that the narrator is no longer sticking to real events, historical or not. We can never quite pin down at what point credulity rebels and we see the narrator, and behind him the author, making mad additions and grotesque embellishments. By raising the question of Oskar's sanity and then refusing to settle it finally, Grass creates a fluidity of perspective, multiplying the possibilities for bizarre incidents by diminishing the differences between sane and insane, subjective and objective, historical and fantastic – a fluidity that proves invaluable in dealing with a period when history was fantastic and behaviour insanity on an international scale. History may explain the causes and effects of the Nazi era, but only madness can catch its flavour.

When we are most forcibly led to suspect that Oskar is confounding plausible reality with insane delusion, the thing at stake for him is always the same: the desire to be master of events rather than victim. His size is a case in point. One version of events which the book makes plausible is that Oskar stopped growing as a result of an accidental fall into the cellar on his third birthday. Oskar is the victim, condemned to life as a dwarf by adult carelessness (Matzerath had left the cellar door open) and bad luck. But the version Oskar would have us believe is that he had a fully developed adult mentality at birth, consciously rejected Matzerath's bourgeois world, and staged the accident carefully and deliberately, thus taking charge of his own destiny and, as a fringe benefit, changing the paternal Matzerath 'into a guilty Matzerath' (p. 63).

Even greater ambiguity surrounds his resumption of growth toward the end of Book Two. In the course of five pages, he twice reverses himself about crucial events he had already narrated, claiming now that Matzerath's death was not an accident but that he, Oskar, had deliberately engineered it because he was 'sick of dragging a father around with him all his life' (p. 404). Then, standing at Matzerath's grave, Oskar tells us, he had decided to grow and replace Matzerath, hoping that Kurt would at last recognise his true father. He threw the drum into the grave and as the pile of sand on it began to grow, 'I too began to grow; the first symptom being a violent nosebleed' (p. 405). Four pages later, however, we get a disingenuous reversal of this account.

It was only when that stone hit me at Matzerath's funeral in Saspe Cemetery that I began to grow.

Stone, Oskar has said. I had better fill in my record of the
events at the cemetery.

(p. 409)

It turns out that while Oskar was reaching his 'decision' to grow,
Kurt, who had been throwing stones at a bird, threw one at Oskar,
hitting him in the head and, in the view of the adults, reversing
the effects of the original accident. Once again, in one version, the
one he would have us believe, Oskar is the magical controller, but
in another, the one that the novel implies, he is the pathetic victim.

The guessing game is even carried over into Grass's later novels.
According to Oskar's account in *The Tin Drum*, his miraculous glass
shattering abilities caused the Dusters to regard him as semi-
divine, and Störtebeker, without argument or hesitation, turned
over leadership of the gang to him. But the youth who led the
gang under the pirate's name, 'Störtebeker', surfaces again as the
narrator of *Local Anaesthetic*, Eberhard Starusch, now a middle-
aged schoolteacher living in West Berlin in the 1960s. According
to his version, he, as Störtebeker, maintained control of the gang
right up till their capture while pillaging a church. By that time
they had taken as a mascot a retarded dwarf with a child's tin
drum who was something of a town character. That they should
victimise such a pathetic creature was taken as a measure of their
depravity, and Störtebeker was packed off to a penal battalion at
the front. Starusch's version is substantiated in *Dog Years* by Harry
Liebenau who claims to have hung around the fringes of the gang,
and in *Cat and Mouse* by Pilenz who had the story second hand
from Hochwürden Gusewski.[11] What is of interest here is not
which version is 'true' but the essential difference that separates
the insane fantasy from the quite possible reality. In one version,
Oskar is a magical, powerful figure who always exercises choice,
controls those around him, and retreats into his disguise (again,
by choice) only to protect himself after the gang is captured. In
the other version, Oskar is a freak, is controlled by those around
him, and is merely a mascot, a kind of grotesque ornament.

But Oskar's possible lunacy is only one element in his idiosyncratic reading of events; for two-thirds of the novel he is also Oskar,
the permanent three-year-old. For Grass, the view from below
seems to have been a most important aspect of the character as a
way of seeing. By the author's own account, Oskar began as a
figure looking down from atop a pillar, a stylite who was to be the

subject of a series of poems, but the undertaking came to nothing. 'One afternoon on a passing occasion, I saw among adults drinking coffee a three-year-old boy who was carrying a tin drum round his neck. What struck me and stayed with me was the total dedication of the three-year-old to his instrument, also the way in which he ignored the adult world.' According to Grass, only Oskar's childish stature offered the right combination of mobility and distance, and made of the narrator a stylite in reverse.[12]

Now, the use of a child as an interpreter of the grown-up world is anything but new in twentieth-century fiction, but it comes new in Grass's hands given his strange and completely unsentimental view of childhood. At Oskar's first day in school, the teacher, Fräulein Spollenhauer, is at first intrigued by the little freak and his toy drum. 'For a moment she became a not unpleasant old maid, who had forgotten her prescribed occupational caricature and became human, that is, childlike, curious, complex and immoral' (p. 80). Curiosity, complexity, and immorality are the defining features of Oskar's viewpoint, and are, in fact, typical of all Grass's demon-children. Childhood, far from being a state of innocence, is in closer touch with the quirkiness, cruelty, and *Schadenfreude* of human nature than is the adult sensibility, encumbered as it is with responsibility and an acquired and often ludicrous moral code: 'Just think of all the innocent grandmothers who were once loathsome, spiteful infants' (p. 499).

In Grass's fiction, especially *The Tin Drum*, the gulf between children's perceptions and those of adults is wider than we are accustomed to finding in modern child-centred novels, and the disparity between the two is relentlessly stressed, largely because the children themselves are so fully aware of it. The child's world is not an analogue of the adult world but a 'cunning little existence' set totally apart. By way of contrast, William Golding has also given us a grim and convincing account of childhood, but in *Lord of the Flies* the child's world is a microcosm of society at large. The child is father of the man, and everything that is wrong with men is wrong in miniature with children. But in Grass, the child is strangely, chillingly autonomous; the child is father of the child and he will brook no other father, not even a presumptive one. In his casual and natural egocentricity, the child is an alien in the adult world, and, in fact, its implacable enemy.

But, of course, Oskar is no ordinary child, even by Grass's standards, and insists he was never a true child at all but was born 'clairaudient', with a fully developed critical awareness of all that was going on around him. Still, in the first two books of the novel, Oskar combines this adult sensibility with ways of seeing and thinking that are characteristically child-like, and it is these ways that literally animate the novel. Jean Piaget tells us that as a child's conception of the world comes to include a differentiation between himself and external reality, 'the self assumes magical powers and . . . in return, things are endowed with consciousness and life'.[13] Moreover, 'the majority of objects or events which the child tries to influence by magic (when he has no other way of acting on them) appear to him to be full of feeling and intentions, either friendly or hostile' (p. 160). Oskar at birth is not only aware of the difference between the self and the external world, he is appalled by it. Attributing to himself the magical powers to understand and evaluate the promises made for him by his parents, he rejects the shopkeeper's world of his father in favour of the three-year-old drummer's world promised by his mother. He is encouraged in this decision by a moth which, like himself, has a secret but urgently busy inner life: 'the moth chattered away as if in haste to unburden itself of its knowledge, as though it had no time for future colloquies with sources of light, as though this dialogue were its last confession; and as though after the kind of absolution that light bulbs confer, there would be no further occasion for sin or folly' (p. 47). Oskar's world is, and continues to be, a child's world largely because it is magical and animistic, because everything in it is conceived of as being alive and possessing a quirky, unmistakably human consciousness, a kind of psychic underground whose existence is not even suspected by stolid adults like Alfred Matzerath.[14] 'Today I know that everything watches, that nothing goes unseen, and that even wallpaper has a better memory than ours. It isn't God in His heaven that sees all. A kitchen chair, a coathanger, a half filled ash tray or the wooden replica of a woman named Niobe, can perfectly well serve as an unforgetting witness to every one of our acts' (pp. 192–3).

Usually when Oskar projects life and consciousness onto an inanimate object, the attitude that he envisions it as having is a reflection of his own attitude toward it or toward his immediate surroundings. On his first day at school, he sees clouds scudding along and observes that clouds obviously have no school that day. When he succeeds in climbing the adult-size stairway of the Stockturm, the stairway has lost the courage of its convictions. A scratched mirror has ceased to take itself seriously. Above all, the zaniness, the casual cruelty, the irresistible attraction of the perverse which characterise so much of human experience as rendered by Oskar is imputed to the inanimate objects he endows with life. For instance, there are the armoured cars that take part in the siege of the Polish Post Office. 'What fun they were having! Back and forth they drove rat-tat-tatting from behind their armour and looking things over: two young ladies intent on culture and so eager to visit the castle, but the castle was still closed. Spoiled young things they were, just couldn't wait to get in. Bursting with impatience, they cast penetrating, lead-grey glances, all of the same calibre, into every visible room in the castle, making things hot, cold and uncomfortable for the castellans' (p. 233). Later in the scene, when a shell mortally wounds Kobyella, it is endowed with a thoroughly Oskarian outlook. 'Lord, what a sense of humor that projectile had: bricks laughed themselves into splinters and splinters into dust, plaster turned to flour, wood found its ax, the whole silly nursery hopped on one foot' (p. 234).

It would be difficult to overemphasise the importance of such animism in creating the idiosyncratic world of *The Tin Drum*. Many critics have noted the emphasis given to objects in Grass's fiction, but 'object fixation' is the wrong way to describe what is happening here.[15] It is not a matter of fascination with objects, but an uncanny ability to capture the child-like intuition of all things possessing a secret life of their own, and to convince us on paper of its imaginative validity.

Another feature of Oskar's child-like point of view is the importance he ascribes to play, not only as an activity in itself, but as a way of coping with experience. When faced with the ghastly, Oskar and, under his influence, other characters devote their full attention and energy to play. The tin drum itself is not an adult-size musical instrument but a child's toy, and Oskar's principal source of power is his ability to use it to captivate his hearers and drum them back to their own childhoods, as he does in the Onion Cellar. Frequently in the novel, play serves as a last refuge when the situation is so hopeless that no serious action could improve things, and reversion to play is no more nor less insane than any other possible course. Such is the case in the basement of the Polish Post Office when the mortally wounded Kobyella, the doomed, hysterical Jan, and the perfectly calm Oskar play a few hands of skat while waiting for the Nazis to storm the building.

But play *can* confer a kind of immunity from disaster on those who, child-like, can enter its magic circle. Kobyella does not die as long as he keeps his mind on the game.

The most striking example of play as a protective rite in a dangerous world occurs in the Niobe episode. The carved figure is one of a series of embodiments of an eternal, destructive female principle, counterbalanced against the eternal, nurturing female principle represented by Anna Bronski. Herbert Truczinski is immune from Niobe, however, as long as he has Oskar along to protect him, and as long as he himself, under Oskar's influence, reverts to childhood, defusing the danger by reducing it to play.

> We felt safe. With a malignant cackle, Herbert drove a nail into her kneecap: my knee hurt at every stroke, she didn't even flick an eyelash. Right under her eyes, we engaged in all sorts of silly horseplay. Herbert put on the overcoat of a British admiral, took up a spyglass, and donned the admiral's hat that went with it. With a little red jacket and full-bottomed wig I transformed myself into the admiral's pageboy. We played Trafalgar, bombarded Copenhagen, dispersed Napoleon's fleet at Aboukir, rounded this cape and that cape, took historical poses, and then again contemporary poses. All this beneath the eyes of Niobe, the figurehead carved after the proportions of a Dutch witch.
>
> (p. 192)

But when Oskar is forbidden to accompany Herbert into the museum, the detachment of play is lost; adult obsession replaces it and Herbert is killed trying to rape the statue.

The Tin Drum, Cat and Mouse, and *Dog Years* continually juxtapose child's play against the fearsome realities of life in Nazi Germany, dramatising the perverse human impulse to perform jigs and cartwheels on the precipice of disaster. Further, such juxtaposition provides the vehicle for the inversion of values that is an essential part of most first rate satire. The momentous events of the adult world are relegated to triviality while the trivialities of childhood are invested with central importance. That Poland is being invaded and the Second World War is breaking out is of no concern; the important thing is getting a new drum, and as far as Oskar is concerned, the drum is every bit as important to the SS Home Guards as it is to him. A sense of such topsy-turvy is crucial to the novel's whole treatment of history. From atop the diving tower (that is, on trial for his life), Oskar has a vision of a world in which the cataclysmic and the trivial exist simultaneously without there being any real difference between them. That aircraft carriers are sinking each other in the Pacific is of no importance to a woman in Lima who is teaching her parrot to say 'Caramba'. In fact, much of the heartlessness and amorality of Oskar's viewpoint arise precisely because he refuses to abandon the detachment of play when disaster overtakes the grown-ups. He has to keep himself from laughing when he sees Herbert impaled on the statue; the grotesque death is just a surprise outcome of their previous games. The fire that consumes Danzig is playing and enjoying itself tremendously. Matzerath's horrible death is merely one incident in an extremely busy world, and Oskar really cannot bother much about it because he has ants to watch and lice to inspect. In a passage I cited in the opening chapter of this study, the massacre of 4000 children is depicted as a ride on the merry-go-round.

This extension of play to ghastly events is not just a quirk of Oskar's, but governs the book's whole treatment of history. In a play situation, the impermissible becomes permissible, and the more deeply we are immersed in play the truer this becomes. In the course of the novel, Grass surprises us at our capacity to snicker at things we know no compassionate or reasonable person should find at all funny. It seems to me that this unpleasant self-discovery, far more than the novel's supposedly obscene or blasphemous content, accounts for the brouhaha, especially in Germany, that greeted the book's publication. We know we cannot sanction Oskar's moral viewpoint; we would like to feel we cannot even imaginatively participate in it. Yet time and time again, at the most brutal parts of the story, it intrigues, amuses, and positively appeals to us. Thus the reader is denied the opportunity to congratulate himself on his capacity to be appalled by the brutality of others. It is precisely that opportunity that dozens of senstive, compassionate, morally anguished accounts of the Nazi era have offered in sodden abundance, and few blandishments are more alluring than an author's invitation to share his moral outrage. Instead, Grass outrages the reader. He does so with great skill and malice aforethought. Sometimes he does so grossly, as in the infamous eel-catching scene, and usually with an infectious *Schadenfreude* that obliterates the position of moral superiority always desired when appraising the monstrosities of others. The ultimate purpose of such *Schadenfreude* is to arrive at horror and aversion by the back door, to take our moral sensibilities by surprise. No one since Swift has done this more daringly or successfully than Günter Grass when he is writing about the real enormities of our century. When his target is mere bourgeois smugness and materialism, something goes wrong with his fiction. The bizarre inventiveness is still there, but the combination of heinous subject matter and shock tactic presentation is not, and things can get a bit turgid. Perversity, obsession, destructiveness, and atrocity are the subjects he deals with best, and no one in our time has dealt with them as well.

In *The Tin Drum*, the child-like perspective is essential to the emergence of the grotesque. The world of the child, like that of the lunatic, is inherently magical, and what most of us like to regard as the laws of causation and the limits of possibility in everyday experience are simply done away with, replaced by forces more powerful and primal. It is in such a world that the grotesque flourishes and has always flourished. It is no accident that the Black Cook, a grotesque symbol for all that is monstrous in human experience, is conjured up from a children's marching game played by Susi Kater and her friends just before they give little Oskar his first taste of gratuitous human cruelty.[16]

The narrator as lunatic, the narrator as child; there is another important aspect of Oskar's viewpoint which we must consider, the narrator as artist/hero, and specifically an artist of the grotesque. The transmutation of the ugly and outlandish into an aesthetic object is the most insistently repeated action in *The Tin Drum*. There is absolutely nothing in the novel which cannot be turned into an art object or at least perceived aesthetically. Even his mother's coffin impresses Oskar because of its exquisite taper at the foot end, and it becomes the standard against which all future coffins are to be measured. His enamel bed in the mental hospital is admired by both Oskar and by Bruno for its ideal whiteness. The adulterous triangle of Agnes, Alfred, and Jan is valued for its symmetry and balance, and Jan's card house, built as World War II begins, strikes Oskar as the architectural ideal, since he can never see a building going up without picturing the same building coming down. The scars on Herbert Truczinki's back become objects of aesthetic appreciation for Oskar and the muse of narration for Herbert. Klepp's revolting spaghetti is 'a culinary ideal, by which from that day on I have measured every menu that is set before me' (p. 505). For Oskar, the severed ring finger in its preserving jar is not only a fetish and an idol, but also a religious art object. His flight to Paris is a movie scenario which he is constantly rewriting.

Oskar is not the only one in this novel who can find art in unlikely places. Greff hangs himself on a drumming potato scale gallows decorated with flowers and pictures of boy scouts. The Dusters are not just juvenile delinquents but devoted art collectors even before Oskar joins them, though his influence, he tells us, brings about an improvement in their taste. Partisans cultivate their terrorism as an art form for its own sake. In the kitchen Matzerath is an artist in the truest sense of the word: he turns feelings into soup. Leo Schugger is the aesthetician of death, and every cemetery in West Germany, we are told, has someone just like him. And then there is Lankes who makes art works of the Normandy fortifications and later transforms his rape of a young nun and her subsequent suicide into a whole series of successful paintings. Dozens of further examples could be cited, but the assertion is everywhere the same. Like play, art is a way of dealing with modern experience, experience that often seems to demolish all other ways of dealing with it.[17]

Oskar, of course, is the most versatile artist in the novel, and his story can be seen as a succession of experiments with various artistic careers – sing-screamer of glass, performing midget with Bebra's troup, tombstone carver particularly noted for his O's, artists' model and subject of *Madonna 49*, of course drummer, and by no means least, writer. It is as drummer and writer that Oskar finds his real artistic fulfilment, the apotheosis of the artist as hero.

The opening pages of *The Tin Drum* depict Oskar laying in a paper supply and contemplating the difficulty of his task. A stupid but fashionable cliché holds that it is no longer possible to write a novel because it is no longer possible to have a hero, individuals in modern society being faceless and alone. Oskar demurs. 'All this may be true. But as far as I and Bruno my keeper are concerned, I beg leave to say that we are both heroes, very different heroes, he on his side of the peephole, and I on my side; and even when he opens the door, the two of us, with all our friendship and loneliness, are still far from being a nameless, heroless mass' (p. 17).

Grass himself rejected the notion that modern life has obliterated differentiation among individuals and reduced everyone to anonymity. Rather, he sees 'originals' all around him, but what defines their originality may be a goiter, a huge Adam's apple, or some peculiar twitch, just as his characters are usually constructed around some quirk, obsession, or perversion.[18] Thus the grotesque may have positive value as an alternative to dehumanisation, an idea we first heard from underground man. We encounter frequently in Grass a figure that can best be described not as an anti-hero but as a grotesque hero – an extraordinary individual whose apartness is emblemised not by handsome looks and nobility of mind but by grotesque appearance and eccentricity.[19] By the single-mindedness of their quest to remain originals and impose their wills upon a murderous world, they are heroes nonetheless.

Mahlke in *Cat and Mouse* is the clearest example of what I mean. He is gangling and ungainly, has protruding ears and a preposterous Adam's apple, a penchant for peculiar dress and odd behaviour. But for all that, he is invested with the traditional attributes of the chivalric hero; extraordinary physical prowess and courage, fame as a warrior and doer of amazing deeds, dedication to an unattainable lady, and a sense of himself as set apart from ordinary men and dedicated to a special quest. It is both his grotesqueness and his heroism that separate him from ordinary boys like Pilenz and pompous functionaries like Klohse, that make him superior to them but particularly vulnerable to their smaller-scaled viciousness. He is a brilliant original in a world that misues brilliance and persecutes originality.

One might argue that Oskar is such a grotesque hero, but how regard his claim that Bruno is a hero too? Besides their relationship as patient and keeper, the one thing that Oskar and Bruno have in common is that they are both artists, transforming the experience of Oskar's life into grotesque art works. Bruno, a dedicated amateur, uses string and plaster to shape 'elaborate contorted spooks' which he mounts on knitting needles. As with Oskar's discussion of the problems of writing a novel, the implication would seem to be that the artist, an original, must find some form in which to render the diverse and often brutal events of modern life into works of art. Given the nature of modern experience and the inappropriateness – indeed, unavailability – of traditional art forms, the new art will find it most characteristic expression in the grotesque.[20]

The point is several times elaborately reiterated and reenforced. In chapter four, Oskar interrupts his chronological narrative to direct our attention to his photograph album, complaining that this once epic art form is now sadly fallen off. 'Yes, gradually the art photo of 1900 degenerates into the utilitarian photo of our day. Take this monument of my grandfather Koljaiczek and this passport photo of my friend Klepp. One need only hold them side by side, the sepia print of my grandfather and his glossy passport phot that seems to cry out for a rubber stamp, to see what progress has brought us to in photography' (p. 50). But even passport photos can be rescued and converted into art works by rendering them grotesque, as Klepp and Oskar used to do with dozens of passport photos they had taken of themselves.

> They gave us a kind of freedom in our dealings with ourselves; we could drink beer, torture our blood sausages, make merry and play. We bent and folded the pictures and cut them up with the little scissors we carried about with us for this precise purpose. We juxtaposed old and new pictures, made ourselves one-eyed or three-eyed, put noses on our ears, made our exposed right ears into organs of speech or silence, combined chins and foreheads. And it was not only each with his own likeness that we made these montages; Klepp borrowed features from me and I from him; thus we succeeded in making new and, we hoped, happier creatures.
>
> (p. 52)

As William Cunliffe has observed, this passage might serve as an epitome of Grass's own artistic methods (*Günter Grass*, p. 58). The point to bear in mind, however, is that this radical procedure has been necessitated by the decline of an older art form from something powerful and original into something mechanical and meaningless. Once again, the assertion is clear: it is better to be grotesque than to be stereotyped, and the mutilated figures in the montages are imagined as happier creatures than the passport photo depictions of Oskar and Klepp.

However, Oskar is not always completely sure that it *is* better to be a grotesque outsider than to be one of the bourgeois smug. His worst doubts assail him at the time of the currency reform and the onset of the economic miracle, and are expressed in the strange revery, 'Fortuna North', a grotesque parody of the graveyard scene from *Hamlet*. Here again, the problem is the inapplicability in the modern world of the traditional ideal of heroism, and the impossibility of art based on such ideals. In the spirit of underground man, Oskar prefers the ugly and degrading to either the heroic in art or the mechanical in life, because at least the ugly and degrading are real; they are not dreams of heroism or illusions of progress, so they take on a beauty and pleasurableness of their own which is also real, though perverse.

Contemplating a decomposed corpse he is helping to exhume near the huge electric power station, Fortuna North, Oskar muses, 'it was reasonably possible to speak of beauty, though on the decline. Moreover, this woman's head and fingers were closer to me, more human, than the beauty of Fortuna North. It seems safe to say that I enjoyed the industrial landscape as I had enjoyed Gustaf Gründgens at the theatre – a surface beauty which I have always distrusted, though assuredly there was art in it, whereas the effect produced by this evacuee was only too natural. Granted that the high-tension lines, like Goethe, gave me a cosmic feeling, but the woman's fingers touched my heart' (pp. 458–9).

As with Oskar's commentary on St Paul's Epistle to the Corinthians at the end of Book One, and the prayer before the preserving jar in Book Three, the Fortuna North revery is tantalisingly obscure, not only because the references are private and cryptic, but also because the correspondences to Hamlet and Yorick keep changing. At first, Hamlet, the power station, and the cadaver are all equated with one another, and suggest simultaneously the decay of art based upon beauty, and the regeneration of West Germany as actually a deepening process of decay. While the power plant was being built, the dead woman was also 'making progress' in her decomposition. It is now Hamlet, not Yorick, who 'lies in the earth ere he rots', and Yorick, the jester, the scoffer, who survives in the person of Oskar, the clown, the artist, the new grotesque hero.[21] But what relationship is this new kind of hero to have with a world that is 'progressively' decaying? 'But for me, Oskar Matzerath Bronski Yorick, a new era was dawning, and scarcely aware of it, I took another quick look at Hamlet's worn out fingers on the blade of the shovel' (p. 459). Rejecting Hamlet's 'absurd formulation' of being versus nonbeing, Oskar contemplates the bizarre events of his past and rejects them also, and resolves to make Yorick a good citizen by marrying Maria, thereby renouncing his roles as artist of the grotesque and grotesque hero. His attempt, however, to normalise his relations with the world turns him not into a good citizen but into a figure we have encountered before in the literature of the modern grotesque, humiliated man. Maria's refusal destroys his new perspective by which Yorick might become a solid burgher, throws him back on his hideous past and ultimately sends him back to work as an artist of the grotesque.

Though the passage is obscure, the polarities seem clear enough: on one hand heroism in a world where heroism has no place, where it is corrupted and serves the ends of corruption; and on the other hand the clown with a knowing and gruesomely comic sense of life and an off-beat genius for depicting it in grotesque forms. This very knowledge and ability make him the new hero without divesting him of his grotesque trappings as clown, and there is no escape for him into the world of bourgeois normality.

Oskar's subsequent career as an artists' model chronicles the demise of several branches of traditional and contemporary art. The school of social protest, motivated by outrage, is so taken with its own indignation that it loses it authenticity as art and becomes merely a furious polemic. Moreover, such art springs from the very rage and violence which spawn atrocity in the first place. Professor Kuchen, the black-haired, black-eyed, charcoal-breathing artist who would have all art an accusation and who assaults white paper with black charcoal, is but another avatar of the Black Cook, the generic symbol of all that is monstrous in the world.

From the art of atrocity, which misses the Goethean serenity of Oskar's Bronski-blue eyes, Oskar passes into the hands of Professor Maruhn, a vapid classicist who cannot finish anything and does not want to work in the grotesque at all. 'It can only have been Oskar's eyes that persuaded this lover of classical harmony to select me as a fit model for sculpture, his sculpture' (p. 465). Maruhn no longer has the courage of his convictions, and his earlier work, from a time when he was as 'vigorous and uninhibited as a young Michelangelo', was all destroyed by the war, implying a similar fate for art based on harmony, proportion, and physical beauty.

Impressionists and cubists all have a fling at Oskar, all with results that disgust him. Success is achieved only when he is discovered by a group of grotesque Surrealists who pair him with the ethereal Ulla in a series of beauty and the beast paintings that serve as a visual synopsis of the novel itself, culminating with Oskar as Christ the Drummer in *Madonna 49*. Once again, as with passport photos, Bruno's string creations, Greff's suicide machine, Lankes' nun pictures, the Dusters' Christmas pageant, and above all, Oskar's continuing act of writing his bizarre memoirs, the creation of a grotesque art work has become a central action of the book.

In every instance, then, the affirmation is made that art is capable of coping with modern experience and of finding forms in which to render it; but, given the nature of that experience, the result will not be art based on an aesthetic of beauty but upon the monstrous, the brutal, the cruelly detached – in short, the modern grotesque. The novel does not merely state this view but embodies it, and, through Oskar's depicted act of creating the novel from his life story, the book dramatises its own epiphany. This self-contained theory of the modern grotesque is, I think, what is really behind the antithesis of Goethe and Rasputin, and the scowling confrontation between Beethoven and Hitler across the Matzerath living room; the sublime artist of the past confronts a figure who epitomises the madness, violence, and upheaval of this century.[22]

I have suggested that Oskar's unique perspective as a point of view character derives from his being simultaneously lunatic, child, and artist of the grotesque. In the novel, of course, these roles are not experienced separately but are parts of a unified character, and the most important instrument of that unity is the central image of the novel, the drum.[23] To the child it is a toy and a refuge from the adult world. To the artist it is both muse and medium of expression. And to the lunatic it is a weapon by which he wields magical control over a world of larger, fiercer beings. Of the characters in the novel, only his presumptive son, Kurt, seems completely immune to its effects. Oskar's second-favourite magical power, the ability to sing-scream glass to pieces, has the same triple function – game, art form, and weapon. Without his magic, Oskar is a pathetic victim, a deformed supernumerary of life. But with his magic – above all the magic of the drum – he is an omnipotent hero, marching through life with the indifference of an *Übermensch* to the destruction of his enemies. His magical powers, however, are the delusions of a madman. If behind the Oskar that Oskar would like us to see there lurks another Oskar, the powerless cripple who is mercilessly trampled by life, we glimpse him only fleetingly between the lines of his own narrative, in much the same way we glimpse the 'real' Kinbote/Botkin through his opaque fantasy in *Pale Fire*.

The two versions of Oskar complement each other, for we can enter the manically inventive world of the Oskar that Oskar presents and delight in the antic parody of our own world that it provides. Yet Oskar is more than the intriguing monster he was taken to be when the novel was first published.[24] We have a continual awareness of the memoir writer himself, an Oskar who is a terrified Oskar, aware of his powerlessness and aware that the issue ultimately at stake is his survival in a monstrously threatening world whose spirit haunts him in the person of the Black Cook. Throughout the novel, the real issue has always been survival in such a world, survival either by hiding in a three-year-old's form or in any number of womb-substitutes, or survival by exerting magical counter-measures. This combination of weakness and omnipotence is what lies behind Oskar's Christ-fixation. Jesus, in the embodiment that Oskar most admires and emulates, is an omnipotent infant, outwardly appearing no different from any human baby, but inwardly knowing all and able to do anything – two qualities Oskar comes close to claiming for himself at birth.

Given the realities of the world as presented in *The Tin Drum*, the individual has only two choices: either find some way of controlling events or find some impregnable refuge. Oskar, an indefatigable reconciler of opposites, tries both control and refuge. In his sense of his failure and in his terror at the possible consequences to himself, he becomes a strangely touching figure, the grotesque artist as vulnerable grotesque hero, about to be thrust out once more unwillingly into the world.

II

At first *The Tin Drum* and *Pale Fire* may seem as dissimilar as the temperaments of the men who wrote them, but despite the obvious differences, there are a number of similarities worth noting because they involve issues central to both novels and to the presence of the grotesque in each. Through a highly erratic, possibly insane first person narrator, each book combines believable, meticulously detailed reality with bizarre events which could not possibly have happened in the world as we know it. Hence, both leave us hesitant to say where reality leaves off and fantasy begins. Both play the radiant, the sublime, the ethereal against the gross, the repugnant, and the grotesque – though Nabokov is a lot gentler about this than Grass. Each contains a self-referential theory of art of which the book itself is a demonstration and realisation. In each, the writing of the book by its first person narrator is a fully dramatised action of the story and constitutes the narrative present. Each narrator–protagonist seems to view himself as a third person, and at times seems to be addressing an audience, presenting his life almost as a case for the defence. In both novels, the narrator presents himself as amoral, self-centred, and supremely confident of his superiority, yet periodically that façade is penetrated to show the real terror, guilt, and despair behind it. At the end of each novel, the narrator–protagonist must head out into a world he finds overwhelmingly frightening, each wondering how he can cope and what his future identity will be. In both *The Tin Drum* and *Pale Fire*, the narrator's bizarre fantasies have been superimposed upon reality expressly so that he can see himself as a powerful, heroic, even tragic figure central to the action of life, rather than as a pathetic freak who might just as well never have lived. Ultimately each seems to sense that he has failed in this attempt. For example, consider the following two statements, the first from Oskar, the second from Kinbote:

> When I considered the miscasting of this tragedy, I had to despair of the theater, for Oskar, the real lead, had been cast in the role of an extra, that might just as well have been dropped.
>
> (p. 287)

> Because of these machinations I was confronted with nightmare problems in my endeavors to make people calmly see – without having them immediately scream and hastle me – the truth of the tragedy – a tragedy in which I had not been a 'chance witness' but the protagonist, and the main if only the potential victim.[25]

Both novels deliberately baffle the reader by raising doubts at certain points about who is actually doing the narrating. As *Pale Fire* progresses, there are vague hints that 'Charles Kinbote' is the fantasy alter ego of V. Botkin, an 'American scholar of Russian descent' (p. 216). About Botkin's character, motives, or sanity we know nothing beyond what we can infer from the possibility that he has taken on the bogus identity of Kinbote who in turn has taken on the bogus identity of King Charles the Beloved. Further, it is not at all certain that the poet, John Shade, or any other of the characters exist as independent entities or whether they are all fantasy creations of the deranged Kinbote or of Botkin.

Of course, any puzzle presents us with the nagging urge to solve it and be done with it for once and for all. This may not be possible or even desirable when the puzzle is also a beautifully wrought, intricate novel about elusive but palely intuited realities and metarealities.[26] The central image of the novel is reflection, particularly one transparent reflection superimposed upon others as in the opening lines of the poem, or an infinite series of mutual self-reflections as in the mirror of Sudarg of Bokay. Now one thing essential to such a series of reflections and reflections of reflections is that each level has a reality of its own which in no way detracts from or invalidates the reality of the other levels. The nearest reflection is no more or less real (as a reflection) than the ninth or tenth down the line, though it is larger, clearer, more accessible to the eye. And so of this novel; we experience it as a series of narrative levels, each one having an artistic reality of its own.

On the first level, it exists most readily as what it appears to be, the story of a deranged academic who takes possession of a posthumous poem and trumps up an absurd edition of it. The next level down, more limpid and elusive, is the story of John Shade, the story told in the poem and the story in the notes about the creation of the poem, including Shade's bemused tolerance, up to a point, of his eccentric neighbour. The next level down (your favourite) is Kinbote's struggle with his madness, his attempt to evade what with one part of his mind he knows to be reality and substitute for it his fantasy of Zembla, and above all, to find King Charles and Zembla in Shade's poem even though he knows they are not there. On the next level down is Zembla itself, the brilliant invention which Kinbote has installed in place of his drab reality. The political and sexual adventures of King Charles make a captivating and amusing story in themselves, a kind of zany fantasy-romance. The story is real because the novel has given it reality in much the same way as Kinbote insisted Shade's poem would give it reality.

Next down in the series of reflections is the more remote, less discernible level at which Shade, Gray, Sybil, Gerald Emerald (and his fantasy Doppelgänger, Izmurudov), Professor Gordon (and his erotic fantasy Doppelgänger, Gordon Krummholz), and perhaps all of New Wye and Wordsmith College are the fantasies of the insane Kinbote. Next, just barely discernible we may see or may just think we see V. Botkin, whose features we cannot make out but who may be creating Kinbote and all the rest too. At this point, the receding images of characters, narrator, possible narrator, and author–artificer Nabokov behind all trail off into infinity, and, as with the receding images in a pair of facing mirrors, we have no choice but to let them do so. To think that by repeated readings, determined anagram solving, and consultation of multilingual dictionaries we can arrive at the nth image down the line and say that this is the *real* image is to treat the novel as merely a puzzle. We could do better to bear in mind Shade's aesthetic credo: 'not text but texture'.

Given the obliqueness of Nabokov's methods, it is inevitable that our sense of the grotesque in *Pale Fire* emerges gradually as the bits and pieces doled out in such precise measure are assembled. The kind of frontal assault on the sensibilities launched in every chapter of *The Tin Drum* is nowhere to be found in Nabokov's novel, but Kinbote himself gradually emerges as a kind of grotesque. By the time we finish the foreword, we know that our editor-narrator is an exceptionally large, full-bearded, and extremely eccentric pederast who has been satirised in a student show, is called 'the Great Beaver', and is considered by at least one acquaintance to be insane. Additional touches are added as the novel accrues – his obsessive mania about Zembla, his conviction that Shade must be writing an epic poem about King Charles the Beloved, his luxuriant and longing fantasies of suicide, his halitosis, his vegetarianism stemming from his having heard about an Italian tyrant who was eaten alive by his subjects. With an air of grievance, Kinbote reports Sybil's description of him as 'an elephantine tick; a king-sized botfly; a macaco worm; the monstrous parasite of a genius' (p. 123).

But the source of the grotesque in *Pale Fire* is not so much Kinbote's physical appearance as his way of seeing and reporting things.[27] The admired poet, John Shade, is a 'fleshy Hogarthian tippler of indeterminate sex. His misshapen body, that gray mop of abundant hair, the yellow nails of his pudgy fingers, the bags under his lusterless eyes, were only intelligible if regarded as waste products eliminated from his intrinsic self by the same forces of perfection which purified and chiseled his verse' (p. 17). The entire novel is a kind of pitched battle between the sublime and the grotesque, with the grotesque having at its disposal the forces of physicality and reality, and the sublime those of fantasy and art. Shade's poem is centrally concerned with the predicament of the ugly and eccentric in a world which values conventional prettiness but in which genuine beauty is difficult to discern and must be accepted in a kind of artistic act of fath. In its way, Shade's poem is as much a commentary on Kinbote's situation as Kinbote's notes are a commentary on the poem. Shade confirms that even as a child he was 'a cloutish freak', and subject to spells or fits, but both his physical and mental peculiarities are linked in some vague but essential way to his poetic talent. The ability to create beauty, however, is not always a concomitant of ugliness and eccentricity. Hazel Shade had the latter but not the former and, in Kinbote's view, deserved admiration for 'having preferred the beauty of death to the ugliness of life' (p. 222). Kinbote's submergence of his ugly life into a brilliant though mad fantasy strikes a position midway between that of Hazel, driven to suicide by the pain of being ugly, and Shade, the conscious artist who can transform even pain and ugliness into a work of beauty.

In *Pale Fire*, ugliness is the usual, spontaneous state of things; beauty must be brought into being by ceaseless imaginative effort. Those unwilling to make the effort, and even more, those incapable of grasping its value, are usually described by Kinbote as being grotesques. Particularly, there is the 'grotesque figure of Gradus, a cross between bat and crab' (p. 111). We first see the would-be regicide as a whimsical cartoon-like figure, scampering through the lines of Shade's poem, but as the poem nears completion and Gradus nears his royal victim, the full power of Kinbote's grotesque imagination is devoted to conjuring up his imaginary nemesis. 'We know already some of his gestures, we know the chimpanzee slouch of his broad body and short hindlegs. . . . We see, rather suddenly, his humid flesh. We can even make out (as head-on but quite safely, phantom-like, we pass through him, through the shimmering propeller of his flying machine, through the delegates waving and grinning at us) his magenta and mulberry insides, and the strange, not so good sea swell undulating in his entrails' (p. 196).

Kinbote's habit of seeing and depicting people in terms of the grotesque extends to many of the minor characters as well. Judge Goldsmith, seen only in his picture, is a 'Medusa-locked hag' (p. 60). A Zemblan psychiatrist has been 'so thoroughly bribed by the Countess as to look, even on the outside, like a putrid pear' (p. 79). Mrs Kaplun, a guest at Shade's birthday party, is 'a dilapidated eagle' (p. 115). Oswin Bretwit is a 'sickly bald-headed man resembling a pallid gland' (p. 126). Thurgus the Third was 'stout and bald, his nose like a congested plum' (p. 223). These are more than metaphors; mad Kinbote is describing the world he lives in and it constitutes in large measure the world of the novel. But Kinbote's madness, like Oskar's, is artistically not clinically conceived. As Shade observes, it is a kind of backhanded art, a system of selection and emphasis, a way of subjectively transforming reality. Moreover, I believe Nabokov is offering here a highly idiosyncratic view of madness, one that controls our way of responding to Kinbote, even though we may not be aware of it, throughout every page of the novel. In a thoroughly Nabokovian cross-reference, Kinbote's condition is prefigured in the poem by that of Maud Shade, the eccentric aunt and connoisseur of the grotesque who had raised the poet.

> I was brought up by dear bizarre Aunt Maud,
> A poet and a painter with a taste
> For realistic objects interlaced
> With grotesque growths and images of doom.

> (ll. 86–9)

Having reached the age of eighty, Aunt Maud (mad?) went insane, apparently from brain damage resulting from a stroke. The passage that describes her condition is a paradigm of Kinbote's.

> There she'd sit
> In the glassed sun and watch the fly that lit
> Upon her dress and then upon her wrist.
> Her mind kept fading in the growing mist.
> She still could speak. She paused, and groped, and found
> What seemed at first a serviceable sound,
> But from adjacent cells impostors took
> The place of words she needed, and her look
> Spelt imploration as she sought in vain
> To reason with the monsters in her brain.

> (ll. 199–208)

The final lines indicate a spark of sanity in an almost totally ravaged mind, a spark that is capable at certain moments of comprehending its plight and struggling to free itself, to fight its way out of the madness that surrounds it. The struggle, however, is futile. Now this, I suggest, is the conception of madness that is at the centre of Kinbote's characterisation.

One of the discarded variants of Shade's poem raises the question of the afterlife of lunatics. Are they still crazy or do they recover their sanity in the hereafter? Kinbote volunteers that Zemblan theology holds that 'even the most demented mind still contains within its diseased mass a sane basic particle . . .' (p. 168). Moreover, at various points we receive clear indications that Kinbote has some inkling of his own madness and that he is wrestling with the monsters in his brain. One note ends with the startling plea, apropos of nothing in particular, 'Dear Jesus, do something' (p. 67). At another point, wishing he could provide the reader with cut out dolls of his boyhood lover, Oleg, he says, 'It would brighten those dark evenings that are destroying my brain' (p. 89). Moreover, throughout all Kinbote's annotations, there is one small part of him that resists what he is doing, a part that knows the poem is not about Zembla, a part that forces him to admit that he may have distorted one variant (p. 162) to make it refer to the King, and finally to admit in the index that he faked all of those variants that seem to substantiate his Zemblan fantasy. That small particle of resistance, however, is not enough to make him stop his mad editorial endeavour.

When Kinbote speaks of the passing of time destroying his brain, he is using neither metaphor nor hyperbole. Like Aunt Maud's, Kinbote's madness is physiological in origin, although Nabokov makes us fish around a bit for this piece of information. We learn in the note to line 287 (pp.130–1) that Shade and Kinbote have the same physician, Dr Ahlert. Kinbote mentions that he was on his way for an appointment, but he does not specify what his complaint was; he says only that he was nervous about going to a doctor. Some thirty-five pages later, in the note to line 691 dealing with Shade's cardiac arrest, Kinbote says, 'Incidentally: the reader should not take too seriously or too literally the passage about the alert [Ahlert?] doctor (an alert doctor, who as I well know once confused neuralgia with cerebral sclerosis)' (p. 177). The inference is that Kinbote went to the doctor complaining of self-diagnosed neuralgia, but was told by Dr Ahlert that he suffered from cerebral sclerosis or hardening of the brain – a diagnosis that Kinbote vigorously rejects. As with Maud Shade, whose momentary sane conceptions were crowded out by impostors from adjacent brain cells, so Kinbote's consciousness is isolated on an ever-shrinking island of sanity, while the surrounding insanity encroaches more and more upon it, luring him toward suicide or threatening him with commitment if he should completely lose the small foothold he has. Whether such a condition is physiologically possible or not is beside the point. It is thoroughly characteristic that Nabokov, whose contempt for modern psychiatry and its practitioners was absolute and uncompromising, should depict his lunatic as suffering from a physiological rather than a psychological disorder.

Ultimately it is this island of frightened sanity isolated in a sea of teeming madness that governs our response to Kinbote's Zemblan fantasy and, indeed, to Kinbote himself. A contrast to Gogol's 'The Diary of a Madman' might be helpful at this point, since it is obviously a prototype of the modern use of a deranged first person narrator, and seems to have had a special place for Nabokov since he used its closing lines as the epigraph for his study of Gogol.[28]

Initially both 'The Diary of a Madman' and *Pale Fire* use the same technique in introducing the deranged narrator, first having him speak in a way that does not strike one as unusual, then introducing an eccentricity or two to let us know that our literary guide is a peculiar one, and then, fairly quickly, introducing a bizarre delusion (the talking dogs in 'Diary', Zembla in *Pale Fire*) that tips us off that the narrator is insane. Both works offer what purports to be an outside text, though in Gogol we know for certain that the narrator has fabricated the correspondence of the dogs, while in Nabokov we do not find out until the index that Kinbote faked some of the variants, and we are never completely certain that he did not invent Shade and Shade's poem. In both stories there are delusions of royalty, Gogol's madman coming to believe that he is Ferdinand VIII of Spain.

However, 'Diary' portrays a linear plunge into insanity, with each entry becoming more and more deranged until finally the narrator is raving in an asylum. Kinbote's condition does not deteriorate but rather fluctuates throughout the novel as he struggles with his mania, and in the end he admits that the poem is not about Zembla at all. Our reaction to Gogol's madman is pathos laced with the grimace of humour provoked by the outlandish inventiveness of his fantasies, the zest with which he takes up new delusions, his sheer manic gusto.

Give me a carriage with horses swift as wind! Drive on, coach-man, let the harness bells ring! Soar upward, my horses, carry me away from this world! Further, further, where I will see nothing, nothing. There is the sky smoking before me. A star twinkles far away, the forest rushes past with its dark trees and the crescent moon. The violet fog is a carpet underfoot. I hear the twanging of a guitar string through the fog; on one side, the sea, and on the other, Italy. Then Russian huts come into sight. Perhaps that's my house over there, looking blue in the distance. And isn't that my mother sitting by the window? Mother, save your wretched son! Let your tears fall on his sick head! See how they torture him! Hold me, a poor waif, in your arms. There's no room for him in this world. They are chasing him. Mother, take pity on your sick child . . .

And, by the way, have you heard that the Dey of Algiers has a wart right under his nose?[29]

Our reaction to Kinbote is more complex, though pathos and humour both play parts in it. Despite his stated loathing for 'human interest' in literature, Nabokov seemed in *Pale Fire*, in *Lolita*, and especially in *Pnin*, to have a literary risk taker's fondness for pushing a character to the very edge of bathos, only to snatch him back again by some deft stroke just as we are about to complain that the novel is becoming sentimental. Many of his characters share with Pnin the more or less justified complaint, 'I haf notink.' So in Kinbote's case, there is pathos too, especially when he prays he will have the strength to resist the allure of suicide.

But there is always in Kinbote that central island of sanity to which we react in ways we cannot to a completely deranged mind, and that island is the habitat of our delight in his picaresque egocentricity, his slyness in his insane pursuit, his indifference to the consternation of his obviously right, completely outraged academic adversaries, his incorrigibility in finding rosy-cheeked 'ingles' wherever he turns and in every grotto of his imagination. There is also a certain inexplicable complicity with Kinbote engen-dered by the game of seeking him out and discovering his 'bunny eggs' secreted throughout the text, as if our opponent in the literary chess game were not Nabokov (which, of course, it is) but Kinbote. Finally, there is the sheer whacky beauty of his creation, Zembla the fair, radiant and diaphanous, with 'that special rich streak of magical madness' (p. 209).[30] Like Shade's poem, it is a beautiful art work created by a grotesque and populated by grotesques, an aesthetic retreat where the painful and the ugly are transformed into the proverbial artificial garden but with *both* real *and* imaginary toads in it.

III

For Oskar and Kinbote, madness is a means of brilliant self-assertion in a world in which they are otherwise despised and powerless. In Samuel Beckett's *Watt*, on the other hand, insanity dramatises the bleakest limits of isolation and psychic stasis. Beckett is working by methods even more oblique that those of Nabokov and Grass. The novel ostensibly opens in the hands of a completely detached narrative persona who for the most part confines himself to reporting the sparse action and choppy dialogue, with only occasional forays into the very limited mind of the hunchback. Mr. Hackett. Not until page seventy-nine does the narrator refer to himself in the first person and hint that Watt had long ago told him of his journey to Mr. Knott's house and his service there. Not until page 125 do we get confirmation that Watt had told the narrator of his experiences over the course of 'some years', and that the narrator, who is now setting his recollections of them down, has long since lost track of Watt. At this time, we are given reason to suspect that the narrator is extremely unreliable: 'And this does not mean either that I may not have left out some of the things that Watt told me or foisted in others that Watt never told me.'[31]

The full narrative situation is not presented until the beginning of Part III, when we find out that the narrator, Sam, and Watt were inmates together at some kind of institution, doubtless an insane asylum, and that Watt, using bizarrely inverted systems of language, pieced out his story to Sam during occasional walks. By this time the reader no longer remembers and no longer cares that the novel opened with events at which neither Watt nor, presumably, Sam was present. But we are left wondering what is the source of the logic-chopping, the preposterous burlesque of epistemology that is the book's most notorious feature. Is it Sam whom we follow through these exhaustive lists of absurd contingencies, or Watt?[32] And what is the source of the grotesque? Is the whole lunatic world of the novel entirely Sam's invention?

Or do Sam and Watt share similar mental aberrations? Do the various footnotes and the addenda of unused fragments come from Sam? Or has Sam Beckett intruded directly into the novel?

Actually, these are questions not to be asked, for Beckett is not playing Nabokovian games but, as several critics have pointed out, is systematically demolishing the form of the novel, deliberately violating all the ground rules and surprising, if not outraging, the readers' expectations. Watt's career as presented by Sam is like the incident of the Galls, 'some story heard long before, an instant in the life of another, ill told, ill heard, and more than half forgotten' (p. 74). Still, the end result is, against all the odds, more than a tedious experiment with language that means nothing and stories that go nowhere, and much of the strange, haunting effect the novel achieves the bleakness of its world, the comic pathos of Watt himself – depends on the double remove of the point of view. What we have here is not a lunatic describing the world as he sees it but a lunatic trying to cope with a world that is every bit as mad as he is. In *The Tin Drum*, and even more in *Pale Fire*, there are clear indications that the world the narrator describes and the real world are two separate things. There is no hint of such separation in *Watt*; the world Sam describes is the only world the novel implies, and hence the inseparability of Sam and Samuel Beckett in the addenda and notes, and even in much of the narration. It is Sam's world that Watt must try to figure out, categorise, and name – a world populated by lunatics and grotesques, operating by the same schizophrenia that is destroying Watt's mind. Sam's viewpoint provides the fittingness between Watt and the world he inhabits.

The fragmented chronology of the story suggests that the place to start an analysis is not at the beginning but at the opening of Part III, the central scene in which Watt and Sam converse and the narrative situation for the first time becomes clear – or, anyhow, as clear as it ever gets in this novel. This is not only the most effective scene in the book (and certainly the most grotesque); it is also the point of emanation for the grotesque transformation of the world which we have experienced for the past 150 pages.[33] As Sam describes the asylum, it is in no way different from the world as a whole, especially the house of Mr. Knott. There is the same almost featureless and hostile landscape: 'Shrubs and bushes, properly so called, were absent from the scene. But thickets rose at every turn, brakes of impenetrable density, and the towering masses of bramble, of a beehive form' (p. 155). The most prominent physical feature of the sanitarium is a maze of wire fences that meander about in so random a fashion as to raise doubts 'in a reasonable mind, regarding the sanity of the person responsible for the layout' (p. 159). Like the house of Mr. Knott, the asylum is full of absurd puzzles which, though entirely meaningless, must nevertheless be solved by the tortuous elimination of 'logical' possibilities. There are identical holes directly opposite each other in two close-set, parallel fences, inviting speculation whether a boar or a sow or a bull or a cow, in flight or in rage or in heat, could have caused them by barging through both fences. After two excruciating pages, Sam abandons the question in all its permutations as impossible.

As in the novel generally, there is insistence in the asylum scene on ugliness and physical disproportion of all people both real and hypothetical. Sam's world, the world of the novel, has been drained of all content except that which is ugly, debasing, and painful. Watt and Sam amuse themselves by killing birds and playing with rats. This is the only glimpse we get of Watt as anything but docile and passive, yet, incongruously, we do not in this passage think of him as cruel in the ordinary sense because there is a total disjunction between the action and attitude taken toward it. The content of cruelty invokes an attitude of serenity.

> Or seizing suddenly a plump young rat, resting in our bosom after its repast, we would feed it to its mother, or its father, or its brother, or its sister, or to some less fortunate relative.
>
> It was on these occasions, we agreed, after an exchange of views, that we came nearest to God.
>
> (p. 156)

This is not the only reference to the Deity in the scene; as Sam sees Watt approaching through the maze of fences, 'His face was bloody, his hands also, and thorns were in his scalp. (His resemblance, at that moment, to the Christ believed by Bosch, then hanging in Trafalgar Square, was so striking, that I remarked it)' (p. 159). The remark has occasioned a flood of interpretations of Watt as a Christ-figure, but a different kind of parallel, I believe, is involved here.

The painting referred to is probably Bosch's *The Crowning With Thorns*, and it is not exactly in Trafalgar Square but in the National

Gallery. Like *Christ Carrying His Cross*, discussed earlier, it is a composition of faces, with four tormentors surrounding Christ in possible parody of the four evangelists. The Christ is facing the viewer directly, and his expression is not of suffering or apprehension as the crown is lowered, but of uncomprehending calm so incongruous as to suggest feeble-mindedness or insanity. But it is the tormentors who arrest our attention, and it is they who have their counterparts in *Watt*: Mr. Hackett who abuses Watt in the opening chapter; Lady McCann who hits him in the head with a stone; Mr. Gorman who soaks him with slops. As in Bosch, suffering is grotesque and is inflicted by grotesques, and the prospect of salvation seems incalculably remote. Watt is the most extreme example of humiliated man as the central figure in the modern grotesque. Yet neither Watt's humiliations nor his physical injuries are the real essence of his suffering. The book seems to be pointing toward some greater horror within, and it is there that we must locate the source of the grotesque.

Whether by conscious design or by intuition, Beckett has built his novel entirely around the symptoms of schizophrenia.[34] In Silvano Arieti's description, schizophrenia is characterised by a widening estrangement of the patient from reality, by the abandonment of normal reasoning processes and the substitution of different methods of thought in their place, by resort to bizarre forms of private and often unintelligible speech, by compulsive, ritualistic movement, and finally in many cases, by complete loss of the sense of the self.[35] It is not simply a question of these symptoms being discernible in *Watt*; the title character is a compendium of them. In the asylum episode at the beginning of Part III, Watt has taken to walking backward, and he and Sam take their strolls breast to breast like partners in some grotesque dance. He has also developed a manic private speech based upon multiple inversion: *'Dis yb dis, nem owt. Yad la, tin fo trap. Skin, skin, skin. Od su did ned taw?'* (p. 168). The effect is similar to what Arieti calls word salad: 'the elements of the sentences, being replaced for others in a unique selection, make up sequences of words that a listener cannot understand or can understand only with great difficulty'.[36]

Though by Part III, Watt has been reduced to complete insanity, his progress through the experiences that have brought him to the asylum can be read as a classic case of a mind plunging into acute schizophrenia complete with auditory, visual and olfactory

hallucinations. According to Arieti, the onset of the disease is often
marked by an individual's seeking a new direction in life, searching
for something without being sure what it is, perhaps without even
being aware that he is searching (Watt's journey to the house of
Mr. Knott to enter service there). This stage is often followed by a
feeling of fundamental displacement. 'It is first experienced as a
sort of strange, emotional resonance between something that is
very clear . . . and something that is unclear and yet gloomy,
horrifying' (Arieti, p. 121). This accurately describes Watt's odd
reaction to the visit of the piano tuners – his conviction that it is
central in some way to the disintegration of all structures and
relationships, the loss of all meaning even the most literal, and the
obliteration of all reliable connection between words and the things
they designate. Arieti reports one case in which the patient found
himself doubting, 'then doubting his doubts, and finally doubting
the doubting of his doubts' (p. 157). That is Watt's situation exactly.
In fact, the endless logic-chopping, the filling of the forms of logic
with the content of insanity which is the novel's most notorious
feature, is itself characteristic of schizophrenic thought. 'The
schizophrenic patient adopts cognitive mechanisms that are different from those used by human beings generally. He does not think
with ordinary logic, but follows different structural organisations
that lead to deductions different from those usually reached by the
healthy person. The schizophrenic is similar to a man who would
solve mathematical problems, not with our decimal system, but
with another hypothetical system, and would consequently reach
different solutions' (p. 220). Arieti is referring here to what he
terms 'paleologic', a primitive system of associative thought. Still,
the description adequately fits Watt's anti-logic which, as John
Mood has shown with Wattian diligence, is filled with internal
inconsistencies and can yield such nonsense formulations as: 'Mr
Knott was not responsible for the arrangement, but knew that he
was responsible for the arrangement, but did not know that any
such arrangement existed, and was content' (p. 90).[37]

Because the world in which Watt must battle his deepening
schizophrenia is the world depicted by Sam, another schizophrenic,
all of the other characters are also presented as behaving in ways
typical of schizophrenia. Lady McCann's unprovoked assault,
Arsene's rambling and often unintelligible monologue punctuated
with pointless guffaws, the compulsive, nonstop eating of Mary,
the maid, are all examples. The elusive Mr. Knott himself, in the

few glimpses we get of him, is portrayed exclusively in the ritualistic behaviour common among schizophrenics: 'Mr. Knott talked often to himself too, with great variety and vehemence of intonation and gesticulation, but this so softly that it came, a wild dim chatter, meaningless to Watt's ears. . . . Knott was also addicted to solitary dactylic ejaculations of extraordinary vigor, accomplished by spasm of the members. The chief of these were: Exelmans! Cavendish! Habbakuk! Ecchymose! (pp. 208–9).

All the foregoing is certainly not to suggest that Samuel Beckett, of all people, has written an old-fashioned psychological novel. The term, 'epistemological farce', that has been often applied to *Watt* fits it well. But just as the paranoid vision charges Kafka's fiction with its power to disturb, so the isolated and joyless world of the schizophrenic gives to the chill universe of *Watt* its combination of compulsion and despair, pathos and disintegration, absurdity and horror.

Moreover, schizophrenia is the most effective embodiment of that sense of cosmic loneliness which it is Beckett's singular power to evoke. 'To be alone as the schizophrenic is, does not mean only to be without others, but to be less himself. . . . Loneliness means fear of losing oneself partially or totally' (Arieti, p. 349). This last, extreme limit of isolation is the condition that overtakes Watt when he must leave the house of Mr. Knott. As he waits in the train station, he has a hallucination of a solitary figure walking down the road but not getting any closer. It finally vanishes altogether. The description of the figure's strange hat, baggy coat, and odd, side-kicking gait suggests that the walker is Watt himself as he was depicted first travelling to the house of Mr. Knott. Now he sees himself as a being apart from himself whom he cannot reach or even identify. It is the ultimate limit of estrangement and, along with his complete passivity to the verbal and physical abuse the station attendants subject him to, constitutes total autistic withdrawal, the bleakest and most acute symptom of advanced schizophrenia. 'But as the illness progresses, even the invasion of social symbols at a paleosymbolic level decreases, and the degree of the mental improverishment of the patient manifests itself in its appalling grandeur. The more he divests himself of common symbols, the more difficult it is for the patient to take roles of other people and the roles that he felt others assigned to him. This improverishment reveals how much of man is actually made of social life. When what was obtained from others is eliminated, man remains an insignificant residue of what he used to be' (Arieti, p. 349). By the time he leaves the service of Mr Knott, with all personal, linguistic, and cognitive links between himself and the surrounding world severed, Watt is an insigificant residue of what he used to be, and considering how little what he used to be was from the beginning, the remnant is nothingness in words enclosed.

5

The Art of Decadence

I

Decadence and the grotesque have long been at home in each other's company, a compatibility that suggests a number of interesting questions. Is grotesque art itself decadent? Is it the product of a decadent society? Does the grotesque flourish in those civilisations that have become jaded, have lost their bearings and their convictions, can no longer take life tragically or even seriously, but have abandoned everything for self-indulgence and are, in fact, grimacing and clowning in the imminence of their own demise? Certainly, many Soviet critics have seen such writers as Kafka and Joyce as examples of bourgeois art and capitalist society falling into decadence.[1] But long before them, John Ruskin clearly linked the emergence of a certain kind of grotesque art and architecture with 'the phases of transition in the moral temper of the falling Venetians, during their fall . . . from pride to infidelity and from infidelity to the unscrupulous *pursuit of pleasure*'. The upshot is that the architecture of the decline 'is among the worst and basest ever built by the hands of men, being especially distinguished by a spirit of brutal mockery and insolent jest, which exhausting itself in deformed and monstrous sculpture, can sometimes be hardly otherwise defined than as the perpetuation in stone of the ribaldries of drunkenness' (*The Stones of Venice*, p. 135).

Most moderns, perhaps as a sign of our decadence, would find Ruskin's attitude typically Victorian and his distinctions between noble and ignoble grotesques specious. But the correlation which he posits between social and moral decay and the emergence of a brutal, mocking, ribald, grotesque art is an intriguing problem, though one that presents its own special difficulties. For one thing, 'decadence', like 'grotesque', is a word about which there is little agreement as to a precise definition. Most discussions of decadence, however, share a number of common themes, above all decline from a past state of health and excellence, decline that may involve any or all of the following: an erosion of previously upheld personal

129

and communal values; a dwindling of energy, or of the will to survive, or of the ability to create; a growing unconcern with the future and concentration on the present moment; a spreading nihilism or cynicism. Some writers also note a proneness to extremes, especially in the pursuit of pleasure or in the lust for destruction.[2] Finally, Lance Morrow, writing, appropriately enough, in *Time*, makes a point that I think is especially true of the twentieth-century notion of decadence: 'To be decadent is not to be just corrupt, but to be *terminally* corrupt.'[3]

I do not think that any consistent cause–effect relationship can be demonstrated between decadence and the emergence of the grotesque in art. One can think of societies that could fairly be called decadent (the Byzantine Empire in its last years, for example) that did not show an increase in taste for the grotesque. Conversely, Ruskin himself points out that the grotesque is present in the art of many healthy societies, and that its very presence is a sign of their creative vigour (p. 187). What can be stated with confidence, however, is that the grotesque can be enormously effective in the *depiction* of decadence. A social condition decadence may be, but when it is deliberately portrayed in art, it is also a perception; its starting place as fiction is in the mind and imagination of the writer who perceives a society as decadent and wishes to portray it as such. Many writers turn instinctively to images of the grotesque to convey a sense of falling off, of lost direction, of empty self-indulgence – of decadence, in a word.

The reasons for this affinity are not difficult to surmise. The depiction of decay has long made use of biological metaphors, and images of biological decay lead straight to the grotesque. Moreover, the grotesque can convey powerful impressions of things having gone out of control, of the animal in man having been given free rein, and of the monstrous forces of the psyche having been loosed. What better way to depict a world in which former beliefs and boundaries have collapsed than by art in which forms have broken down, categories have lost their separateness, and the world is perceived as anarchic?

It is symptomatic of our time that the feeling of exhaustion is most readily engendered not by the old but by the new. The most conspicuous use of the grotesque in modern fiction to depict a state of moral and cultural depletion occurs not in the literature of Europe (where the conjunction of decadence and the grotesque reached its peak in the work of such late nineteenth-century writers as J. K. Huysmans), but in the Anglo-American and Spanish–American writing of the New World. Alan Spiegel makes a provocative distinction between two characteristic uses of the grotesque in the literature of the United States: the Southern writer gives us the everyday world as it is experienced by a person who is mentally or physically deformed, while the Northern (that is, non-Southern) writer gives us a normal individual who is beset by a surrounding world that is grotesque.[4] While I would not push the distinction quite as far as Spiegel does, the general pattern does seem to prevail, with Nathanael West and Flannery O'Connor providing particularly clear examples of each type.

For all their differences in locale and technique, they share a similar sense of decadence in the modern world and both use the grotesque primarily as a radical attack upon the normal. For both, the central problem is that modern life has found no substitute for a lost or failing belief in myth or in God, and culture is uninhabitable without such belief at its centre. Both seem to share the view of decadence given its most elaborate articulation by Oswald Spengler.[5] The human community, in its youthful, healthy state, lives close to the land, and the bond of shared beliefs is so strong that individual members are not even aware of the cohesion because no other way of living would occur to them. In its late phase, however, culture becomes civilisation, its habitat the world-city or megapolis. Roots wither, the arts die, and all that remains is the possibility of control over the material world. 'Culture and civilization – the living body and the mummy of it. For Western existence, the distinction lies about the year 1800 – on the one side of that frontier life in fullness and sureness of itself, formed by growth from within . . . and on the other the autumnal, artificial, rootless life of our great cities, under forms fashioned by the intellect. . . . Culture-man lives inwards, Civilization-man outwards in space and amongst bodies and "facts".'[6]

In two of West's four novels, life in the countryside is represented as a lost and irrecoverable idyll juxtaposed against the brutal, illusion-sated life of the metropolis. Indeed, West's New York and Los Angeles are the very incarnations of Spengler's soulless world-city. In both of O'Connor's novels as well as in many of her short stories, the deep country is the reservoir of enthusiastic, fundamentalist religion, which in the strange world of her fiction is modern man's principal, if not only, remaining path of access to God. The city or the town in her fiction is the domain of the social scientist and the habitat of vapid urbanites for whom the mere surface of reality is enough.

Though both West and O'Connor seemed to find decadence in the same features of modern life, in their reactions to what they saw, and in their views of possible alternatives, they could hardly have been more different from each other, and their differences are especially striking in their individual uses of the grotesque.

West's grotesques are passive and hopeless; they are crippled, deformed, or maimed because of what life has done to them, and there is no way of much improving their situations. The most characteristic grotesque figure in West is the beaten clown, a figure who appears in various forms in all four of the novels. His pain is real, but it is also part of a theatrical act and is perceived by the audience as hilarious not because it is sham but because it *is* real. In *The Dream Life of Balso Snell*, Beagle Darwin imagines himself as a clown performing before an audience of clowns and is tempted to cut his throat before their eyes with 'a last terrific laugh'.[7] In *Miss Lonelyhearts*, when the jealous Doyle remarks that he is pimping for his own wife, she furiously assaults him with a rolled newspaper. 'He surprised her by playing the fool. He growled like a dog and caught the paper in his teeth. When she let go of her end, he dropped to his hands and knees and continued the imitation on the floor. Miss Lonelyhearts tried to get the cripple to stand up and bent to lift him; but as he did so, Doyle tore open Miss Lonelyheart's fly, then rolled over on his back, laughing wildly' (p. 128).

A rolled newspaper is also the weapon in *A Cool Million*, which presents the most elaborate treatment of the beaten clown as archetypal man. In his quest for the American dream of making his fortune by hard work and honesty, Lemuel Pitkin has lost successively his teeth, an eye, a thumb, a leg, and his scalp. What is left of him is hired as a stooge by the vaudeville team of Riley and Robbins. Outlandishly dressed by trying to maintain dignity, he stands silently by while the two comics trade jokes. At each punch line, they take out rolls of newspaper and clobber him so that his false teeth and glass eye pop out and his toupee is knocked off revealing his naked skull. The audience goes wild as he replaces the false parts and solemnly awaits the next beating. 'For a final curtain, they brought out an enormous wooden mallet labelled 'The Works' and with it completely demolished our hero. His toupee flew off, his eye and teeth popped out, and his wooden leg was knocked into the audience. At the sight of the wooden leg, the presence of which they had not even suspected, the spectators were convulsed with joy. They laughed heartily until the curtain came down and for some time afterward' (p. 250).

Rather than resenting this abuse, Lem is grateful for the job, obligingly fashions the clubs that will be used to beat him, and is pleased that he is allowed to read the newspapers afterward as he can afford no other amusement. It is fatal, however, for clowns to become serious. One night the comedians do not appear; Lem goes on stage not in his usual costume but in the uniform of Shagpoke Whipple's Leather Shirts to make a political speech. '"I am a clown," he began, "but there are times when even clowns must grow serious. This is such a time. I . . ." Lem got no further. A shot rang out and he fell dead, drilled through the heart by an assassin's bullet' (p. 252).

In *The Day of the Locust*, Harry Greener, the ageing vaudevillian, scored the one success of his career in a similar routine in which he was worked over by a family of flying oriental acrobats. Once again, the clowning spills over grimly into real life; Harry enjoys aping all the stock grimaces and groans a very hammy actor might use to play a man dying of heart failure – except Harry actually *is* dying of heart failure.

The beaten clown in an appropriate type for modern man as seen in West's fiction. He is a pathetic victim, rendered ludicrous and grotesque by forces over which he has no control and for whose existence he is in no way to blame. But at the same time, his very helplessness and bumbling good intentions are primarily what make him the object of abuse and sadistic glee. In both of West's successful novels, *Miss Lonelyhearts* and *The Day of the Locust*, we are consistently presented with situations of a kind we have encountered in Kafka, especially in 'The Metamorphosis': pity or compassion shown toward a person in misery is invariably accompanied by a wave of irritation at the same person for being in need of pity, especially if he is abject and the situation is hopeless. When prolonged, such irritation can build to positive hatred which vents itself in sadistic enjoyment of the very misery that had cried out for pity in the first place. Helplessness invites violence, and the victim, whether he complains or tries doggedly to carry on, is just asking for more abuse by his very vulnerability to it.

Miss Lonelyhearts finds that against his own will he is concerned, eventually obsessed, about the suffering of those who write for his advice. He comes to realise that the letters are 'profoundly humble pleas for moral and spiritual advice, that they are inarticulate expressions of genuine suffering' (p. 106). Eventually the cries of 'help me' drive him desperate, and he takes out his fury on an old man he and a friend take captive in a public toilet. 'Miss Lonelyhearts felt as he had felt years before, when he had accidentally stepped on a small frog. Its spilled guts had filled him with pity, but when its suffering had become real to his senses, his pity had turned to rage and he had beaten it frantically until it was dead' (p. 87). As he mocks and finally assaults the helpless old man, he comes to realise that it is the grotesque, complaining letter-writers he is tormenting with sadistic pleasure: 'He was twisting the arm of all the sick and miserable, broken and betrayed, inarticulate and impotent. He was twisting the arm of Desperate, Broken-hearted, Sick-of-it-all, Disillusioned-with-tubercular-husband' (p. 88).[8]

In *Miss Lonelyhearts*, the letter-writers, whose pleas and laments are distributed throughout the novel, are like a grotesque chorus before whom the sordid little tragedy of the protagonist is played out. It is not just a matter of there being no helping them; far worse in the eyes of Miss Lonelyhearts, there is no escaping them. The plot, in so far as this novel can be said to have a plot at all, consists of the exploration of a succession of dead ends, the most desperately pursued being romantic love and sex, escape to an older, simpler way of life in the country, and amelioration of suffering through Christian faith, hope, and charity. All fail; there is no way out. That is the absolute condition of the world of West's fiction, as it was later to be in the work of another creator of clowns, Samuel Beckett. Retreat to Walden will not work because the decadent urban reality is still there waiting for one to come back. Christianity will not work because the confident faith that must underlie the hope and charity is no longer possible. The problem is not merely disbelief; in fact, complete disbelief like Shrike's can encase one in an armour of cynicism which, if ugly, is at least protective. But in Miss Lonelyhearts, the psychic need to believe confronts the intellectual incapacity to do so. The figure of Christ detached from the cross and nailed directly to the wall of Miss Lonelyheart's room ceases to be a religious symbol and becomes but one more emblem of grotesque mutilation and suffering.

So too in the secular realm: the problem is not that the myths are dead and buried; the problem is that they are dead but *not* buried, and their remains contaminate the environment, poisoning those who try still to live by them. Their patent falsehood is ludicrously inadequate to the solace people seek from them. A dying man staggers into a movie to see *Blonde Beauty*, while a diseased and ugly woman is delighted to find a romance magazine in a garbage can. 'Men have always fought their misery with dreams. Although dreams were once powerful, they have been made puerile by the movies, radio and newspapers. Among many betrayals, this one is the worst' (p. 115).

With charity cut loose from faith, with sex divorced from the capacity to love, with compassion stifled by the contempt that abject suffering provokes, attempts to establish any emotional communion between people end in failure, usually ludicrous failure. The epitome, of course, is the tableau at the end of the novel, when, Miss Lonelyhearts, determined to practice the love and humility of a Christ in whom he does not believe, rushes to offer sympathy and comfort to the petulant cripple, Doyle. Doyle attempts to flee the embrace, shoots Miss Lonelyhearts accidentally, and the two roll clasped together down the stairs.

A number of years ago, Stanley Edgar Hyman created a controversy by suggesting a Freudian reading of *Miss Lonelyhearts* as a story of repressed homosexuality, resting his case primarily on the relationship between the title character and Doyle.[9] I fear the critic may have fallen into exactly the trap that West set for the characters: an attempt by one man to offer sympathy to another is likely to be interpreted as a sexual advance. 'Miss Lonelyhearts went over to the cripple and smiled at him with the same smile he had used in the speak-easy. The cripple returned the smile and stuck out his hand, Miss Lonelyhearts clasped it, and they stood this way, smiling and holding hands, until Mrs Doyle reentered the room. "What a sweet pair of fairies you guys are," she said' (pp. 128–9). The handclasp in the speakeasy, however, had not been erotic but had been an attempt to establish some form of sympathetic contact after language had proved capable only of endless complaint. (There is a nearly identical incident of misunderstood motives in *The Day of the Locust*. In the course of a long, wretched complaint to Tod Hackett, Homer Simpson begins calling him 'Toddie' and tries to clasp his hand, much to the artist's annoyance. Yet Faye's taunting of him in the night club makes clear that, far from having sexual designs, Homer does not even know what a 'fairy' or a 'homo' is.)

In both novels, the mistaken imputation of homosexual advances is but part of a larger pattern; *any* attempt to extend solace or feeling is transmuted into something perverse by 'those who stare'. Miss Lonelyheart's distress at the woes of the letter-writers indicated to Shrike only that he is a 'leper licker'. 'Barkeep, a leper for the gent' (p. 83). To Betty, his painful concern is morbid and sick. That compassion can make a difference is not an illusion that West long allows his characters – nor, for that matter, his readers. In the absence of any real hope for improvement, there is something embarrassing and pathetic about Doyle's pleas for affection and Miss Lonelyheart's attempt to bestow it. In the absence of any larger frame of values to give it significance, Miss Lonelyheart's desire for saint-like humility is both self-delusion and self-indulgence. The letters themselves may indeed be 'profoundly humble pleas', but they are also grotesque parodies of human suffering. Jay Martin points out that the real-life version of the first letter in *Miss Lonelyhearts* was from a girl who had a weak knee and had to use a cane.[10] West makes her fictional counterpart a girl who was born without a nose '. . . although I am a good dancer' (p. 67). West goes out of his way to make unhappiness ludicrous and degrading so that his sufferers become, by the sheer volume of their woes, gruesomely comic.

By the time we arrive at *The Day of the Locust*, the search for alternatives has become moribund. Walden has become southern California and the quest for God has degenerated into faddish cults that Tod Hackett can imagine best in terms of artists like Goya, Daumier, and Desiderio, 'the painters of Decay and Mystery' (p. 352). The background figures are not the pathetic, complaining victims of misfortune, but the ugly hoards of people who have come to California to die, 'torn, emotion-starved masses whose fury borders on holocaust'.[11] Their rage, however, is really an outgrowth of their passivity, and they are as much helpless victims as the letter-writers and beaten clowns in the earlier works. They have believed the illusions that were peddled to them, but now know that a romance plucked out of a trash can is not enough to sustain them. They have come to California to die and their boredom while waiting to do so makes them deadly. Their obsession with celebrities and movie stars is actually sublimated hatred, their adulation a form of aggression and frustrated desire for revenge.

Though West consistently writes of people driven by anguish and rage, there is little of either quality in his writing itself. Genuine indignation, like genuine compassion, may well be impossible for a writer as coolly and wholly cynical as West appears to have been. For all the pessimism of his vision, there is something playful, even downright cheerful about West's nihilism and he seems to view the apocalypse he creates with a certain gratification. It is a quality he projects onto his final protagonist. Tod Hackett – whose first name means death and whose last name is obviously appropriate for a serious artist who earns his living at the studios – has only two desires in the world: to have sex with Faye Greener on any terms whatsoever, not excluding rape or prostitution, and to finish his panoramic painting, *The Burning of Los Angeles*. He fails at the former, but from first to last he always contemplates the latter with relish, indeed, with affection. 'He wanted the city to have quite a gala air as it burned, to appear almost gay. And the people who set it on fire would be a holiday crowd' (p. 334). At one point, having failed in his only attempt to take Faye by force, he questions his own pessimism as reflected in the painting. Perhaps he has made too much of the people who have come to California to die; perhaps their murderous lunacy is not the wave of the future. But after a moment's hesitation he decides his nihilism is better for his art. 'The Angelenos would be first, but their comrades all over the country would follow. There would be civil war. He was amused by the strong feeling of satisfaction this dire conclusion gave him. Were all prophets of doom and destruction such happy men?' (p. 335). It is a moment similar to the one in which Miss Lonelyhearts, back from the country, gives up any hope that either marriage to Betty or a simple, secluded life could provide any real alternative to the ugliness and anguish of the city; he immediately feels a sense of relief. West, like his French contemporary, Céline, seemed to enjoy his own misanthropy.

He also seemed to enjoy his own grotesques. Norman Podhoretz has suggested that the trouble with *The Dream Life of Balso Snell* stems from West's fondness of the grotesque for its own sake. 'Mocking his own work . . . was West's way of telling himself that merely to indulge his feeling for the grotesque and the diseased was morbid sentimentality, that he had to do more with this feeling than take it at face value if he were going to produce mature fiction.'[12] Podhoretz is surely right about *Balso Snell*, in which the sniggering of small boys writing obscenities on the schoolhouse wall is hard to miss. But I think the critic overestimates the degree to which West disciplined the excesses of his youth. West's small canon is, as has been widely noted, very uneven, but it is uneven in a strangely cyclic way. The sophomoric *Balso Snell* is followed by the intensity and clear focus of *Miss Lonelyhearts*, in which the use of the grotesque is controlled and never gratuitous. Then comes a great leap backward, *A Cool Million*, whole stretches of which could be out of a school humour magazine; the use of the grotesque is relentless and deliberately outrageous. Then comes West's most ambitious and, I would say, finest novel, in which the grotesque is used sparingly at first, then with greater insistence, building through the cockfight and the party to the destructive frenzy of the riot scenes, West's most effective picture of a decadent society mired and thrashing about.

In West's fiction, the grotesque is an irrepressible force threatening to run out of control. He uses it to mock a decadent society, but his involvement with it does not end there. In *Balso Snell* there is a fantasy in which an audience in a theatre is reminded that the author is always the implacable enemy of the middle class. Then, to preclude any misunderstanding, the roof of the theatre opens and those below are bombarded with excrement. It is a fantasy of the author's relation to his audience that West never wholly relinquished.[13] For Tod Hackett, a serious artist from the East forced to eke out a living in Hollywood, *The Burning of Los Angeles* will be not only masterpiece but wish-fulfilment and revenge. For West, a New York writer who went to California to die, *The Day of the Locust* serves similar functions.

All of West's novels, especially the last, are much like the phantasmagoric movie lot he so brilliantly describes – a wild, improbable jumble of incongruously mixed façades with nothing behind them. In the vacuity the empty joke resides, but West, in contrast, say, to Beckett, enjoys the possibility of grotesque play with the surface so much that the chill loneliness and despair that are central to our experience of Beckett are somewhat attenuated; hence, West's beaten clowns are more comic than pathetic. In the closing passage of *The Day of the Locust*, Tod Hackett, having been nearly dismembered by the mob, is being driven from the scene of the riot by the police when he breaks into a howling imitation of their siren. Are his wails hysteria? Desperation? Madness? Or just another irresistible, spur-of-the-moment impulse to clown around?

In West's fiction, there is no alternative to decadence; in that of Flannery O'Connor there is, but the alternative is even more bizarre and disturbing than West's vision of apocalypse. By her own account, the grotesque was for her a shock tactic to jar the reader into seeing reality from an eternal, spiritual perspective incompatible with the modern temper: 'to the hard of hearing you shout, and for the almost blind you draw large and startling figures'.[14] Most of her fiction moves along a bilevel path that is neither traditional symbolism nor allegory exactly, but an elaborate system of encryption, a sustained double entendre. Seen in one way, she is writing about farm women, hired hands, children, and criminals; seen in another she is writing about God, the devil, sin, grace, and redemption. In *The Violent Bear It Away*, Tarwater's friend and counsellor may be a figment of his imagination; Mr. Meeks may be just a travelling salesman, and the pervert may be just a pervert. There is nothing that forces the reader to accept them as incarnations of the devil, though various clues and codes in the text indicate that that is what they are intended to be. When Tarwater has his Old Testament-style revelation and God speaks to him from a burning tree, we recall that a short while before, the hysterical boy had set the woods on fire. O'Connor always offers the reader an escape hatch while trying to persuade him not to use it.

The surprising thing is not that a writer whose subject is religion should employ the grotesque; there is ample precedent for that. The surprising thing is the number of writers of the modern grotesque besides O'Connor who make religion a central concern of their work. Just look at the fiction considered in this study: *Ulysses*, with its opening parody of the Mass and its elaborate religious cross-references; *The Tin Drum*, with Oskar's Christ fixation; *V.*, with its title character's obsession about Roman Catholicism, her conviction that she is literally the bride of Christ and that all her lovers are His substitutes; *Pale Fire*, with Shade's preoccupation with the immortality of the soul; *Miss Lonelyhearts*, with the columnist's aspiration toward sainthood. Certainly there are works of the modern grotesque that are not concerned with religion, but the preeminence of the above works in the fiction of the modern grotesque argues that the connection between religious themes and the modern grotesque is more than coincidental.

O'Connor herself may have given us part of the reason when she said, 'We live in an unbelieving age, but one which is markedly and lopsidedly spiritual' (*Myster and Manners*, p. 159). It is an astute comment about a modern world in which God may be dead for the intelligentsia, but religious wars flare in both East and West, and bizarre cults number their collective membership in millions. Religion has long mediated between man and those areas of his life he experiences as profoundly mysterious, full of sacred awe but also of primal terror. Such areas are also the natural breeding ground of the grotesque, and religious art, from ceremonial masks to gargoyles, has always included it in abundance. In the margin of her copy of Eliade's *Patterns of Comparative Religion*, O'Connor wrote, 'the grotesque is naturally the bearer of mystery; is dangerous'.[15] She, of course, is different from the other writers considered here in that she was the only one who wanted to be understood as a person of faith who made her faith central to her art. The others depict the religious experience of modern man through pseudo-religions or parodies of religion, and through characters like Stephen and Oskar who would agree with Hazel Motes that blasphemy is the only way to truth but experience no change of heart.

What makes religious experience in O'Connor's work so stark and intense is that alternative methods of dealing with reality are caricatured with such contempt and aversion that only messianic religious fervour can serve as an antidote. West's characters are helpless before powers that make them grotesque; O'Connor has given us a whole gallery of characters who take up ugliness and perversity as their banners of rebellion, who refuse to be normalised out of sheer contempt for normality. A clear example is Rufus Johnson, the crippled juvenile delinquent in 'The Lame Shall Enter First'. He uses his deformed foot as both weapon and badge of defiance, and he refuses Sheppard's offer of an orthopaedic shoe. The guidance counsellor is convinced that Rufus' antisocial behaviour is caused by insecurity over his deformity: Rufus has a different explanation: '"Satan," he said. "He has me in his power."'[16] He places the conflict between good and evil exactly where O'Connor wants it, in the struggle between God and the devil, and it makes no difference whether or not Sheppard is 'good' if he is not also 'right'.

O'Connor's fiction is full of characters who flaunt their deformity to make a point. Joy Hopewell changes her name to Hulga because it is the ugliest one she can find. She exaggerates the clumping of her artificial leg, dresses in castoff children's clothing, and cultivates ugliness the way some people cultivate beauty – all to declare her contempt for her vacuous mother and good country people. Mrs. Turpin feels sorry for the extremely ugly Mary Grace, but Mary Grace accentuates her ugliness by making hideous faces at Mrs. Turpin. O. E. Parker covers his entire body except his back with tattoos, trying to fill an emptiness that ultimately can be filled only by Christ.

In O'Connor's fiction, decadence is epitomised by the pat and trivial substitutes modern society offers for the eternal, spiritual, mysterious dimension of man in his relationship to God. On the one hand there are the social scientists and well-intending secularists who have boundless faith in psychological testing and personality adjustment. On the other there are those for whom surface propriety is enough, whose self-congratulation is based upon a conviction that Christ, a staunch admirer of middle-class values, is as pleased with them as they are with themselves. Both types are guilty of the same sin: failure to recognise the essential fallenness of human nature and hence the need for grace and redemption.[17] It is not primarily their materialism or secularism that make them the objects of O'Connor's wry ire; it is their unwarranted optimism she is out to get.

In previous religiously inspired art, the grotesque was most often used to depict the enemies of God, but O'Connor exactly reverses this. The antagonists have none of the mystery, the isolated integrity that the grotesque often assumes in her fiction. The devil is represented by a succession of seedy hucksters and small-time con artists, while the secular is tawdry and comical, what one might call the mock-grotesque. Enoch Emery's pseudo-meta-morphosis into a movie gorilla is its epitome. The genuine grotesque is reserved for the spiritual, the mysterious, the extreme, what Frederick Asals has called 'the grotesque luminosity of the divine'.[18] When Hazel Motes ends his furious crusade against Christ and accepts his own 'uncleanness', he blinds himself with lime, puts glass fragments in his shoes, and wears strands of barbed wire around his chest. '"It's not natural,"' his landlady complains.

"It's natural," he said.

"Well it's not normal. It's like one of them gory stories, it's something that people have quit doing – like boiling in oil or

being a saint or walling up cats," she said. "There's no reason
for it. People have quit doing it."

"They ain't quit doing it as long as I'm doing it," he said.[19]

One critic has called Hazel Motes a 'grotesque saint', hitting the
mark exactly.[20] An admiration for martyrdom, the more gruesome
the better, is at the centre of a lot of O'Connor's fiction. The Christ
who haunts her South has a lot in common with her revivalist
preachers and self-made grotesques. He is 'the ragged figure who
moves from tree to tree' in the back of Hazel Motes's mind (*Three*,
p. 8). He is 'the bleeding stinking mad shadow of Jesus' whom
Tarwater tries futilely to avoid (*Three*, p. 357). He is the stern
Byzantine Christ whose all-demanding eyes fixate Parker as he
pages through the book of tattoo designs. Only late in her short
career did O'Connor explicitly state something implicit in much of
her fiction all along: that the face of good can be grotesque too,
'that in us the good is something under construction' (*Mystery and
Manners*, p. 226).[21]

If O'Connor's highly individual religious outlook can account
for the genesis of the grotesque in her work, it can not by itself
account for the effect of that work on the reader. Were her stories
no more than the elaborate encryption of religious messages, they
could not speak so powerfully and memorably to a large audience
most of whom do not share her religious convictions. Though
O'Connor professed to despise 'psychological novels', it is, at the
most immediate level, the psychological validity of her fiction that
accounts for much of its power, especially when she is delineating
a recurring, archetypal situation. O'Connor is first and foremost a
chronicler of the dissatisfied spirit in a decayed society, of characters
whose day-to-day address to the world is a more or less belligerent
refusal to be fobbed off by half-way measures. Much of her best
writing is done in the depiction of personal antagonisms that
spring up spontaneously and may endure for years, becoming so
deeply embedded as to be the most reliable constant of the
relationship, almost a way of life. The particulars of the basic
situation may vary: a strong-willed child versus a strong-willed
adult, a more docile child who intuitively senses that his elders
cannot or will not give him what he needs, a grown offspring
almost desperate with exasperation at the vacuity of an ageing
parent, a lone farm woman who feels that others do not appreciate
her struggles or accomplishments, a deep-dyed believer rebelling

against religion, or an inverted saint who casually slaughters a prattling old woman and her entire family. Such antagonism arises not from 'personality conflict' but from spiritual deprivation which one character cannot tolerate and the other will not acknowledge. Thus the fundamental conflict is between the incomplete and the uncomprehending.

The results are often comic, frequently violent, sometimes lethal. Time and again her characters are forced into situations in which there is nothing left except recourse to extreme measures which are attractive precisely because they *are* extreme. The antithesis is Reyber, the psychologist in *The Violent Bear It Away*, who deliberately stifles the religious, mystical, enthusiastic side of himself because from its furthest reaches he feels the terrifying pull of madness. But spiritual hunger is not to be satisfied with stale cake, peanut butter, and ketchup. O'Connor's characters, like many of Dostoyevsky's, reject an unmysterious world and *demand* the ineffable, even if mutilation, horror, and madness are the price of having it.

II

Thomas Pychon's fiction is centrally concerned with decadence, and the grotesque is one of the means used to portray it. In his first novel, *V.*, Pynchon is very clear – I think a bit too clear – about what he means by decadence. 'Decadence, decadence. What is it?' asks Fausto Maijstral rhetorically. 'Only a clear movement toward death, or, preferably, non-humanity. As Fausto II and III, like their island, became more inanimate, they moved closer to the time when like a dead leaf or fragment of metal they'd be finally subject to the laws of physics. All the time pretending it was a great struggle between the laws of man and the laws of God.'[22] The same idea is repeated by Itague: 'A Decadence . . . is a falling-away from what is human, and the further we fall the less human we become. Because we are less human, we foist off the humanity we have lost on inanimate objects and abstract theories' (p. 380).

The problem I find with this definition is that Pynchon's *sense* of the decadent is far richer and more complex than the repeatedly offered abstract theory about it. In place of the mechanistic definition offered by this novel, consider the following as a description of decadence as portrayed by Pynchon in *V.* and in *Gravity's Rainbow*:

> The style inadequately called of decadence is nothing but art arrived at the point of extreme maturity yielded by the slanting suns of aged civilizations: an ingenious, complicated style, full of shades and of research, constantly pushing back the boundaries of speech, borrowing from all technical vocabularies, taking color from all palettes and notes from all keyboards, struggling to render what is most inexpressible in thought, what is vague and most elusive in the outlines of form, listening to translate the subtle confidences of neurosis, the dying confessions of passion grown depraved, the strange hallucinations of obsession which is turning to madness.

Complicated style – full of research – borrowings from technical vocabularies – subtle confidences of neurosis – dying confessions of passion grown depraved – strange hallucinations – obsessions turning to madness: yes, that's Pynchon all right; I can imagine no more evocative description of his fiction, though the comment was written in the nineteenth century by Theophile Gautier with reference to the work of Baudelaire.[23]

The brilliance of *V.*, and even more of *Gravity's Rainbow*, is in the way they convey the *feel* a culture whose moral, emotional, and aesthetic atmosphere is becoming positively viscous. The inhabitants of such worlds react with nothing like the appropriate panic, but with a lassitude approaching torpor, as they turn to narcissism or the cultivation of cruel pleasures, – the siege party at Foppl's, the voyage of the *Anubis* – or as, like Slothrop, they simply lose interest and dissolve. 'But nowadays, some kind of space he cannot go against has opened behind Slothrop, bridges that might have led back are down now for good. He is growing less anxious about betraying those who trust him. He feels obligations less immediately. There is, in fact, a general loss of emotion, a numbness he ought to be alarmed at, but can't quite. . . . Can't . . .'.[24]

The earlier novel takes place in a world in which illusion is not the mask of reality but a substitute for it, sometimes willed consciously into being, sometimes imposed by madness or fever. It is a bizarre but aesthetically intriguing alternative to the terror and pity reality should inspire if the events transpiring were faced without the veil. The purest example is Vheissu, the technicolour nightmare Hugh Godolphin hallucinates after witnessing the atrocities of the Mahdist uprising at Khartoum. The other-worldliness of Vheissu, its ghastly, frightening beauty, its genesis in apparent madness, signal that reality has passed beyond what can be expressed in terms of human behaviour, and experience is now strangeness fuelled by itself, by its own very strangeness. Aesthetics are governed by deformity and cruelty which have reached the rarefied precincts of the sublime. Vheissu lies at the centre of Pynchon's vision of fascinating horror, like the rainbow-coloured spider monkey buried beneath the South Pole, the zero point of absolute stasis.[25]

In a world in which fantasy is given a privileged place over reality, civilisation itself becomes a kind of elaborate collective illusion, little more than the elegant attire of barbarism. The title character is a walking demonstration of underground man's contention that societies do not become more civilised and humane as they grow more advanced, but become barbaric and cruel in direct proportion to their sophistication and boredom. V. is the ultimate combination of elegance and violence; she is the complete sophisticate who moves with ease through the various cultivated international settings of the novel, but she is also some kind of catalyst that makes atrocity possible. She does little herself, but terrible things happen when she is around, and the novel is purposely vague about whether or not she is causing them.[26] What she facilitates is not just violence, but love of violence for its own sake, its cultivation as an art form (literally, in the Paris chapter), its delectation as fare for the connoisseur. The novel abounds with characters who are enamoured of slow apocalypse, from Bongo-Shaftesbury with his dictum, 'Humanity is something to destroy' (p. 69), to Foppl with his nostalgia for genocide. V. shares this taste herself, though her preference is to enjoy all things, from sex to cruelty, vicariously; hence her seduction of Hugh Godolphin to take part in the atrocities of the siege party.

By 1919, V. clearly *wants* to be dehumanised. She has acquired a mechanical eye and a sapphire in her navel is an anatomical part of her. She has even more drastic modifications in mind. 'See my lovely shoes. . . . I would like to have an entire foot that way, a foot of amber and gold, with veins, perhaps in intaglio instead of bas-relief. How tiresome to have the same feet: one can only change one's shoes. But if a girl could have, oh, a lovely rainbow

or wardrobe of different-hued, different-sized and -shaped feet'
(p. 459). Stencil's final vision of her is as a beautiful, ageless
automaton living in Sweden, or somewhere, the still-surviving
object of his endless fantasy/quest.

But if V. is a force of destruction, allied in shadowy ways with
declining Empire and rising fascism, she is also at the same time a
victim of modern experience – uprooted, dehumanised, transformed from the lovely Victoria Wren into the grotesque automaton,
the 'bad priest', and finally disassembled.[27] It is her role as victim
that is emphasised in Fausto Maijstral's confession. What makes
the scene of her dismantling so macabre is the matter-of fact way
in which the children of Malta discover that the 'bad priest' is
composed of mechanical parts that can be removed, and the
insouciance with which they ignore her pleas for help, ignore even
the blood that wells when they cut out the sapphire. The children
are by that point products of the very force V. represents; their
coldness duplicates her coldness; they have become as remote and
crystalline as the 'bad priest' urged them to be. They are, in a
sense, *her* children. Brought up in sewers as the city above them
was being pulverised, they made war into a game, structured it
like a fantasy, and hence are no longer capable of responding to
real horror when they encounter it. The result is the combination
of emotional atrophy and physical mutilation that is both decadence
and the grotesque in *V.*

The gradual metamorphosis of V. from Victoria Wren to the 'bad
priest' is made to correspond to the decline of humanity in this
century. However one defines decadence, it is surely not only a
moral or physical condition; it is also a process, and the great
chroniclers of decline – Gibbon, Ruskin, Spengler – have all
emphasised its historical, developmental character. But the historical nature of decadence poses, I think, a problem in the
ideational structure of the novel, a conflict between its historical
settings and its governing metaphor, entropy as the inevitable
nature of things. A decline necessarily implies a decline *from*
something – an ideal or at least a preferable state in the past. In
V., it is difficult to imagine what the past might be. Though the
first avatar of V. is named for Queen Victoria, Victorianism is
certainly not being offered as a state of health in contrast to the
undiagnosed disease that, according to Sidney Stencil, afflicted
Europe sometime between 1859 and 1919. Rather, the Victorians
caused all the problems, putting people where they did not belong,

creating Baedekerland, and bringing about the conditions of the apocalyptic wars of this century. If decadence is a falling away from what is human, at what period were people supposed to have been more human? The novel does not specify. It is not, in contrast to *Miss Lonelyhearts*, nostalgic about any pre-industrial past. If it is nostalgic about anything, it is not a period but a state of mind in which it was still possible for men to believe fully their own explanations of things, still possible to entertain a conviction of their own well-being. Such characters as Sidney Stencil, Fausto Maijstral, Hugh Godolphin, and, in a way, V. herself all pine for a world which has been taken away from them. As will be that case with the self-exiled Argentineans, the gaucho-submariners of *Gravity's Rainbow*, 'nostalgia is like seasickness: only the hope of dying from it is keeping them alive' (*GR*, pp. 383–84). Fragments of old beliefs, explanations that have lost their power to explain, are still around and are still clung to, but they have begun to putrefy and spread disease. The successive, self-created personalities of Fausto Maijstral, Herbert Stencil's quest for V., Hugh Godolphin's Vheissu, Mondaugen's dream-living of the 1904 massacre, Father Fairing's mission to the rats – all are variations of the same process. These characters fabricate their beliefs like fantasies and then proceed to believe in them, or half-believe in them, or half-believe in them for as long as they can.

Moreover, it is in creating the relationship between the characters' fantasies and the reality of violence and decay that Pynchon achieves his most daring and ingenious effect in this novel, building up with one hand what he has just torn down with the other. Herbert Stencil does not himself know how much of his inference about V. he believes and how much is pure fantasy. The narrative voice, the other characters, even Stencil himself, constantly warn that what he knows about V. is almost all conjecture and may have no basis at all in reality. Eigenvalue even stops Stencil's account of the events in Southwest Africa to point out that he could not possibly know the minute details he claims to based on Mondaugen's recollection from a distance of over thirty years. But while Pynchon is busy discrediting Stencil as a witness, he is equally busy substantiating everything Stencil says. Though many of the V. episodes are supposedly being told by Stencil to Eigenvalue or Benny Profane, they are not presented to us by Stencil as narrator but are given the objectivity of the detached narrative voice of the novel. This in itself confers a certain reality upon them.

Moreover, Profane *does* find Father Fairing's parish in the sewer, Fausto Maijstral *does* confirm the existence of the 'bad priest', Paola *does* have V.'s comb, and finally, after Herbert Stencil has left the scene, the epilogue (which stands apart from the novel rather like the period does from the V in the title) confirms not only V.'s existence but many of the previous events of the narrative, all without the least intimation that past events have been 'Stencilised'. Thus Pynchon is eating his cake and having it too, conferring the reality of objective fact upon V. and her career, while still insisting that her reality, like all 'realities', is contingent upon the eccentric and biased interpretation of incomplete and unreliable evidence. It is a remarkable effect, and brought off so adroitly that the reader is not even aware that he is being offered two incompatible sets of assertions about reality in the novel and is accepting both of them.

The simultaneous insistence on two incompatible views of reality, that everything is part of some vast, international plot, and that everything is a random event unconnected to anything else, is the cornerstone of Pynchon's fiction, and a failure to grasp *both* sides of it while ignoring the incompatibility between them leads to a fundamental misreading of his work, especially of *Gravity's Rainbow*, but also of *V.* For instance, consider the usual interpretation of the concluding episode of *V.*, that Sidney Stencil's death in a water spout is a purely chance event, and that his son's search for evidence linking his death to V. is just more making cabals out of random caries.[28] A good portion of the epilogue is devoted to the seemingly irrelevant story of Mara (Maltese for 'woman', so we are told), a medieval witch with a talent for making strange things happen.[29] She is described as inhabiting the peninsula whose tip is Valletta, which is apparently also the location of V.'s villa, but her influence extends over a circle that has Valleta as its centre and Lampadusa as its edge (p. 434). The final paragraph, in which the water spout appears, begins, 'Draw a line from Malta to Lampadusa. Call it a radius' (p. 463). Mara had been taken prisoner by the Turks and used by them as the figurehead on the prow of a ship. Enslaved by a Sultan, she had brought havoc to his harem by introducing bisexuality, and had made her escape dressed as a cabin boy. 'Disguise is one of her attributes' (p. 434). The exact same words are used by Herbert Stencil with reference to V. (p. 363), who is bisexual and a transvestite. Mara had the power to control the elements; of V. it is said, 'Giving tango lessons in Rotterdam she commanded the rain to stop; it had' (p. 464). All these lines, if they do not quite converge, seem to point to a single female figure, the destructive side of the White Goddess. One is reminded of Grass's Niobe, another medieval witch immortalised as a figurehead, whose mere presence was enough to unleash murder and mayhem.

I am puzzled by one odd detail in the closing paragraphs of *V*. As Sidney Stencil sets sail from Malta, never to be heard of again, Veronica Manganese, with whom he has resumed his affair of twenty years before (when she was Victoria Wren), does not come to the harbour to see him off. 'But as the xebec was passing Fort St. Elmo or thereabouts, a shining Benz was observed to pull up near the wharf and a black-liveried driver with a mutilated face came to the harbour's edge to gaze out at the ship. After a moment he raised his hand; waved with a curiously sentimental feminine motion of the wrist. He called something in English, which none of the observers understood. He was crying' (p. 463). Why should Evan Godolphin, of all people, be in tears at Stencil's departure? Why the 'curiously sentimental, feminine motion'? One possible answer is that the figure is not Evan at all but Veronica Manganese, that is, V. 'Disguise is one of her attributes.' And if the figure at the harbour is V., and V. is an avatar of Mara, then the appearance of the water spout out of a perfectly cloudless sky may not be a random event. Caries or cabals? In a novel that leaves so much to the inference of the reader, it is difficult to tell, and Sidney Stencil's death presents the reader with what Sidney himself would have described as a Situation.

What makes Thomas Pynchon and Günter Grass among the most formidable of contemporary novelists is their willingness to take on the most enormous events and issues of our century – World War II, genocide, power wielded by ideological lunatics, the development of weapons whose power for destruction is limited only by technical considerations we do not fully understand – and the ability to deal with such issues and events in imaginative terms that approach being commensurate with the events themselves.[30] Both authors are masters of the grotesque, a fact in no way coincidental to their immense success in a task that many modern authors consider impossible. There have been countless novels about the Nazi era and the devastation of European civilisation that it encompassed, but *The Tin Drum* and *Gravity's Rainbow*, sprawling, complex, often revolting by design, seem more than any others to approach sufficiency to the task.

The source of the grotesque in *Gravity's Rainbow* is the unseen narrator himself. Now, we have encountered grotesque narrators before, most notably in *The Tin Drum*, but they have been characters in the novels that they narrate. The most tantalising question about *Gravity's Rainbow* is exactly who or what is telling the story. There seems, rather than one narrator, to be a medley, a cacophony, of narrative voices – scientist, poet, mocking hipster, pedant, singer, orchestra, movie buff, trivia champion, stand-up comedian, professor of history, doper – all competing and trading off with each other at the most unexpected moments. What, if anything, holds it all together and generates the world of the novel?

Recall that in the Southwest Africa chapter of *V.*, characters had the capacity to participate in each other's fantasies, and much of the story seemed to consist of Mondaugen's living in someone else's consciousness. Pirate Prentiss in *Gravity's Rainbow* has the same power, but it is given only perfunctory mention and plays no part in the narrative, as if an original and intriguing possibility of viewpoint had ceased to interest the author. What we get instead of multiple fantasy as a narrative technique is multiple hallucination, that is, fantasy completely out of control, the process of combining elements run amok, synthesis gone berserk. *V.* combined disparate elements, especially the dark seriousness and sinister beauty of the Paris and Southwest Africa episodes with the adolescent clowning of the Benny Profane chapters. Whether by default or by design, however, the seams are so plainly visible that for much of its length, the book seems to be two different novels that do not belong together. But in *Gravity's Rainbow*, the synthesis of an even wider range of disparate elements is absolutely complete, brought about by the hallucinating consciousness of the disembodied narrator. The net effect is that the narrative becomes a kind of palimpsest, offering layers of hallucination which can only be viewed *through* each other. Or, perhaps a different, though related, comparison might be to that kind of decorative Venetian glass in which layers of colour seem to recede toward the centre of the piece. We seem to see each one through the other, but, of course, to appear true, the colours must in actuality be distorted so that the yellow will look yellow when viewed through the red on top of it, and so forth.

The narrative consciousness hallucinates the grotesque world of the novel. But how describe the qualities of a world which is, by design, never clearly visible in itself and is in a wild state of flux?

Indeed, *should* those qualities be defined, or does such a critical inventory contravene everything *Gravity's Rainbow* is trying to say and do? The novel defies all critical approaches, both traditional and contemporary. One certainly cannot attempt biographical criticism, since no one (at least no one who is talking) knows anything much about Thomas Pynchon, the man. Historical placement stumbles upon the wild anachronisms that are part of the basic point of view, which seems to treat World War II as if it had occurred in the 1960s rather than the 1940s. If one proceeds along the most usual lines of analysis, dividing the work into categories or constituent elements, one may be blundering into exactly the kind of thinking that the novel is out to expose as not only specious but pernicious.[31] But if, in the other direction, one attempts to deconstruct the text, pointing to its self-referentiality, plurality of meaning, radical reversal of reader expectations, indeterminacy, and profound scepticism about the reliability of language, then one is merely doing what Pynchon has already done with incomparably greater brilliance.[32] This is a pre-deconstructed novel. In fact, in *Gravity's Rainbow*, Pynchon may well have written exactly what he no doubt set out to write: a novel that is simply *beyond* criticism.

Having noted this, the critic can either walk away with a shrug, despairing of the enterprise, or else proceed knowing that the results are likely to be even more partial and provisional than usual, and may even violate the design of the novel itself. These are always the risks of criticism, but with no other novel do they seem as inimical to confidence as they do with *Gravity's Rainbow*.

A major difficulty in coming to grips with this novel is not that it is anarchic or even disorganised, however much it might try to give that impression, especially in its final section. Rather, the problem arises from its being such an intricately organised book, perhaps even an over-organised book. Once again, the image of a palimpsest comes to mind, with systems of organisation superimposed upon each other, and visible only through each other. But if *Gravity's Rainbow's* self-deconstruction is as much a product of artifice and design as, say, a carefully constructed plot or a unifying point of view would be in conventional fiction, then one way of dealing with the novel might be to seek out the structures of its apparent disorder. The one that is most immediately visible, by its insistent repetition if nothing else, is the pairing of binary opposites, particularly the binary numbers, the 1 and the 0. Time and again characters, topics (the word 'theme' seems wholly inappropriate to this novel), and events are faced with the equal possibility of their own nonexistence, the most pervasive example being the nature of paranoia.[33]

'Paranoia', is, of course, a word we have encountered before in connection with fiction of the modern grotesque, but Kafka and Pynchon are not really comparable in their concepts of what the word means nor in their ways of incorporating it into the worlds of their fiction. In fact, Kafka does not even have a *concept* of paranoia; rather he has an intuition of the world experienced in paranoia, and uses its features, especially projective thinking, as the basis of his work. But in *Gravity's Rainbow*, Pynchon does have a concept of paranoia, and it is more a social concept than a clinical one. The ubiquitous 'They' are linked in a gigantic conspiracy of miltinational cartels, secret government agencies, and a sinister scientific/business community that controls the war, controls the buying and selling which are the real business of the war, and condition the individual for Their purposes from infancy onward. No event, no matter how remote from Them or how seemingly gratuitous, can be assumed simply to have happened without the work of Their hands behind it. Yet the novel allows neither the characters nor the reader to be sure to what extent this mega-conspiracy actually exists outside the minds of those who feel themselves controlled by it. Opposed to the possibility of a world controlled by the few who stand above nationality, above ideology, and serve only power, profit, and death is the complementary alternative: randomness and uncertainty in which even those like Pointsman, who do aim for total control by surreptitious means, are undone by absurd mishaps, and are trying to exert their control in a world that runs by the logic of a lunatic asylum. The White Visitation, the central headquarters for many of the conspirators, actually *is* a mad house, as well as a grotesque architectural conglomeration whose overall effect is chaos: '. . . no two observers, no matter how close they stand see quite same building in that orgy of self-expression, added to by each succeeding owner, until the present War's requisitioning' (p. 83). Pointsman himself, the arch-Pavlovian and Slothrop's behind-the-scenes nemesis, is ultimately discredited because of a preposterous series of events which results in Major Marvy's being surgically castrated instead of Slothrop. Pointsman's binary opposite, the statistician Roger Mexico, acknowledges only distribution, and suggests that perhaps science should abandon cause and effect and strike off at some other angle (p. 89). 'What if Mexico's whole generation have turned out like this', wonders a rattled Pointsman. 'Will Postwar be nothing but "events" newly created one moment to the next? Is it the end of history?' (p. 56).

Even Slothrop, who is convinced that everything that happens to him happens because 'They' have arranged it that way, has his moments of doubt.

> If there is something comforting – religious, if you want – about paranoia, there is still also anti-paranoia, where nothing is connected to anything, a condition not many of us can bear for long. Well right now Slothrop feels himself sliding into the anti-paranoid part of his cycle, feels the whole city around him going back roofless, vulnerable, uncentered as he is, and only pasteboard images now of the Lasting Enemy left between him and the wet sky.
>
> Either They have put him here for a reason, or he's just here. He isn't sure that he wouldn't actually rather have that *reason* . . .
>
> (p. 434)

As the book and its central character self-deconstruct, it becomes hard to imagine how conspiracies such as Slothrop believes in could operate, especially in the Zone, in which all is reduced to randomness and chaos, and master operators like der Springer all seem to operate on their own in a vacuum. Here, as in *V.*, on the matter of sinister international conspiracies versus a world governed by random chance, Pynchon seems determined to have things both ways.

The same binary opposition between an entity and its own negation exists in many other areas of the novel – the Elect and the Preterite, black and white as forces of life and death (but with the customary Western colour values reversed), the Schwarzkommando and the Empty Ones, film and reality (again with the values reversed because in this novel film is more real than 'reality'), target and anti-target, time and the delta-t, and, as we shall see, the wartime world and the Zone. But there also exists a second kind of opposition, not the 1 and the 0, entity and negation, but something more like the pairing of binary stars, two bodies orbiting around a single centre of gravity.

The clearest example is provided by the half-brothers, Enzian and Tchitcherine. In many ways they are diametrical opposites: black and white, African and European, prey and hunter; but at the same time they are inextricably linked to each other, even though they appear together in only one very brief episode at the end of the book. They are both briefly introduced in adjacent episodes, Enzian encountering Slothrop on the roof of a train to Nordhausen, then Tchitcherine described by his girl friend, Geli Tripping, to the panicky Slothrop. They both make their first substantial appearances in adjacent episodes, and their common centre of gravity is, of course, the Rocket. Both are colonels in armed forces from which they are estranged, and Tchitcherine, considering that his difficulties have arisen from the very existence of the brother whom he has never seen, comes to regard Enzian as an actual part of himself, 'a black version of something inside *himself*. A something he needs to . . . liquidate' (p. 499). But ultimately their dual orbits only take them silently past each other, 'not the first time a man has passed his brother by, at the edge of the evening, often forever, without knowing it' (p. 735).

Similar forces of attraction and identity between separate and totally different entities proliferate in the novel, either between characters who may never actually encounter each other, or even between inanimate objects. Gottfried and Katje are male and female, soldier and double agent, yet almost twins in their bondage to Blicero, who turns them into Hansel and Gretel and occasionally cross-dresses them. Ilse and Bianca never encounter each other or even appear in the same episode, but both are phantom-children, begotten from the same pornographic film, *Alpdrücken*, made by Gerhardt von Göll. In long debates between Säure and Gustav, Beethoven and Rossini are advanced as creators of the perfect music. Slothrop's ancestor, William Slothrop, saw Christ and Judas as a necessary binary pair: 'Everything in Creation has its equal and opposite counterpart' (p. 555). For Pökler, the Rocket itself is an 'Aggregat' that unites in combustion the eternal opposites of experience: 'he seemed to look at fuel and oxidizer as paired opposites, male and female principles uniting in the mystical egg of the combustion chamber: creation and destruction, fire and water, chemical plus and chemical minus –' (p. 403). A similar view of the guidance system and its relation to the mystical symbol, the mandala, is explained by Andreas to Slothrop. 'The four fins of the Rocket made a cross, another mandala. . . . Each opposite pair of vanes worked together, and moved in opposite senses. Opposites together' (p. 563).

The mightiest of these 'opposites together' are those which figure largest in creating the world of the novel itself. Like Grass, Pynchon has created a fusion of history and fantasy. His methods of doing so are very different, but the constituent elements are basically the same: the literal facts of wartime Europe and the hallucinations of a unique mind for whom the distinctions between physical reality and fantastic embellishment simply do not exist. One may not think of literal reality as playing much part in *Gravity's Rainbow* at all, but indirectly it does. We are all familiar with the devastated Europe of 1945, most of us, like Pynchon no doubt, through newsreel footage as well as dramtic recreation in films. This literal depiction of life in the rubble of a incredibly large and complex civilisation brought to an even more incredible state of devastation is a basic reference point of the book. It is the bottom layer of the palimpsest, and if we seldom see it directly, it is always there as a component of what we do see, a historical reference point, however obliquely referred to. The rest of the novel, bizarre as it is, would be inaccessible, incapable of producing any effect except random lunacy, if we did not have that abiding awareness of what happened and what the aftermath looked like. Indeed, conjuring up the sense of life in England under the terror of the European war's most fearsome weapon is one of the distinguished accomplishments of the novel's opening section, and for all the grotesque embellishment, a good deal of time and effort is expended on establishing the underlying reality.

The long section entitled 'The War's Evensong', occurs when Roger Mexico and Jessica Swanlake visit a small chapel to hear Christmas music being sung by a choir lead by a black countertenor. The passage can be seen in one way as a kind of prose poem which owes a good deal in its tone and technique to *The Wasteland*. But it can perhaps be more accurately described as a prose movie, for here, as in much of the novel, Pynchon's approach is predominantly visual and overtly cinematic. The basic pattern is to start out with a long, panoramic shot of England, especially the coastal areas, and then to cut rapidly to a series of individual vignettes that are linked by association rather than being chronological or contiguous. To indulge in exactly the kind of division the novel deplores (and uses itself), we can see the reel as composed of ten sequences, each containing from one to five shots, the average being three.

I. The first panorama begins over the coast, where warships are being built or refitted, and huge piles of discarded toothpaste tubes are waiting to be returned to the war, that is, recycled so that the metal can be reused. By association, we focus in on domestic scenes of individual children and adults brushing their teeth. They dream of eating decent meals instead of subsisting on 'the week's offal in gland pies, Household Milk, broken biscuits at half the usual points' (p. 130). When the toothpaste tubes of the British children have been melted down and recast as weapons, they will be used against 'the children of that other domestic incarnation'; thus, the war is the great divider, and the need to make divisions even while calling for solidarity and *volk* is its only true need. 'Yet who can say *what* the War wants, so vast and aloof is it . . . so *absentee*. Perhaps the War isn't even an awareness – not a life at all, really. There may be some cruel, accidental resemblance to life' (p. 131).

II. This abstraction leads away from the mundane to the fantastic, and the sound is raised on the sardonic voice of the narrator recalling the schizophrenic patient at the White Visitation who thought he *was* the War, whose temperature shot up to 104° on D-Day, and who would die on V–E Day. This projected death recalls by association the tribal practice of killing the venerated king at a predetermined time, and kings are now shown venerating the Christ child at Bethlehem by bringing Him gifts of war munitions.

III. Fast cut now, back to another panorama over England, moving in from the coast to view a collection of the abandoned – women who have postponed their weddings for another year and hung up their mouldering wedding dresses: Asian refugees wandering through a city that is unrelated to them, or huddled in an underground that cannot afford the protection from the Rocket that it did from the Blitz; Italian prisoners of war set to work in the post office trying to cope with the blitz of Christmas mail. By contrast, the English have 'no *play*, for God's sake, about life and death' (p. 132).

IV. The cut is now to more scenes of mundane frustration, as people wish for the pleasures of Christmas without the war, such as children playing with electric trains, an image suggested by the shot of the underground station in the preceding segment. But now the children play with toy war weapons fashioned from old Spam tins which, like the toothpaste tubes, have been recycled.

The scene at Bethlehem is introduced once again by way of the manger sets in the homes. The children still believe that 'on the magic night before, the animals will talk, and the sky will be milk', but their grandparents are 'watching again for the yearly impossible not to occur . . .' (p. 133).

V. The mention of the elderly leads into the bitterest sequence of the Evensong; the hopeless old live in cold poverty because 'the War needs coal'. Faceless powers running the grid tamper with the voltage ('the War needs electricity'), so that the electric clocks go haywire, whirling toward the Nativity in 'the Night's Mad Carnival' (p. 133).

VI. The camera draws back again to a high panorama, and for the remainder of the prose film the view is more remote, zooming in only momentarily to pick out fragmented images. On the sea shore, the pleasure boats of prewar years have been abandoned, and the beach is strewn with barbed wire put there to repel the German invasion that never came. The city streets are blacked out, even the headlamps of the high, red buses. Birds, confused by the anti-aircraft search lights, fly until they drop like rain on the people below.

VII. Back in the church, the choir intones 'Where are the joys?' The voice of the narrator fades in, admonishing the soldier to give over the war, as he did when he left his heart at the stage door canteen. The title of the popular 1940s tune prompts the only piece of grotesque clowning in the footage, as AFI girls are pictured sorting out aorta of real flesh and blood left at the night club. The continuing sardonic voice insists that 'Everybody you don't suspect is in on this', even Walt Disney, whose Dumbo is like the body of the fallen soldier at the Battle of the Bulge that lies in the snow clutching a religious medal.

VII. At the climax, or rather the apex, of the piece the camera tilts back suddenly to the sky, where the Rocket is poised in the measureless instant before it begins the descent half of its arc, 'a Christmas star in helpless plunge to Earth' (p. 135). The singing angels are V–1 buzz-bombs coming in below.

VIII. The scene switches for a third time to Bethlehem, now a Roman version of the Zone, with bookmakers, hookers, hustlers, double agents, and Roman census takers who are thinking about assigning a number to everyone.

IX. The ancient analogy produces another fast cut to a heckled chaplain at the Bulge, drawing a parallel between Herod and Hitler in what turns out to be a sermon delivered in jive talk on the insanity of salvation.

X. The voice of the narrator fades in again to conclude with what is one of the very few tender passages in the novel, as the reader is seen to be the failed saviour of the infant Christ, Himself in need of salvation.

Like the concluding verses of the novel, 'The War's Evensong' is a hymn of the Preterite, an empty gesture before the even emptier one of continuing the war. (There is a similar, though much shorter, prose movie later in the book, 'Nationalities on the Move', a slow-motion migration of Europe's refugees down the roadways of the continent, a passage probably suggested by the newsreels which were the daily fare of neighbourhood movie houses in 1945 and 1946. Consisting mostly of long strings of adjectives and participial phrases, the passage is strung out like the endless lines of refugees themselves. It is a junk inventory of European civilisation – tools, clothes, random possessions, 'the detritus of an order, a European and bourgeois order they don't yet know is destroyed forever' [p. 551]). Such passages, taken by themselves, can lead one to suspect that under all the hip and mockery, Pynchon is a crypto-humanist at heart, just as other passages might portray him as a touchingly old-fashioned agrarian anarchist. But as usual with a very complicated writer, one should be careful about staking too much on any individual passage.[34] 'The War's Evensong' is a moving, even a beautiful piece of writing, but it is only one element, and a rather rare one, in Pynchon's world of binary opposition. The zero is the Zone.[35]

By definition, a zone is demarcated, set off, defined by boundaries; yet, within the Zone, there is anarchic freedom, all boundaries, like all restraints on behaviour, having collapsed with civilisation. The previous order, or more exactly, the previous specific kind of disorder, has vanished, and the restricted spheres of authority and systems of exclusion have yet to appear. Russians and Americans swill beer together in the underground SS rocket factory, and the Schwarzkommando set up in business for themselves. In Berlin, outside has become inside and vice-versa; the straight boulevards have become winding trails through the rubble and 'Earth has turned over in its sleep, and the tropics are reversed' (p. 373). Action in the Zone is dominated not by vast unseen conspiracies, but by dope dealers, hipsters, and free wheeling super-operators like der Springer, Wimpe, Enzian, Tchitcherine

Major Marvy, and sometimes even Rocketman himself.[36] The Zone is, above all, motion – frenetic, aimless motion, nothing at rest. 'All anyone knows about you is that you keep showing up', Enzian tells Slothrop (p. 364). Slothrop himself comes to view the situation as a kind of mass transit system of conspiracies which converge and digress along lines even more complex than the design of a modern subway system. You can transfer from one to another and keep going endlessly (p. 603). But the transport image that more accurately describes the Zone is offered elsewhere in the book (p. 412): a tour bus driven by an affable lunatic, talking fast as he gleefully careens toward random destruction. 'We all just keep moving, that's all. In the end it doesn't matter', explains Ensign Morituri aboard the *Anubis*, giving voice to the first law of the Zone.[37]

Even the slow-moving *Anubis* is speeded up; the ship may be on a leisurely cruise to nowhere, but life on board is very fast indeed. The orgy, initiated by Greta's and Bianca's studio mother/screen moppet spanking routine, is not so much a piece of calculated obscenity (though it is that) as frenetic sexual anarchy, in which all practices are rather like the notes in Webbern's music, 'an expansion of music's polymorphous perversity till all notes were truly equal at last' (p. 440). The *Anubis* is the most accessible image of decadence in the novel because it is the most obvious, the floating equivalent of Foppl's seige party during the Black uprising in *V.*, jaded gaiety surrounded on all sides by death. The white pleasure ship is bracketed by two other unusual vessels in the episodes immediately preceding and following its appearance: the toilet ship, *Rücksichtslos*, to which the Schwarzkommando abduct Achtfaden, and the sea-going drag-racer of Frau Gnahb, with which she ultimately rams the fantasy-yacht. The *Anubis* is decadent not so much because of its hedonism or the brittle cruelty of its passengers; it epitomises decadence in the novel because those on board are oblivious to being on a death-ship, sailing out of disaster to nowhere in particular.

This frenetic energy devoted to aimless movement propels the novel itself to its anti-conclusion. One thing about *Gravity's Rainbow* that not even its most avid admirers have much commented on is that it is such a superbly paced novel, a major consideration for so long and dense and difficult a book. A plot it may not have in the usual sense (or it may have so many of them that they get lost in each others' debris), but it surely does have a climax. The very pace and energy of the prose seem to increase as the coherence and structure, such of they have been, are deliberately thinned and finally sabotaged. With the increasing velocity and energy of the ride, the Zone periodically metamorphoses into *Raketen-Stadt*.

Raketen-Stadt is not really a locale; the action seldom fully shifts there. Rather its coming, its epiphany, is repeatedly announced, and it fades in and out of sight like a mirage or, more exactly, like this hallucinating novel's ultimate hallucination. It is first envisioned by Slothrop as he approaches the underground SS-shaped rocket factory at Nordhausen; he sees it as a kind of world's fair exhibit, with unauthorised guided tours being offered on the sly by a carnival hustler named 'Micro' Graham. Besides showing the slave labour camp, Dora, and the former quarters of the Schwarzkommando, 'Micro' also takes spectators to the remotest area of the caves to a model city of the future, where everything is based on The Promise of Space Travel. But instead of being the highly organised, hi-tech Utopia usually offered at fairs and trade shows, it is a vision of futuristic chaos. 'No, this Rocket-City, so whitely lit against the calm dimness of space, is set up deliberately To Avoid Symmetry, Allow Complexity, Introduce Terror (from the Preamble to the Articles of Immachination) – but tourists have to connect the look of it back to things they remember from their own times and planet . . .' (p. 297). A futurist vision of terror based on the memory of past experience is what *Raketen-Stadt* is for Enzian. A model like a vast toy train set which he views from the isolation of a balcony, the ultimate limit of his own estrangement from the world of both Africa and Europe – so he envisions it when Katje asks him what Blicero still means to him. For Blicero, the Rocket was transcendence; for Enzian, it is merly elevation.

At other points in the novel, especially in part four, *Raketen-Stadt*, like most illusions in *Gravity's Rainbow*, acutally materialises filled with bizarre characters and events, including Slothrop's father, who is springing endless ingenious plots to kill him. Action has become even more frenetic and disjointed than in the Zone 'Decisions are never really *made* – at best they manage to emerge from a chaos of peeves, whims, hallucinations and all-round assholery' (p. 676). *Raketen-Stadt* is everything and nothing. It i the world disintegrating in disintegrating minds. The dopers, fas talkers, and con men are back in force with renewed energy, thu accentuating the pun on the English 'Rocket' and the Germa 'Racket' city, the building of the rocket, like all the war, havin been an international scam of the I. G., G. E., and Siemens A. G., the shell game of Shell Mex. It is Fritz Lang's underground metropolis, and Buck Roger's twenty-fifth century, with elevators as large and comfortable as airliners providing a 'Vertical Solution' to the problem of getting around the ever-growing rocket capitol. It seems also to owe something to the 'Interzone' in a number of Burroughs novels, especially in the manic energy and malicious glee of the narrative tone.[38] Yet another affinity is the California of Richard M. Zlubb, in which the novel spends its final moments. But mostly it is composed of hallucinations even more densely concentrated than those in the rest of the novel. It is the Rocket-cartel, the ultimate conspiracy, 'and the Rocket is its soul' (p. 566).

A grotesque, hallucinated world, energetic though dying, popu-lated by characters who are themselves often extreme grotesques, such is the world of *Gravity's Rainbow*.[39] Yet the characters are not merely *in* the setting; to a great extent, they constitute it, the common bond being that they and it are all hallucinated by the narrator. More than in any other novel I know, one is aware of the characters as being figments of the narrative persona.[40] He even endows them intermittently with his own mannerisms – the slight stammer, especially on the word 'and', the tendency to lapse into jive talk or the radio and movie stereotype of teenage talk in the 1930s, a fondness for tossing off one-liners based on pop culture – whether such mannerisms are appropriate to their characters or not. The most grotesque of these creations is Captain Blicero, and he dominates the novel all the more because ultimately he turns out to be its principal spokesman.

'Blicero' is one of several characters who are carryovers from *V.*, where he was a minor but sinister figure in the most powerful single episode Pynchon has written to date, the Southwest Africa chapter. In the earlier novel, he is not so much a character as a presence, a foreshadow as early as 1922 of what lay ahead for Germany, a reincarnation of the anonymous soldier (Foppl as a young man?) whose experiences during von Trotha's massacre of the Herero's Mondaugen experiences as a feverish dream/fantasy. The events are more than a preview of militarism and racism combining to produce genocide. By some deepening malaise born out of boredom and displacement, as well as from the freedom to do anything here thousands of miles from 'civilisation', cruelty becomes not only a sadistic pleasure but an absolute aesthetic, closely allied to the most tender feelings of love. Cruelty is the inspiring force behind all culture and personal life, dominating gaiety, love-making, art, even nostalgia. '"I loved the man"', Foppl recalls of von Trotha. '"He taught us not to fear. It's impossible to describe the sudden release; the comfort, the luxury; when you knew you could safely forget all the rote lessons you'd had to learn about the value and dignity of human life. . . . Till we've done it, we're taught that it's evil. Having done it, then's the struggle: to admit to yourself that its not really evil at all. That like forbidden sex, it's enjoyable"' (*V.*, p. 234).

That combination of refined sadism and an exquisite aesthetic sense puts one in mind of Kafka's Officer in 'In the Penal Colony', with his sensitive appreciation for the subtle embellishments of the machine. In *Gravity's Rainbow*, our first introduction to Weissmann/Blicero, Captain 'White Death', is by way of his fondness for Rilke's poetry, and his equally delicate appreciation of the tortures he inflicts upon his 'children', Katje and Gottfried. But the oblique, veiled quality that characterises the Duino Elegies, governs the presentation of Blicero as well. A half-dozen pages in the first section of the novel constitute the only direct access the narrator gives us into the officer's mind; in contrast to other major characters, Weissmann is seen almost entirely through the eyes of others – Katje, Gottfried, Thanatz, Margherita Erdman, Pökler, and Enzian. Moreover, many of these second-hand protrayals are couched in terms that might best be called 'the borrowed grotesque'. In Pynchon's depiction of Blicero, there is no attempt, as there is, say, in William Styron's characterisation of Rudolf Höss, to understand the psychology of atrocity.[41] Pynchon is more interested in finding metaphors for it, predominantly visual metaphors, and in his search for them, he ransacks the culture, from fairy tales, to movies, to opera, to science, to poetry. What makes Blicero such a compelling villain is that he is such a patently artificial one, but at the same time, so immediate, strange to the point of outlandish fantasy but instantly recognisable. Pynchon is here treading the same no-man's-land as Grass: is it *possible* to exaggerate anything about the Nazis? Perhaps, but Pynchon insists time and again that they must be exaggerations drawn from recognisable portions of our culture. For him, the decadence of a society is most visible in its artefacts, and of these, none is more telling than the images it creates. Hence, the preoccupation with film throughout *Gravity's Rainbow*, especially with such films as *King Kong* and *Bride of Frankenstein*, and with art and sub-art in general. Hence, his construction of elaborate systems of images superimposed upon history and overlaid across each other. Blicero is not so much a character as a series of transformations into monstrosities born out of all areas of modern culture.

For example, in Katje's recollection after she has fled to the White Visitation, he is first presented as the witch from Hansel and Gretel, as she remembers his teeth, 'long, terrible, veined with bright brown as he speaks these words, the yellow teeth of Captain Blicero, the network of stained cracks, and back in his nightbreath, in the dark oven himself, always the coiled whispers of decay' (p. 94). But Katje suspected, and Blicero confirms in his own reverie, that the game drawn from the fairy tale is itself an elaborate screen from the truth, that the 'little Oven-state', grotesque and sadistic as it is, 'shall be their preserving routine, their shelter, against what outside none of them can bear – the War, the absolute rule of chance, their own pitiable contingency here, in its midst . . .' (p. 96).

The most powerful and unnerving of the depictions of Blicero both occur during the voyage of the *Anubis*, when first Thanatz, and then Margherita desribe their meeting with him. Their tour on 'the barbed wire circuit', presenting pornographic shows for the SS men at the death camps, finally took them to the Schwarzgerät launch-site on the Lünenberg Heath. Once again, the image of him is borrowed, this time from opera. '"The battery commander had become a screaming maniac. . . . He'd begun to talk the way the captain in *Wozzeck* sings, his voice breaking suddenly up into the higher registers of hysteria. Things were falling apart, and he reverted to some ancestral version of himself, screamed at the sky, sat hours in a rigid trance, with his eyes rolled clear up into his head. Breaking without warning into that ungodly coloratura"' (p. 465) [42] For Thanatz, the transformation constitutes not just madness but a primal reversion to the 'Urstoff' of pagan Germany, and perhaps a necessary, or at any rate, exciting corrective to the Christianised world, with its obligation to the 'Contract' which never did exist; '". . . we are appalled by reversions like that. But deep, out of its silence, the Urstoff wakes and sings"'.

Later in the episode, Margherita, herself hysterical to the point of madness, and perhaps having killed her daughter, also sees Blicero as living in mythical rather than real space and time. Her image of him, drawn ultimately from folklore but immediately from the horror movies with which she is so intimately familiar, is of a werewolf, who, in a shriek so quiet it is almost a whisper, describes his own grotesque, dehumanised face as the map of his Ur-Heimat, the land of the Lord Blicero. 'I had an understanding: he was seeing the world now in *mythical regions*: they had their maps, real mountains, rivers, and colours. It was not Germany he moved through. It was his own space' (p. 486). Like von Göll, Blicero has the power to bring his private myths of torture and destruction into actual reality. Upon first arriving at the site, Thanatz and Greta walk through what they first think are ancient ruins, but as they walk on, filled with growing and inexplicable terror, they come to recognise the ruin as a recently destroyed city, and the destruction was not wrought by the wartime means that have now become routine. 'In the middle of the road, giant turds showed up, fresh laid in twists like strands of rope – dark and knotted. What could have left them? . . . Ahead of them, the path curved on, into trees. But something stood now between them and whatever lay around the curve: invisible, impalpable . . . some *monitor*. Saying, "Not one step farther. That's all. Not one. Go back now"' (p. 485). The 'monitor' suggests 'Minotaur', the mythical beast Pointsman dreams of in part one, and whose labyrinth is mentioned several times throughout the novel. As with Vheissu in *V.*, horror has passed beyond the real and possible terrors of war even at its worst, and has assumed the aura of hallucination, the mythical terror that is the native habitat of the grotesque. There are also resonances of Vheissu in Greta's recollection of having been dressed by Blicero's henchmen in a costume of Imipolex G, presumably while the S-Gerät was being fired. 'Great curtains of styrene or vinyl, in all colors, opaque and transparent, hung row after row from overhead. They flared like the northern lights' (p. 487). As always, the reaction to Blicero is ultimately one of uncontrollable erotic arousal, and Greta's description of her plastic ecstasy parallels Gottfried's immolation taking place simulataneously but not described until the closing pages of the novel.

Pökler, an enthusiast, though not a poet, where rockets are concerned, provides no mythical dimension for Blicero, nor any image consciously borrowed directly from other art to epitomise what the Captain has become. Why, then, does the Blicero we see through Pokler's eyes seem at once remote and yet familiar? Where do we recognise him from? The answer, I think, is in a feverish mental picture Slothrop has during his bout with dysentery:

' – lost, alone with that sovereign Nazi movie-villain fist clamping in his bowels ja – you vill *shit* now, ja?' (p. 360). For Pökler, Blicero is an unimposing man endowed with complete inscrutability and complete omnipotence, solely because he has control of the only thing in life Pökler any longer values, the chance of seeing, for two weeks a year, his daughter Ilse – though he fears that this too is a cinematic sort of illusion manufactured by substituting a different child each year. Aside from this power, Blicero is small, greying, wears thick bottle-glass spectacles, but seems to be contemplating his virtual ownership of a good plastics man with confidence that derives from being in complete control of a game, the other party not even being sure of what the rules are. Blicero as seen by Pökler is the sum total of dozens of cruelly smiling Hollywood SS men, all of whom probably had their genesis in the newsreel footage of Dr. Joseph Goebbels. Many critics have marvelled at Pynchon's ability to create with almost palpable reality events and settings which he could never have personally seen. In the case of the Nazis, I think perhaps the opposite may be the case. He can create characters like Blicero precisely because he had *no* experience with their real life counterparts, his sources, like his methods, being largely cinematic. Blicero as stock movie SS man is something within our experience, though carried in the novel to extremes that the movies of the 1940s could not imagine, let alone dramatise.

Several of the most complex and ambivalent views we get of Weissmann are from the vantage of the Schwarzkommando leader, Enzian, the German's protege, former lover, and ersatz son. Interestingly, it is this relationship that we see first through Blicero's own mind during the short passage for which the novel is situated in his consciousness. Blicero, like Enzian, is strangely unsure whether he was victimiser or victim, corruptor or corrupted, creator or destroyer. As agent of the former colonial power, Weissmann tainted the young Herero with European culture, displaced him from Africa, made him into 'Weissmann's monster', and an acolyte of the Rocket. But Weissmann himself had been infected, and the bizarre career which reaches its climax on the Lünenberg Heath had its beginnings in Southwest Africa. 'Among the abrading fires of the Kalahari, under the broadly-sheeted coastal sky, fire and water, he learned' (p. 99). The first thing that the Herero had done was to destroy the possibilities of keeping things within well-separated categories. When Enzian used the native word for god to ask for sex, Blicero was terrified for he still believed in blasphemy; '. . . but to the boy, Ndjambi Karunga is what happens when they couple, that's all: God is creator and destroyer, sun and darkness, all sets of opposites brought together, including black and white, male and female . . .' (p. 100). For Blicero back in Europe, the Europe of the dying Reich with all categories in shambles, the means of reconciling those opposites – black and white, male and female, creation and destruction – are his sadistic sex games with the interchangeable 'twins', Katje and Gottfried, Hansel and Gretel, and finally the firing of the oven itself, the Schwarzgerät. Moreover, it was Enzian who taught him that every god *must* be both organiser and destroyer, and it is such a god whose identity Weissmann attempts to assume in his demented self-transformation into Dominus Blicero.

Enzian himself is attempting to imitate the final action of his ersatz father, mentor, and lover, asembling a unique version of the Rocket, the 00001, and firing it to nowhere. The novel never makes clear (even by its own standards of what might pass for clarity) why Enzian, like Slothrop, Tchitcherine, and Marvy, is hunting the S-Gerät, or whether he and the Schwarzkommando ever do launch their scavenged A4. On issues of real importance, Enzian does not think in terms of reasons, but in terms of associations; he is the most poetic of the characters in his habits of thought, and his poetry springs not from a cultivated aesthetic but from an inner urgency that he does not try to articulate in any terms other than those that have immediacy to him. He is no less a puzzlement to the other characters of the novel than he is to a reader.

What is clear, if by nothing more than constant association, is that the assembly and launch of the last rocket is closely identified in his own mind with resistance to the Empty Ones, and their advice, tribal suicide.[43] Ombindi riddles with Enzian about the most erotic of all things, a non-repeatable act. 'Firing a rocket', suggests Enzian, but Ombindi demurs because there will always be another rocket. His answer, of course, is suicide, because it includes, at least by analogy, all possible sex acts, including the 'Deviations' (319). Enzian in turn declines to be convinced, and presumably sticks to his original answer. For him, there are really only two choices: to risk probable death by doing the one thing that will assure that all the whites, regardless of nation or ideology, will implacably pursue his death and the destruction of the

Schwarzkommando; that is, he will arm his sub-state with a working A4. The alternative is accepting passive death by attrition, completing the work that von Trotha and his troops left not quite finished forty years before. The point is made explicit by Andreas when he is explaining to Slothrop the relation between the Rocket's fins and the mandala-shaped village of the Hereros: 'But [the Rocket] was waiting for us when we came north to Germany so long ago . . . even confused and uprooted as we were then, we *knew* that our destiny was tied up with its own. That we had been passed over by von Trotha's army so that we would find the Aggregat' (p. 563). For Enzian, the only choice is between activity and passivity; the successful launch will, in some way that seems apparent only to him, achieve the transcendence he ascribes to Blicero – the separation from the European amalgam of time, death, and the Rocket – that the Empty Ones themselves see as the promise of tribal self-annihilation. 'What Enzian wants to create will have no history. It will never need a design change. Time, as time is known to the other nations, will wither away inside this new one. The Erdschweinhohle will not be bound, like the Rocket, to time. The people will find the Centre again, the Centre without time, the journey without hysteresis, where every departure is a return to the same place . . .' (pp. 318–19).

As for Weissmann himself, at least seen in retrospect by the Enzian of 1945, 'The man's thirst for guilt was insatiable as the desert's for water', and his real love was for 'the last explosion' (p. 324). Nevertheless, Enzian is trying to become Weissmann in reverse, Schwarz Weissmann, as if the Rocket could provide the same centre of identity for him that it had for Blicero, as if he could resolve the binary opposition, the 00001 facing the 00000. When he finally hears from Thanatz what happened on the Lünenberg Heath, he feels somehow his own sense of transcendence, not so much a reconciliation with the Empty Ones as a fulfilment within his own soul of the mystical *something* which has always united him, even against his will, with the Rocket and with Weissmann, its high priest, its magician, even its theologian. But as with all quests in the Zone, it comes to nothing. In his few remaining appearances, Enzian dissolves almost as helplessly as Slothrop; the 00001 may or may not be launched, and he and Ombindi are as much irreconcilable opposites as ever.

By the time he talks to the Schwarzkommando, Thanatz is convinced that Blicero is still alive, but the novel leaves us a good deal less certain.[44] The borrowed image at this point is of a ghost: 'He is the Zone's worst specter. . . . Weissmann/Blicero's presence crossed the wall, warping, shivering into the fetid bunkrooms, with the same reach toward another shape as words trying to make their way through dreams' (p. 666). He presides over a 'phantom SS command' which the 175's, the homosexuals of Dora Camp, the outcasts from even the damned, have set up after their liberation because they could not live without their oppressors. As always with Blicero, his madness and grotesqueness produce not revulsion in those he encounters, but identification and uncontrollable sexual arousal, as Thanatz, the only outsider to see the launch of the S-Gerät, admits (to himself? to the Schwarzkommando? to the spectral Blicero?) that he too had desired to murder the child he loved, Bianca, as some kind of primal or biblical sacrifice, and the ultimate ecstasy of self-imposed pain.

By this time, something of the mesmerising effect that Blicero has exerted over all the characters of the novel has begun to rub off on the reader. In part, this is because we are finally on the brink of the launch of the S-Gerät, one expectation that the author does not thwart. Blicero himself has become a kind of male V., fascinating because of his monstrosity, the quintessential grotesque. He has also become the supreme artist, the Rilke of rocketry, the aesthete of atrocity. He commits atrocities not in the name of war, but in the name of beauty; he has gone mad, not because of what he has seen or endured, but because he is following his own artistic principles to their conclusion. He also becomes the closest thing that the novel has to a spokesman for the central conception that has been its fuel and oxodiser from the beginning.

And sometimes I dream of discovering the edge of the World. Finding there *is* an end. My mountain gentian always knew. But it cost me so much.

America *was* the edge of the world. A message for Europe, continent-sized, inescapable. Europe had found the site for its Kingdom of Death, that special Death the West had invented. Savages had their waste regions, Kalaharis, lakes so misty they could not see the other side. But Europe had gone deeper – into obsession, addiction, away from all the savage innocences. America was a gift from the invisible powers, a way of returning. But Europe refused it. It wasn't Europe's Original Sin – the latest name for that is Modern Analysis – but it happens that Subsequent Sin is harder to atone for.

In Africa, Asia, Amerindia, Oceania, Europe came and established its order of Analysis and Death. What it could not use, it killed or altered. In time the death-colonies grew strong enough to break away. But the impulse to empire, the mission to propagate death, the structure of it kept on. Now we are in the last phase. American Death has come to occupy Europe. It has learned empire from its old metropolis. But now we have *only* the structure left us, none of the great rainbow plumes, no fittings of gold, no epic marches over alkali seas. The savages of the other continents, corrupted but still resisting in the name of life, have gone on despite everything . . . while Death and Europe are separate as ever, their love still unconsummated. Death only rules here. It has never, in love, become *one with* . . .

(pp. 722–23)

Here is, I believe, what I observed at the start of this essay was lacking in *V.*, a conception of the process of decadence commensurate with Pynchon's sense of its symptoms and his ability find fictions in which to embody them. Decadence for the West is the death-love of Europe transported to its colonies, from whence it returns as the final stage of the terminal infection. That relationship is the riddle of Wiessmann and Enzian as creators and destroyers of each other. 'Fathers are carriers of the virus of Death, and sons are infected . . . and, so that the infection may be more certain, Death in its ingenuity has contrived to make the father and son beautiful to each other as Life has made male and female' (p. 723). So Blicero croons to Gottfried, the lover and ersatz son, as white as the first had been black, whom he is about to immolate by launching him not so much into death as into an indefinite and hopeless future. The S-Gerät is aimed southward, the one direction in which the Nazis did not fire it. But it comes down in the Los Angeles of the Nixon era, the new-world *Raketenstadt* – except that it does not land; the perfect rocket never does. It is poised for infinity in the delta-t, the moment that never arrives. The 'Ascent' section ends 'Now – ' as the 'Descent' ends 'Now everybody – ', but the now can never arrive; it is suspended like the Rocket, shaved to ever narrower slivers of non-time, as the Preterite join hands and sing.

The very name of this rocket-grail, the object of so many and such varied quests, is, I think, significant. 'Gerät' means apparatus, or, as Pynchon opts, instrument. But there is also the German verb, 'geraten' (third person singular, 'gerät'), meaning to turn out or, particularly, to succeed. Finally, there is the verb 'raten', to advise or counsel, the past participle of which is 'gerat', the same word without the umlaut. The launching of the S-Gerät is a final outcome or success, but it is a success of madness and an impulse toward death. The Empty Ones have all along been formally counselling death, and Enzian's quest had been for the Rocket as an antidote to that black counsel. The usual western colour associations of black with death and white with life have throughout the novel been reversed, but now they are combined, as the extremely pale-skinned, white-haired Gottfried, clad in white lace and the white shroud, is immolated in the black instrument fabricated for only that purpose. That these multiple puns – Gerät, geraten/gerät, and raten/gerat are intentional is signalled, I think, by the presence a bit earlier in the subsection entitled 'On the Phrase "Ass Backwards"', of a little disquisition on German umlaut puns. Säure recalls a woman, Minne Klaetch (whose name could have an umlaut instead of the diphthong), who could not pronounce umlauted vowels, and so when calling for defence from a 'cute thief' (hübsch Räuber) seems to be exclaiming about a helicopter (Hubschrauber, literally 'lift screwer').

The Schwarzgerät itself is a multiple image of Europe and America as mutual infectors of each other. It is a ballistic missile, of a kind which will become the ultimate engine of death, but it is also a parody of a space ship, of a kind that will (as Blicero foresaw) go to the edge beyond America, the moon, and become the ultimate conqueror of gravity. It is a conjunction of science, eros, cruelty, and art, the four main driving forces of the novel itself. It unifies both sexes, the phallic rocket with a womb and foetus inside, the foetus wrapped in a placenta. But it is a man-made, plastic placenta, constructed by Pökler out of Imipolex G (as good a hint as the novel gives us about why Slothrop, with his mammoth Oedipal problems, had his unique sexual relationship with the 00000's siblings). This womb bears not the beginning of life, but the infinite plunge into death.

The launch of the Rocket stands in binary relation to another climactic scene in the novel, Slothrop's liaison with and abandonment of Bianca back on the *Anubis*.[45] In his imagination, Slothrop had seemed to be inside his own penis, and his orgasm was the firing of a rocket. Now the metaphor has become literal, as metaphors tend to do in fiction of the modern grotesque. It is characteristic of this novel, in which all values are pushed beyond the zero, that in a scene which out-Humberts Humbert, the erotic act conventional society most despises and condemns, sex between an adult and a child, is presented as a lost opportunity for salvation. Slothrop's crime is not that he has vigorous intercourse with a girl of eleven or twelve, but that he does not persevere in the relationship. 'We can get away. I'm a child, I know how to hide. I can hide you too', Bianca offers, but, knowing she can succeed, he leaves her, 'and for this he is to be counted after all, among the Zone's lost' (p. 470). Even when he comes to realise, through Ensign Morituri's story, that Bianca may be in danger from her homicidal mother, Slothrop fails to save her because he is engulfed, literally, by the perpetual party going on aboard the ship. The beginning of his eventual dissolution is later dated to this moment when he killed his love-child just as surely as Blicero is killing his.

The Schwarzgerät has been further modified so that voice radio messages can be received but not sent. In his final words to the launched Gottfried, Blicero again becomes spokesman for the vision of the novel. His message is not about a social situation but of a planetary one, the situation of the planet we inhabit and we who inhabit it. '"The edge of evening . . . the long course of people all wishing on the first star. . . . Always remember those men and women along the thousands of miles of land and sea. The true moment of shadow is the moment in which you see the point of light in the sky. The single point and the Shadow that has just gathered you in its sweep . . ."' (pp. 759–60). The evening star upon which the masses make their wishes (cf. p. 553), is visible only as the shadow line demarcating day from night, passes along the face of the earth just where those hopers are situated. 'The first star hangs between his feet', the narrator says of Gottfried, and the Rocket turns from its apex as the force of gravity takes over.

Pynchon's vision of modern decadence, when extrapolated from the novel, seems unbearably bleak even by the standards of modern fiction. 'So generation after generation of men in love with pain and passivity serve out their time in the Zone, silent, redolent of faded sperm, terrified of dying, desperately addicted to the comforts others sell them, however useless ugly or shallow, willing to have life defined for them by men whose only talent is for death' (p. 747). Yet, far from being a universal shrug, the novel itself is more like a high-powered rocket ride into regions undreamt of, complete with on-board movies and all sorts of hijinx to ward off boredom on a very long trip. Pynchon's is a particularly ebullient apocalypse.

The most astonishing thing about his writing is the length to which he will go in creating depictions of modern experience as serious as those of any living writer, while undermining that same purpose with more deliberate low-grade clowning than any serious contemporary writer, even Heller or Vonnegut, has attempted, let alone gotten away with.[46] Like any truly original work, *Gravity's Rainbow* challenges us to take it on its own terms, and those terms are not just black comedy (what are we more used to than that?), but a combination of the most complex and erudite mind in current American literature with the narrative voice and sense of humour of an obstreperous, ebullient, and frequently exasperating adolescent. An early comment often made about *V.* was that Pynchon would be among the most brilliant writers of his generation if he would only cut the horsing around, interspersing masterpieces like the Southwest Africa chapter with Benny Profane's misadventures, episodes which often read like material from a college humour magazine.[47] Pynchon's response has been neither to increase nor decrease the adolescent clowning, but to integrate it fully into the texture of his fiction. In *Gravity's Rainbow*, the relation between the cataclysmic and the sophomoric is not one of juxtaposition or contrast or mere proximity. Nor can the two be said to be identical. Rather we are constantly seeing one through the other. There are so many different voices, with different attitudes and areas of knowledge, that it is not only impossible to sort them out; it is often impossible to decide the composition of the mix we are listening to at any given point. But the one that carries most strongly, that forms the largest part of our reaction to the work, is the voice of the contemptuous adolescent. That is the top layer of the palimpsest. The Schwarzgerät is the most complex and brilliant image of the novel, but the book's spirit is epitomised by Tchitcherine's youthful plot to throw a custard pie at Stalin. The rocketry may be drawn from von Braun and Dornberger, but the outlook is straight from the Spike Jones record of the 1940s (mentioned on page 678), 'Hi-yo Pffffffft! Right in der Fuhrer's Face.'

No assumption makes sense except that this combination is a

deliberate device of a very deliberate artist.[48] If much of the success of *The Tin Drum* derives from Grass's ability to convey the experience of the Nazi era through the eyes of a narrator who is simultaneously lunatic, child, artist, and hero, Pynchon achieves a comparable tour de force by convincing us that his narrator can be genius and goof-off, and can serve by turns (or often simultaneously) as tour director, technical director, movie director, music director, voyeur, put-on artist, Slothrop's alter ego, hipster, doper, and smart-ass kid.[49] Thus the narrator is not a unifying point of view as in traditional fiction, or even as in so unconventional a work as *The Tin Drum*. Rather we have here the narrator as multiple personality, reminding us that rockets and toilets are both human inventions which speak with equal importance about the nature of their inventor. (One section is actually entitled, 'Listening to the Toilet'.) Moreover, there is a kind of zestful glee about *both* the major incompatible elements of the novel. Nobody learns as much about science as Pynchon has without having feelings for it besides apprehension and revulsion, just as no one writes a seven hundred plus page book with a Rocket as its central character if he does not share something of Pökler's fascination with rockets as rockets, quite apart from their employment as engines of death. Conversely, the relentless vulgarity of the novel, its obsession with toilets and what goes into them, its sexual anarchy, its hype for the drug culture, its insistence on the appropriateness of low humour in *any* context whatsoever, all have about them something of the adolescent's desire to use the outrageous to advantage while also having a laugh out of it himself.

Pynchon is not the first writer to portray World War II (America's 'good war') anachronistically as if it had taken place in the counterculture of the 1960s; Heller had already done that. But what we get in Pynchon, at least by inference, is a sense of how much the 1960s were a product of World War II. The violent rejection of Western culture by the young, especially the privileged, gifted, educated young, the universal suspicion of Them and disposition to find Their hand in the working of all social evils, the 'Vietnam Era' itself, were not just the immediate effects of Vietnam, but also the delayed effect of events which the dissidents had not experienced first hand, or, like those Americans of Pynchon's age, had experienced as the remote background of their childhoods. The period of the late 1960s, when *Gravity's Rainbow* was being written, may have been a product of Vietnam, but it was just as much an attitude waiting for Vietnam or something like it to happen. The most sweeping and, in the long run, most powerful reaction was the vindication of a style and culture that was not just a protest against the established order, but a calculated insult to it.

Gravity's Rainbow is, among a great many other things, such a deliberate affront, sometimes even an overt attack upon the reader. The novel does not so much use the grotesque to depict decadence, or portray the grotesque in a decadent society; by the way of the narrator's hallucinating mind, the novel willfully becomes in itself a grotesque object. Both parts of the relationship, the one and the zero, are essential to the ultimate effect; in contrast to *V.* it is impossible to imagine the novel as existing without both the epic scope that chronicles the death-throes of an era, and the layer of adolescent mockery through which the cataclysm is viewed. One cannot wish (if one is going to read this book at all) that Pynchon had either better taste or less complicated intellectual designs.[50] The final impression, achieved by a nearly impossible synthesis of that which cannot be combined, is that the most momentous events of our time, or of all recorded time, are being run through the mind of a brilliant, incredibly gifted adolescent who, zonked on something, is listening to junk music on the radio, eating bananas, reading comic books, and, from time to time, jerking off.

III

In the opening pages of Gabriel García Márquez, *One Hundred Years of Solitude*, José Arcadio Buendía, armed with the magnets he had bought from Melquíades, rushes off into the jungle in search of gold, ignoring the gypsy's advice that magnets are no good for that. Instead of gold, he finds only a rusted suit of armour inside of which is 'a calcified skeleton with a copper locket containing a woman's hair around its neck'.[51] The chivalric favour, uncovered hundreds of years after the lovers are dead, circles with perfect fatuity the grotesque that time and decay have made of the adventurer. Moreover, behind the discovery lies a story that is implied but deliberately left untold. We never learn how the amorous conquistador met his end, but we have a distinct sense of the little joke that nature has in store for those who, full of bravado, go clanking off into the jungle.

The episode is emblematic of the meeting between Old and New World in this novel. In many North American writers such as West, the primitive, natural state of pre-industrial America is something that has been lost or betrayed. In Márquez, such paradisiacal antecedents never existed; the attempt to transplant European culture to the jungles of Macondo is a perverse joke, an enterprise that none but lunatics could have undertaken in the first place.

Too much of the commentary on Marquez' fiction, especially *One Hundred Years of Solitude*, has centred on his rendering of political, economic, and social conditions in Latin America.[52] Certainly, they are an important aspect of his work, and without them as a starting point, it probably could not have come into being. But ultimately Marquez is casting a wider net; his topic in this book is nothing less than the invention and disintegration of culture itself. The history of the Buendía family and the inseparable history of Macondo are the story of man's struggle to create and sustain culture against the enormous odds posed by both an absolutely hostile external world, and by man's own perverse tendency to destroy everything he has built.

In Macondo, practically everything taken for granted in Western civilisation must either be rediscovered or reinvented, not just initially but on an almost daily basis. 'The world was so recent that many things lacked names and in order to indicate them it was necessary to point' (p. 11). Of course, it is not the *whole* world that is new. The world outside Macondo is old and highly developed, with both Eastern and Western cultures long established. But in Macondo only the basic skills of language and housekeeping have been transplanted. The town is initially a kind of virgin territory of the mind where strains of the European civilisation of imperial Spain and the arcane mysticism and magic of Melquíades and the East commingle, causing bizarre permutations of each other. Science, religion, commerce, government, music, drama, war, literature, imperialism, architecture, aviation – all are either rediscovered or reinvented by Macondan man, with awe and wonder, and most of the time with a penchant for extremism that can lead to insanity, chaos, and annihilation. This antic replay of the development of human culture takes place, moreover, in an environment which, because of its climate, isolation, and ruggedness, is totally inimical to civilisation. Nature, here identified with the swamp and jungle that surround the town, is a welter of fecundity and putrescence, and its very richness is the most dangerous, anarchic thing about it. What Macondo represents is the encroachment of human culture upon a particularly inhospitable nature, its subsequent growth in conflict with nature, its advances, declines, and ultimate destruction.

Part of the reason for this failure is that in reinventing the culture of Europe, Macondons seem doomed to repeat all the earlier mistakes of Europeans. But an even more important reason is the fragility of culture itself – its dependence on memory and language, its vulnerability to both the hostile environment and man's erratic nature. Early in the novel, Rebecca brings with her the insomnia sickness which frees people from the need to sleep but gradually obliterates their memories, so that signs have to be hung on everything to recall what they are. 'Thus they went on living in a reality that was slipping away, momentarily captured by words, but which would escape irremediably when they forgot the values of the written letters' (p. 53). José Arcadio Buendía hits upon a solution that combines his characteristic practicality and extravagance; the whole of human knowledge must be relearned every day. He designs a kind of gigantic circular file to assist in the process. Nothing less than this kind of heroic diligence will suffice to keep culture alive.

The problem is that few of the characters are capable of such sustained effort for long. Mostly they alternate between enthusiasm and narcissism which, predictably in this novel, turn out to be two versions of the same thing. Ursula alone seems to have the stamina and determination equal to the task but time defeats her. In her prime, she makes the Buendía household a kind of European oasis, filled with Dutch linen and Viennese furniture, a citadel of culture where the arts are cultivated and hospitality flourishes. Even after the ten-year deluge has ravaged the house and old age has reduced her to the children's grotesque plaything, she rallies her energy for one last try: '"Open the windows and the doors," she shouted. "Cook some meat and fish, buy the largest turtles around, let's reinstate the old conviviality, even if on a coarser level . . . because that's the only way to drive off ruin"' (p. 311).

As time passes, culture fails, and what invariably supplants it is the grotesque. In this novel the grotesque is primarily something that people are turned *into*, and the process of that change, repeated over and over, is one of the main narrative patterns of the book. The grotesque is a kind of natural principle in Macondo, alway ready to emerge with the passage of time as the merciless jungle environment reduces all encroachments which the foreign culture has managed to make. Many characters live to incredible age, and hence become fantastically decrepit; exaggeration in one sphere produces exaggeration in the other. In the old age of his second life, Melquíades seems to combine with the eternal wilderness itself. 'His skin became covered with a thin moss similar to that which flourished on the antique vest that he never took off, and his breath exhaled the odor of a sleeping animal' (p. 75). So too, José Arcadio Buendía seems almost to become part of the chestnut tree to which he is bound for years after he goes mad. Well into her second century of life, the shrunken Ursula becomes the favourite toy of little Aureliano and Amaranta Ursula who paint her with soot, bedeck her with dead lizards, and carry her about like a broken doll. Even Petra Cotes, the inexhaustibly fertile mistress of Aureliano Segundo, is found by him after the deluge 'green, disheveled, with sunken eyelids and skin spangled with mange, but she was writing out numbers on small pieces of paper to make a raffle' (p. 307).

But the passage of time in the jungle environment is not the only thing that can turn men and women into grotesques; they are quite capable of doing that for themselves by the extravagance of their passions, their penchant for following one bent to outlandish extremes. The opposite poles of such extremity are dramatised most particularly in the recurring sets of José Arcadios and Aurelianos, the former being enormous, robust, extroverted, and the latter lean, withdrawn, mystical. But either type can meta- morphose into the other, as happens several times, and both types through extremism can become grotesques. The clearest example is the case of the identical twins, José Arcadio Segundo and Aureliano Segundo. The latter in his youth was introverted and studious, spending his days pouring over the indecipherable manuscripts of Melquíades, but he changes, becoming a prodigious gormandiser and womaniser; he 'grew fat, purple colored, turtle shaped, because of an appetite comparable only to that of José Arcadio when he came back from travelling around the world' (p. 239). At the height of his prowess and prosperity, he nearly kills himself in an eating contest with Camila Sagastume, 'the Elephant'. His identical twin, on the other hand, José Arcadio Segundo, starts out life with youthful exploits that culminate with his bringing the first railroad to Macondo. After seeing an execution, however, he changes, becomes morose, takes up the same manuscripts his brother had abandoned, and vanishes so completely into the room of Melquíades that the other inhabitants of the house forget he is there. One day Ursula finally discovers him.

> The only thing visible in the intricate tangle of hair was the teeth striped with green slime and his motionless eyes. When he recognized his great-grand-mother's voice he turned his head toward the door, tried to smile, and without knowing it repeated an old phrase of Ursula's.
> "What did you expect?" he murmured. "Time passes."
> "That's how it goes," Ursula said, "but not so much."
>
> (pp. 309–10)

'But not so much' might well be the universal plea of all those trying to maintain order and sanity in Macondo. Time and again the emergence of the grotesque in this novel is the visual symptom of the failure of culture, or at least of the transplanted European culture, in the New World tropics. Some of the characters after Ursula's heyday have a similar sense of the importance of maintaining the human superimposition upon the creeping jungle, but all are deeply flawed products of the very culture they are championing. Fernanda lives in the chill orthodoxy of strict Catholicism and aspires to the splendour of the old viceregal administration. She tries to keep up appearances, not sensing, as Amaranta and, finally, Meme do, that appearances are all she is capable of. Even appearances are swept away by the deluge, and after venting her frustration in a four-page diatribe against Macondo, the Beundías, and, in particular, her husband, she retreats into the oblivion of dreams, gradually becoming a costume parody of the queen she was raised to be.

Civilisation of a sort is briefly restored when Fernanda's son returns from Rome and finds Ursula's buried gold. But he uses the treasure to turn part of the house into a luxurious realisation of his pederast fantasies, and his brief regime ends when four of the debauched children with whom he has surrounded himself drown him in his bath and make off with what remains of the gold. A more determined and longer-lived effort is made when Amaranta Ursula, the last of the Buendía women, returns from Europe with a rich Belgian husband on a silken leash, and completely restores the house to its former splendour. But the Belgian grows bored with Macondo and returns to Europe as Amaranta Ursula and Aureliano Babilonia lose themselves in incestuous passion, and the jungle reclaims its own. The weeds grow so fast they can actually be heard, and the ultimate nemesis of the Buendía family, the giant red ants, take over the house room by room. Making love in this 'paradise of disaster', Amaranta Ursula laughs, '"Who would have thought that we really would end up living like cannibals?"' (p. 377).

Toward the end of the story, portents of the demise of culture are everywhere. The old Catalan, a former classics professor and proprietor of the only bookstore in town, gives up on Macondo and returns to Europe, severing the last link between the New World and the Old World culture. His protégé, Gabriel, a descendant of Colonel Gerinaldo Márquez, is last seen headed for Paris with a big copy of Rabelais under his arm. (Márquez, like Grass and Nabokov, is fond of jokes.)

The final demise of civilisation and civilisers is announced by the birth of the last Buendía, a child with the tail of a pig. All along, this aberration, nature's laugh at the incestuous passions of the Buendías, has been the grotesque symbol at the novel's centre.[53] It was the cause of Macondo's having been founded in the first place, and throughout the novel, Ursula has sensed some connection between the tail of the pig and the Buendía penchant for extremisim. '"You shouldn't complain," Ursula told her husband. "Children inherit their parents' madness."' And as she was lamenting her misfortune, convinced that the wild behaviour of her children was something as fearful as a pig tail, Aureliano gave her a look that wrapped her in an atmosphere of uncertainty' (p. 46). The final appearance of the 'mythological animal' is the grotesque herald of civilisation's overthrow. The red ants claim the freak as their prize, and the prophetic manuscripts of Melquíades become easily readable as the apocalyptic whirlwind descends on Macondo.

A story of failure and annihilation *One Hundred Years of Solitude* certainly is, and yet it is among the most unstintingly comic of modern novels, and the lingering impression is more of exuberance than of futility. The novel in effect short-circuits its own pessimistic appraisal of the human endeavour. One reason for this is the way in which Márquez leads us away from our historical world only to bring us back to it from an altogether different perspective. Dostoyevsky posited fantastic realism; the true nature of mundane reality is revealed only in the extraordinary, the extreme, the uncanny. Márquez has reversed the polarity and given us what might be called realistic fantasy; the miraculous is narrated with all the unshakability of the matter-of-fact.[54] The effect is to expand the realm of the everyday to include the fantastic while imbuing the most literal things of modern life with the wonder of fantasy. To the residents of Macondo, people flying about on magic carpets become routine, but a train seen for the first time is 'like a kitchen dragging a village behind it' (p. 210). Márquez makes us catch ourselves looking at commonplace things anew, and recognising as we usually do not their wild improbability.[55] Science and magic are so confounded as to be identical; in fact, magic more often seems to provide the more reasonable explanations. Faced with a mechanical contraption, a pianola, José Arcadio Buendía deduces the principle of its operation: there must be an invisible player. To prove his theory scientifically, he will use another technical gadget, the camera, to catch the spectral musician unaware and snap his picture. The confounding of science and magic could not possibly be more complete, and each becomes a point of vantage from which the other is viewed. Not in the incongruity but in the ease and plausibility of the mental operation for the characters lies the joke.

Second, the grotesque itself, even at its most gruesome, is always basically a comic convention in Márquez' handling. Whether used to portray the outcome of extremism in human behaviour, or to dramatise the way that time and nature always turn the tables on man, the grotesque appears suddenly, is always outlandish and frequently outrageous, and is introduced with the imperturbable deadpan that is Márquez' principal technique. Fernanda's father, Don Fernando del Carpio, always sends a large package of Christmas gifts to his grandchildren. One year when the oblong box is opened it is found to contain nothing other than the exceedingly ripe corpse of Don Fernando himself. How such a thing could happen is never gone into; the outlandish in human affairs is left to speak for itself. At the same time, we realise that it is not Don Fernando who has had a grotesque joke on his family, but Márquez who has had one on us – again.

Finally, in a way most fitting for this novel of opposites that prove to be identical, the passionate extremism that causes men to destroy all they have built in Macondo is the same force that enables them to create in the first place. When the Buendías are at the height of the prosperity, Ursula buys the pianola so that music and dancing may be brought to Macondo. Pietro Crespi arrives from Italy to assemble and tune the instrument, but no sooner has he departed than José Arcadio Buendía, in a fever of curiosity (and without Ursula's knowledge) takes it apart to investigate further 'its magical secret'. He manages to reassemble it, after a fashion, but on the night of the grand party to dedicate the new house, it refuses to work. Both Ursula and Melquíades tinker with it but to no effect. 'Finally José Arcadio Buendía managed, by mistake, to move a device that was stuck and music came out, first in a burst and then in a flow of mixed notes. Beating against strings that had been put in without order or concert and had been tuned with timerity, the hammers let go. But the stubborn descendants of the twenty-one intrepid people who plowed through the mountains in search of the sea to the west avoided the reefs of the melodic mixup and the dancing went on until dawn' (p. 66). Dauntless revellers dancing to cacophony, that is the epitome of Márquez' comic vision of the making of culture in Macondo.

Postscript

A cartoon which appeared a number of years ago in *The New Yorker* depicts the workshop of a medieval sculptor. In the foreground sits the somewhat tipsy-looking artist chipping away at a monstrous gargoyle, and throughout the shop are other figures of gargoyles, griffins, and chimeras in various stages of completion. Behind the sculptor stands his perplexed patron who is asking: 'Where *do* you get your ideas?' This study has in essence asked that question about a variety of works in twentieth-century fiction. How *account* for the grotesque as a perennial strain in the human imagination, and how account for its particular prevalence in much of this century's best fiction, and for the variegated forms it has there assumed?

Grotesque art did not originate in an aesthetic theory or artistic movement: it antedates all theories and all movements. In individual experience, the grotesque is first encountered in the dreams and fantasies of childhood; in culture, grotesque art appears in the earliest and most primitive societies and its history goes back to the dawn, the very first light of artistic creation. Paleolithic caves throughout Europe and Africa, but especially in southern France and northern Spain, are now the galleries for some of the earliest known paintings and carvings, art works that date from 10,000 B.C. to 30,000 B.C. or earlier. For the most part, the pictures are more or less realistic portrayals of bison, horses, and bulls; but several depict creatures which never inhabited this world or any other except the world of the human imagination.[1] The most spectacular is a figure (see p. xii) that seems to preside over a jumbled hunt in the Cave of Trois Frères at Montesquieu Avantes (Ariège). Joseph Campbell describes it as –

> poised in profile in a dancing movement that is similar . . . to a step in the cakewalk; but the antlered head is turned to face the room. The pricked ears are those of a stag; the round eyes suggest an owl; the full beard descending to the deep animal chest is that of a man, as are likewise the dancing legs; the apparition has the bushy tail of a wolf or wild horse, and the

182

position of the prominent sexual organ, placed beneath the tail, is that of the feline species – perhaps a lion.

The hands are the paws of a bear. The figure is two and half feet high, fifteen inches across. 'An eerie, thrilling picture,' wrote Professor Kuhn. Moreover, it is the only picture in the whole sanctuary bearing paint – black paint – which gives it an accent stronger than all the rest.[2]

The apparition has been variously interpreted as a spirit or god controlling the hunt, a sorcerer or shaman performing a ritual dance, or a hunter costumed and masked to beguile the prey. In any case, what is striking is that here, fully seven thousand years or more before the dawn of anything we might care to call civilisation, is a figure which, in modern terminology, would have to be called grotesque. By a strange coincidence of history and language, 'grotesque' is exactly the right word for the kind of art we are considering, but the *grotte* in question have nothing to do with ancient Rome; they were themselves ancient before Rome was built.

Of course, we do not known what significance such cave paintings had for their creators and we shall probably never have any way of knowing. We may, I think, be certain that our modern idea of the grotesque would have had no meaning to a Stone Age carver, any more than it would to a modern-day aborigine in a ceremonial mask. The inclination to view the mythical or supernatural figure as something set apart, aberrant, outside the realm of the normal or even the possible implies a high degree of specifically modern acculturation. Hence the comparatively recent origin of the term. But the earliest paintings share much in common with art that we would term grotesque; they are not rudimentary or borderline examples either, but complete and fully developed. There is the contravention of what is experienced as possible, the flight into a realm of fantasy and magic, the suggestion of the dream world. There is the combination of disparate elements, animal and human, the deliberate ungainliness and outlandishness, the affront to physical consistency or predictability. Further, there is the suggestion of the frightful, summoning up the world of irrational fear or nightmare in which such creatures might exist. Finally there appears to the modern eye to be a certain wry playfulness, whimsicality, or perverse glee. The fact that there has been art of this peculiar kind for as long as there has been any kind of art at all is impressive, and argues that the grotesque is not a genre or mode of representation, still less an artistic theory or school, but rather a spontaneous intuition of the world, a version of reality, a way of responding to experience. It is the synthesis of animalism, magic, and play in the intuition of the world as monstrous, as capable of efficacy or aggression in magic, fantastic ways.

It is, I think, possible to tell a good deal about the fears and obsessions that characterise a particular age, its most dreaded sense of its own vulnerabilities, by examing the grotesque in its art. For instance, men of the late Middle Ages were preoccupied by the malevolent presence of the demonic; they theorised and wrote about it at obsessive length, and employed the most drastic means, both religious and secular, to protect themselves against it. Can it be coincidence that the demonic in the painting, sculpture, and literature of the period is one of the richest veins in the whole history of the grotesque in art?

In the modern grotesque, we are not invited to ask what power might change a man into an insect or a woman into a machine as some kind of cosmic joke. The attention, rather, is directed to the predicament of the besieged and humiliated self in its struggle with the brutal and brutalising other. In his autobiography, *Counting My Steps*, Jakov Lind recounts his escape from the Holocaust as a teenager and his wanderings through the collapsing Reich. Toward the end of the book, he reproduces a diary entry he had made in 1945: 'The new Christians are the survivors of Hiroshima. Survivors and disciples. I will start this new Church. The fashion in 1975 will be to look as *maimed* and as *ugly* as possible. Millions of dollars to be earned for the Helena Rubinstein of ugliness. Young men should look like Frankenstein, and the chicks will have plastic surgery to look deformed.'[3] Nineteen seventy-five has come and gone, and the transformation, at least on the literal level, has not been quite so complete as the teenager just through World War II envisioned. But the statement accurately reflects the problem of much modern art: to find terms that seem equal to the enormity of twentieth-century experience. To give form to the unspeakable has always been a function of the grotesque. Its enduring power resides in man's capacity for being fascinated by the monstrousness that besets him.[4] As for twentieth-century man, a sense of power-lessness in the world without, a fear of collapse of the psyche within, the premonition that the present culture, the only home afforded him, has already embarked irreversibly on the path to some hideous or merely ludicrous demise – these are the spawning grounds of his monsters. He proceeds to play with them, to make them grotesquely dance.

Notes

Chapter 1: THE GROTESQUE AND THE MODERN GROTESQUE

1. For a history of the use of the term 'grotesque', see Frances Barasch, *The Grotesque: a Study in Meanings* (The Hague: Mouton, 1971).
2. Lee Byron Jennings, *The Ludicrous Demon* (Berkeley: University of California Press, 1963), pp. 3–5, compiles an interesting and amusing list of various modern uses of the term.
3. Wolfgang Kayser, *The Grotesque in Art and Literature*, trans. Ulrich Weisstein (Bloomington: University of Indiana Press, 1963); Mikhail Bakhtin, *Rabelais and His World*, trans. Helene Iswolsky (Cambridge, Mass.: MIT Press, 1968). A very useful summary of theories on the grotesque through Kayser is in Arthur Clayborough, *The Grotesque in English Literature* (Oxford: Clarendon Press, 1965) pp. 1–69. For a discussion of more recent work, especially among German critics, see Fritz Gysin, *The Grotesque in American Negro Fiction*, The Cooper Monographs on English and American Language and Literature, 22 (Bern: Francke, 1975) pp. 21–34. Not surprisingly, the presuppositions of each of these studies, whether Marxist, Jungian, or structuralist, largely shape the definition of the grotesque which each critic formulates.
4. *The Works of John Ruskin*, ed. E. T. Cook and Alexander Wedderburn (London: George Allen, 1904) XI, 45.
5. On pp. 72–76 of *The Grotesque in Art and Literature*, Kayser analyses 'The Sandman' within the framework of his theory of the grotesque, seeing the work as a story of estrangement from the world.
6. 'The "Uncanny"', *The Standard Edition of the Complete Psychological Works of Sigmund Freud*, ed. James Strachey (London: Hogarth Press, 1955) XVII, 240.
7. Jean Paul Sartre, *Sketch for a Theory of the Emotions*, trans. Philip Mairet (London: Methuen, 1962).
8. This point is very well made by Nadia Khouri in 'The Grotesque: Archeology of an Anti-Code', *Zagadnienia Rodzajow Literackich* 23.2 [45] (1980) 5–24. 'Concordantly, "grotesque" denotes a specific attitude which has been set within a vertical system of values' (p. 6). Her essay includes a discussion of the status of grotesque art created before the word was coined.
9. In a short but stimulating article, M. B. v. Buren argues that criticism of the grotesque in art and in literature has followed two different paths, the former being almost exclusively descriptive and the latter largely theoretical. Literary studies seem more concerned with the effect of the grotesque than with what it represents. 'The Grotesque in Visual Art and Literature', *Dutch Quarterly Review of Anglo-American Letters*, 12 [1] (1982) 42–53.

10. Jennings makes the point that much confusion has arisen from trying to apply the term 'grotesque' to the non-visual. *The Ludicrous Demon*, p. 22.
11. Geoffrey Harpham, *On the Grotesque* (Princeton University Press, 1982).
12. Tzvetan Todorov, *The Fantastic: a Structural Approach to a Literary Genre*, trans. Richard Howard (Ithaca, N.Y.: Cornell University Press, 1970). By declaring that the fantastic encompasses only those novels that will not let us decide whether or not the supernatural is being evoked, Todorov does not so much define or describe a genre as he attempts to dictate one into existence.
13. 'The dividing line is the blackness in the middle, which has no distinctive features, but a number of analogues. It is a spatial equivalent of "paradigm confusion"; or the conceptual leap of metaphor, in which unlike elements are yoked by violence together; or of the "river" of death we cross at the margin of time and eternity. Or, finally, of the mental crisis of the interval of the grotesque, that we must suffer through on the way to the discovery of a radical new insight . . .' (p. 46).
14. 'Totem and Taboo', *The Standard Edition*, XIII, 125–32.
15. For a discussion of such innate releasing mechanisms and their possible effect on the formation of myth, see Joseph Campbell, *The Masks of God: Primitive Mythology* (New York: Viking, 1959) pp. 34–49.
16. In the nineteenth century, Charles Gould was so struck by the coincidence that he theorised that dragons (about which he had encyclopedic knowledge) must have originated in man's dim memory of now extinct creatures which perished in the Deluge. *Mythical Monsters* (London: A. H. Allen, 1886) pp. 132–5. Even today, Carl Sagan has speculated that there may have been some overlap between the last of the dinosaurs and the early protohuman ancestors, and that the world-wide phenomenon of dragon lore is a result. *The Dragons of Eden: Speculations on the Evolution of Human Intelligence* (New York: Ballantine, 1978) p. 150.
17. *Freaks: Myths and Images of the Secret Self* (New York: Simon & Schuster, 1978) p. 24.
18. Freud discusses the world transforming power of the uncanny in literature; 'The "Uncanny"', pp. 249–50.
19. Jennings bases his theory of the grotesque on the balance between the fearful and ludicrous, suggesting that the latter somehow 'disarms' the former. *The Ludicrous Demon*, pp. 10–15. A similar theory is offered by Philip Tomson, *The Grotesque*, The Critical Idiom, 24 (London: Methuen, 1972); and Michael Steig, 'Defining the Grotesque: an Attempt at Synthesis', *Journal of Aesthetics and Art Criticism*, No. 2 (Winter, 1970) 253–60. Such theories seem to confine the grotesque to a narrow and characteristically modern range of tragi-comedy.
20. *Homo Ludens*, trans. R. F. C. Hull (Boston: Beacon Press, 1955) p. 8. The semantics of the word 'play' are discussed in detail on pp. 28–45.
21. *The Masks of God: Primitive Mythology*, pp. 22–9. ·
22. *The Grotesque in Art and Literature*, p. 187.
23. *Rabelais and His World*, p. 91. For discussions of Bakhtin's theory of the carnival grotesque in the light of contemporary criticism, see

Michael André Bernstein, 'When the Carnival Turns Bitter: Preliminary Reflections on the Abject Hero', *Critical Inquiry*, 10 (1983) 283–305; and David Hayman, 'Toward a Mechanics of Mode: Beyond Bakhtin', *Novel*, 16 (1983) 101–20.

24. Sylvia Henning, in *'La Forme in-formante:* a Reconsideration of the Grotesque', *Mosaic*, 14 (1981) 107–21, notes this shortcoming in both Kayser and Bakhtin, but her solution is the same post-structuralist formulation that Harpham was to elaborate a year later: 'The grotesque . . . might more appropriately be called a play with the very indeterminacy of existence' (p. 107).

25. *English Drama from the Early Times to the Elizabethans* (London: Hutchinson's University Library, 1950) pp. 73–4.

26. 'Childhood Terror and the Grotesque', *Contemporary Review*, 104 (July–Dec., 1914) 101–8.

27. *Past Masters*, trans. H. T. Lowe Porter (New York: Alfred Knopf, 1933) pp. 240–1.

28. Jean Paul Sartre, *Nausea*, trans. Lloyd Alexander (New York: New Directions, 1964) p. 78.

29. Günter Grass, *The Tin Drum*, trans. Ralph Manheim (New York: Vintage, 1963) p. 411.

30. *Dickens and Kafka* (Bloomington: University of Indiana Press, 1963).

31. Doestoyevsky, *Notes from Underground*, trans. Andrew R. MacAndrew (New York: Signet, 1961).

Chapter 2: THE PARANOID VISION

1. For a discussion of some of the methods employed, see Roy Pascal, 'Critical Approaches to Kafka' in *The Kafka Debate*, ed. Angel Flores (New York: Gordian, 1977) pp. 42–50.

2. *The Diaries of Franz Kafka 1910–1913*, ed. Max Brod, trans. Joseph Kresh (New York: Schocken, 1948) p. 288.

3. W. J. Dodd, in 'Varieties of Influence: On Kafka's Indebtedness to Dostoevskii', *Journal of European Studies*, 14 (1984) 257–68, takes the whole matter of the Russian writer's influence far beyond the widely recognised hint of 'Metamorphosis' in *Notes from Underground*. He cites especially *The Double* as influencing Kafka from as early as *The Trial*, not the least resemblance being 'a sharp sense of grotesque humor' (p. 260).

4. *General Psychopathology*, trans. J. Hoenig and Marion Hamilton, 7th ed. (University of Manchester Press, 1962) p. 28.

5. *Dearest Father: Stories and Other Writings*, trans. Ernst Kaiser and Eithne Wilkins (New York: Schocken, 1954) p. 148.

6. *Letters to Melina*, ed. Willi Haas, trans. Tania and James Stern (1953; rpt. New York: Schocken, 1962) p. 79. For a recent account of the writing of the letter, see Ronald Hayman, *Kafka: A Biography* (New York: Oxford University Press, 1982) pp. 244–6.

7. David Swanson, Philip Bohnert and Jackson Smith, *The Paranoid* (Boston: Little, Brown, 1970) p. 8. Referred to hereafter as Swanson.

8. Walter Sokel, 'Freud and the Magic of Kafka's Writing' in *The World of Franz Kafka*, ed. J. P. Stern (New York: Holt, 1980) pp. 145–58, discusses the role of both repression and projection in Kafka's fiction, but he sees both as elements of characterisation rather than as a fundamental technique used directly by Kafka himself to invent a fictive world. 'The fantastic in Kafka is a projection or prolongation of psychic tendencies in the protagonist, a fact which is clearly hinted at by the text. . . . It is the function of Kafka's miracles to make the external world of his fiction conform to the unacknowledged wishes of his characters' (pp. 154–5).

9. The extraordinary critical activity this story has generated is examined in *The Problem of "The Judgment": Eleven Approaches to Kafka's Story*, ed. Angel Flores (New York: Gordian, 1977). In that collection, Stanley Corngold, 'The Hermenuetic of "The Judgement"', notes that over 100 interpretations have been offered and that no ten-page story outside religious or classical canons has prompted so much exegesis (p. 39).

10. Franz Kafka, *The Complete Stories*, ed. Nahum N. Glatzer (New York: Schocken, 1972) pp. 79–80.

11. This ingenious reading was put forward by Kate Flores in *Franz Kafka Today*, eds. Angel Flores and Homer Swandor (Madison: University of Wisconsin Press, 1958) pp. 5–24, and was recently reprinted in *Explain to Me Some Stories of Kafka*, ed. Angel Flores (New York: Gordian, 1983) pp. 34–53.

12. 'The Metamorphosis' in *Complete Stories*, p. 97.

13. *Diaries 1910–1913*, p. 291.

14. Kafka, *The Castle*, trans. Willa and Edwin Muir, additional material trans. Eithne Wilkins and Ernst Kaiser (New York: Vintage, 1974) p. 81.

15. Claude Magny also cites this sketch as a particularly clear example of how the seemingly mundane is bordered by the horrible. 'The Objective Depiction of Absurdity', trans. Angel Flores, *The Kafka Problem*, ed. Angel Flores (1946; rpt. New York: Octagon, 1963) p. 95.

16. *The Trial*, trans. Willa and Edwin Muir, rev. trans. E. M. Butler (New York: Vintage, 1969) p. 286.

17. 'The Burrow' in *Complete Stories*, p. 339.

18. Norbert Kassel, in his structuralist study of the grotesque in Kafka, also concentrates on the short stories and journals. *Das Groteske bei Franz Kafka* (Munchen: Wilhelm Fink, 1969).

19. See Stanley Corngold, *The Commentator's Despair: the Interpretation of Kafka's Metamorphosis*, National University Publications Series on Literary Criticism (Port Washington, N.Y.: Kennikat Press, 1973).

20. The most ambitious attempt to explain it with regard to Kafka is Karl-Heinz Fingerhut, *Die Funktionen der Tierfiguren im Werke Franz Kafkas* (Bonn: Bouvier, 1969). See esp. pp. 84–157. More recently, Peter Stine, working in the context of Walter Benjamin's essay on Kafka, explores a variety of the animal stories as versions of the lost self. 'Franz Kafka and Animals, *Contemporary Literature* 22 (1981) 58–80. For 'Metamorphosis', see pp. 62–6.

21. 'Kafka's "Metamorphosis" and the Beauty and the Beast Tale', *JEGP*, 53 (Jan. 1954) 69–71.
22. 'The Cockroach as Identification, with Reference to Kafka's *Metamorphosis*', *American Imago*, 16 (spring 1959) 69.
23. 'The Objective Depiction of Absurdity', p. 95.
24. In some recent criticism, the machine has been abstracted almost out of existence. For E. R. Davey, 'The Broken Engine: a Study of Franz Kafka's *In der Straf Kolonie*', *Journal of European Studies* 14 (1984) 271–83, the apparatus represents the breakdown between the spiritual and the physical, between the Idea and its realisation in time and space. The 'Schriften' of the Old Commandant can no longer control the operation of the Harrow (p. 282). The connection with writing is even more explicit for Arnold Weinstein, who repeats the dismally predictable threnody of much contemporary criticism; 'It registers at all levels the failure of communication, the falling short of language, the unrelated and uncomprehending selves'. 'Kafka's Writing Machine: Metamorphosis in The Penal Colony', *Studies in Twentieth Century Literature*, 7 (1982) 21–33.
25. A detailed and perceptive analysis of the narrative situation is given by Roy Pascal in 'Kafka's "In der Strafkolonie"': Narrative Structure and Interpretation', *Oxford German Studies*, 11 (1980) 123–45. See esp. 125–9.
26. 'Trotzdem zögerte er jetz im Anblick des Soldaten und Verurteilten einem Atemzug lang. Schliesslich aber sagte er, wie er musste: "Nein".' Franz Kafka, *Samtlicke Erzahlungen*, ed. Paul Raabe (Frankfurt am Main und Hamburg: Fischer, 1970) p. 116.
27. Marjorie Gelus, in 'Notes on Kafka's "Der Bau"', *Colloquia Germanica*, 15 (1982) 98–111, gives a fascinating account of the relation between external and internal reality in this story, noting the similarity to the three-part world Kafka described in the letter for his father, as discussed above.
28. For a full analysis of tense in the story see J. M. Coetzee, 'Time, Tense, and Aspect in Kafka's "The Burrow"', *MLN*, 96 (1981) 556–79. Coetzee concludes that narrative time itself collapses. My analysis is based on the text of 'Der Bau' in *Beim Bau der Chinesischen Mauer*, eds Max Brod and Hans Joachim Schoeps (Berlin: Gustav Kiepenheuer, 1931) pp. 90–102.
29. 'Ich habe wohl sehr lange geschlafen . . . was fur ein unaufhörlich tätiges Volk das ist und wie lästig sein Fleiss!' (pp. 105–6).
30. 'Franz Kafka's "The Burrow": an Analytical Essay,' *PMLA*, 87 (1972) 152–66.
31. Henry Sussman, in 'The All-Embracing Metaphor: Reflections on Kafka's "The Burrow", *Glyph*, 1 (1977) 100–31, ingeniously suggests that the animal becomes panic-stricken at the sound of its own digging (p. 119). But in this desconstructive reading, the existence of the beast is beside the point; the interpretive act is the real subject of the story. 'In the conjunction of death, writing, and duplicity which it stages, the all embracing metaphor, the construction, serves as a setting for the discovery of textual limit' (p. 120).

32. 'Die Arbeit war vollendet; es fehlt in den erhalten gebliebenen Blättern nicht mehr viel bis zum Schluss gespannter Kampfstellung in unmittelbar Erwartung des Tieres und des entscheisdenden Kampfes, in dem der Held unterliegen wird. (Diese Angaben verdanken wir der liebenswürdigen Mitteilung von Dora Dymant, der hinterlassenen Lebensgefährtin des Vorstorbenen.)', *Beim Bau der Chinesischen Mauer*, p. 261. Mark Boulby and Britta Mache, in separate articles in the same volume of *German Quarterly* (55 [1982]), give two variations of the biographical argument based on Brod's assertion that Kafka himself equated the beast with his own terminal disease. Boulby, 'Kafka's End: a Reassessment of "The Burrow"' (pp. 175–85), argues that Kafka could not and would not finish the story because he could not write to his satisfaction about his own death (p. 181). Mache, 'The Noise in the Burrow: Kafka's Final Dilemma' (p. 526–40), equates the burrow itself with Kafka's respiratory system, while stipulating that this interpretation does not preclude its being also the real burrow of a real animal. She likens the story to a cubist painting that can be seen from several perspectives at once (p. 527).

33. Weigand suggests that the animal dies from a heart attack caused by his self-induced fright, but continues to speak to his last heartbeat, knowing it is his last (p. 165).

34. *The Diaries of Franz Kafka 1914–1923*, ed. Max Brod, trans. Martin Greenberg and Hannah Arendt (New York: Schocken, 1940) p. 102.

35. If 'Der Bau' was originally inspired by Kafka's own illness, then the story represents the fulfilment of his prophecy and is a kind of artistic playing with his own impending death.

Chapter 3: BLOOMSBODY

1. There have been two studies in recent years that discuss the grotesque in *Ulysses*. One is Eliot Gose's *The Transformation Process in Joyce's Ulysses* (University of Toronto Press, 1980), and the other Patrick Parrinder's general study, *James Joyce* (Cambridge University Press, 1984). Both came to my attention after the present essay was completed in draft form. Though there are some cases in which the studies touch on the same points, ultimately each takes a quite different view of the nature and function of the grotesque in this novel. I shall comment in notes when appropriate on similarities and differences.

2. The scheme of correspondences was published in 1930 by Stuart Gilbert claiming Joyce's authority. See Gilbert's *James Joyce's Ulysses*, 2nd ed (New York: Alfred Knopf, 1952) pp. 40–42. See also, Richard Ellman, *James Joyce* (New York: Oxford University Press, 1959) p. 450.

3. Parrinder (p. 9) notes that Bakhtin's concept of the grotesque body in Rabelais has affinities with Joyce. He seems, however, to find the congruence between the two more complete than I do. I shall argue that the Rabelaisian sense of the indefatigable and joyous body is only one side of Joyce's far more ambivalent attitude toward physicality and sexuality.

4. The importance of food in *Ulysses* is the subject of a recent book-length study, Lindsey Tucker's *Stephen and Bloom at Life's Feast: Alimentary Symbolism in James Joyce's* Ulysses (Columbus: Ohio State University Press, 1984).

5. See above, p. 15.

6. James Joyce, *Portrait of the Artist as a Young Man* (New York: Viking, 1956) p. 90.

7. Morris Beja, in 'The Joyce of Sex: Sexual Relationship in *Ulysses*' in *The Seventh of Joyce*, ed. Bernard Benstock (Bloomington: University of Indiana Press, 1982) pp. 259, analyses Stephen's apparent aversion to sex in *Ulysses* in terms of his relationship to his mother in *Portrait*.

8. *Ulysses* (New York: Modern Library, 1961) p. 5. I regret that the newly corrected edition published jointly by The Bodley Head and Penguin became available only as the present book was already in press. I would much prefer to have used it. Throughout his chapter, I am indebted to Don Gifford and Robert J. Seidman, *Notes for Joyce: An Annotation of James Joyce's* Ulysses (New York: Dutton, 1974).

9. Parrinder, *James Joyce* (pp. 146–7), analyses Bloom's rejection of the spiritual implications of death and his insistence on its complete physicality.

10. *James Joyce and the Making of Ulysses* (New York: Harrison Smith and Robert Haas, 1934) p. 106.

11. Gose in *The Transformation Process in Joyce's* Ulysses, makes an eloquent and long-overdue case that *Ulysses* should be read as more of a 'joyful comedy' than has been usual. Though in the course of his examination of the grotesque in the novel, Gose draws upon the theories of Kayser, Jennings, Steig, and Victor Hugo, he does not seem familiar with Bakhtin, whose notion of the grotesque most substantiates the comic view. Gose argues that the comic and the grotesque are a continuum, but spends much of his chapter on the grotesque in 'Circe' (pp. 153–66) trying to differentiate between comic grotesques and fantastic or fearsome grotesques, always a difficult distinction to make, perhaps because it may be specious to begin with.

12. '"Circe"' in *James Joyce's* Ulysses, eds Clive Hart and David Hyman (Berkeley: University of California Press, 1974) p. 357. Kenner elaborates his original argument in *Joyce's Voices* (London: Faber & Faber, 1978) pp. 91–3; and *Ulysses* (London: Allen & Unwin, 1980) pp. 123–7. Marilyn French, *The Book as World: James Joyce's* Ulysses (Cambridge: Harvard University Press, 1976), suggested the word 'hypostatisations' to describe the 'production numbers staged by the author for the audience' (p. 187).

13. David Hayman in Ulysses: *The Mechanics of Meaning*, rev. ed (Madison: University of Wisconsin Press, 1982), distinguishes between the 'narrator' and the 'arranger' in the novel, and concludes 'Joyce seems to have taken the whole book, jumbled it together in a giant mixer and then rearranged its elements in a monster pantomime which, as proper, includes every imaginable form of foolery but which may well be the most serious chapter in the book, a true rite of passage' (p. 102). In an even more engaging conceit than the literary mix-master, Richard

Pearce likens the narrative technique of the chapter to Bella Cohen's pianola: 'all the keys are moving and nobody is playing'. ('Experimenting with the Grotesque: Comic Collisions in the Grotesque World of *Ulysses*'. *Modern Fiction Studies*, 20 [1974] 381).

14. A. Walton Litz, *The Art of James Joyce: Method and Design in* Ulysses *and* Finnegan's Wake (London: Oxford University Press, 1961) pp. 24–9, argues that 'Cyclops' and 'Circe' are closely related in composition since many of the 'gigantic' parodies of the former were late insertions at the time the latter was being written. This account has been modified somewhat by Michael Gordon, Ulysses *in Progress* (Princeton University Press, 1977) pp. 115–65.

15. French, p. 186.

16. Marie Delcourt, *Hermaphrodite: Myths and Rites of the Bisexual Figure in Classical Antiquity*, trans. Jennifer Nicholson (London: Studio Books, 1961) p. 45.

17. Dorothy Price, *A Historical Review of Embryology and Intersexuality: Fact and Fancy* (Leiden: E. J. Brill, 1967) p. 13.

18. Mark Schechner, *Joyce in Nighttown* (Berkeley: University of California Press, 1974) p. 115, suggests that the whole Bella Cohen sequence has the form of a medieval *auto-de-fe*. 'The torture, the charge, the confession of guilt, the imposition of cruel penance, the final judgment, and final despair form an identifiable pattern.'

19. Not surprisingly, the question of Bloom's androgyny has become an issue of wide interest and lively debate in recent years. In 1964, Stanley Sultan could argue, in *The Argument of* Ulysses (Columbus: Ohio State University Press), that Bloom lacked masculinity in managing his home life, and his ordeal in 'Circe' allowed him to find his manhood and assert proper control by demanding breakfast in bed the following morning (pp. 321–30). Since then, the argument has become more heated. Marilyn French argues that aggressive masculinity is presented in the novel as unacceptable and Bloom is to be admired for showing his feminine side (*The Book as World*, pp. 46–8). Carolyn Heilbrun has argued that as both man and woman, Bloom is sympathetic man and woman as hero (*Towards Androgyny: Aspects of Male and Female in Literature* [London: Victor Gollanz, 1973] p. 95). Sandra Gilbert argues that Bloom has wrongly succumbed to female attire and 'his clothing tells us, accordingly not of his large androgynous soul but of his complete degradation', thus reflecting Joyce's opinion that to *be* a woman is to be degraded ('Costumes of the Mind: Transvestism as Metaphor in Modern Literature', *Critical Inquiry*, 7 [1980] 396). Cheryl Herr's argument, in 'One Good Turn Deserves Another: Theatrical Cross Dressing in Joyce's "Circe" Episode', *Journal of Modern Literature*, 2 (1984) 263–76, is that Bloom does not change sex at all. His apparent change derives from a long tradition of comic cross-dressing in music hall routines – an interesting idea, but one that puts Herr in the position of having to explain away rather lamely Bloom's explicity mentioned physiological change and his motherhood as 'little more than stage props' (p. 274). On the other hand, Joseph Boone, in 'A New Approach to Bloom as "Womanly Man": the Mixed Middling's

Progress in *Ulysses'*, *James Joyce Quarterly*, 20 (1982) 67–85, argues that Bloom's 'feminine' qualities become a source of distress only when confronted by a society that demands stereotyping. Mary Burgan, in 'Androgynous Fatherhood in *Ulysses* and *Women in Love'*, *Modern Language Quarterly*, 44 (1983) 178–97, argues that in Joyce (and Lawrence too), androgyny and male motherhood involve 'the arrogation to the male of even the most basic of femine attributes – the attribute of giving birth' (p. 197), and signal the desire of both writers 'for a kind of 'obstetrical' status in their roles as artists' (p. 180). I suspect that the argument is far from over.

20. In a letter to Harriet Weaver on 24 June 1921 (Ellman, p. 525). He later seems to have changed his view.

21. Gose, who considers Virag the most fully developed grotesque character in 'Circe', notes that one of his (its?) exclamations is 'Locomotor ataxy'. The critic observes that locomotor ataxia is a spinal disease usually caused by syphilis, and is characterised by an inability to control muscle movements. 'Joyce remarked to Budgen that "the rhythm" of the Circe episode "is the rhythm of locomotor ataxia"' (*The Transformation Process in Joyce's* Ulysses, p. 157).

Chapter 4: INSANITY AS A POINT OF VIEW

1. For an impressively wide-ranging study of literary madness, though one with some curious omissions (no Cervantes, no Dostoyevsky), see Lillian Feder, *Madness in Literature* (Princeton University Press, 1980) esp. pp. 203–86. See also Theodor Ziolkowski, *Dimensions of the Modern Novel: German Texts and European Contexts* (Princeton University Press, 1969) pp. 332–61.

2. Seventh verse in the 'Argument of the Frontispiece', eds Floyd Dell and Paul Jordon-Smith (New York: Tudor, 1941) p. 2.

3. *The Divided Self* (New York: Pantheon, 1960) pp. 27–28.

4. Cf. comments on the relation of madness to the grotesque in Kayser, *The Grotesque in Art and Literature*, p. 184; and Bakhtin, *Rabelais and His World*, p. 39.

5. *Madness and Civilization: a History of Insanity in the Age of Reason*, trans. Richard Howard (New York: Pantheon, 1965) pp. 72–4.

6. Volker Neuhaus, *Günter Grass*, Die Blechtrommel: *Interpretation* (Munchen: Oldenbourg, 1982) pp. 25–6, discusses the effect on the narrative situation of the phrase 'Insasse einer Heil- und Pflegeanstalt.'

7. Georg Just, *Darstellung und Appel in der* 'Blechtrommel' *von Günter Grass: Darstellungsästhetik Versus Wirkungsästhetik*, Literatur und Reflexion, 10 (Frankfurt: Athenäum, 1972) pp. 91–9, examines the fantastic episodes from the viewpoint of their effect on reader response.

8. H. E. Beyersdorf, 'The Narrator as Artful Deceiver: Aspects of Narrative Perspective in *Die Blechtrommel'*, *Germanic Review*, 55 (1980) 129–38, categorises the shifting perspectives of the novel as follows: (a) Oskar the uncertain narrator; (b) Oskar the lying narrator; (c) Oskar the narrator of unlikely events; (d) Oskar's perspective as alienation

of the normal world; (e) changes in narrative perspective; and (f) Oskar as omniscient and omnipotent narrator.

9. *Günter Grass*, Twayne's World Author's Series, 65 (New York: Twayne, 1969) p. 80. Cunliffe explains the similarities by speculating that in an absurd world only an ironic attitude is appropriate.

10. Cf. Beyersdorf, p. 135, who takes both Bruno's and Vittlar's testimony at face value, arguing that each shows us a less grandiose view of Oskar than Oskar himself does, and that each reenforces the impression that Oskar is an unreliable narrator – as if that were in need of reenforcement!

11. *Local Anaesthetic*, trans. Ralph Manheim (New York: Harcourt, Brace and World, 1969) pp. 10, 138; *Dog Years*, trans. Ralph Manheim (New York: Harcourt, Brace and World, 1965) p. 325; *Cat and Mouse*, trans. Ralph Manheim (New York: Signet, 1963) p. 80.

12. Günter Grass, 'Looking Back at *The Tin Drum*', *Encounter*, (July 1976) p. 85. Grass gave a similar account of Oskar's inception in an interview in *Frankfurter Neue Presse*, 14. Nov. 1959, as excerpted in Kurt Lothar Tank, *Günter Grass, Köpfe des XX Jahrhunderts*, Band 38 (Berlin: Colloquium, 1965) p. 57. Despite Grass's claim that in order to deny German teachers variants to play with he had burned all previous drafts of the novel, an early version was discovered in Paris and substantiates that Oskar developed largely as an idiosyncratic way of looking at things. See Silke Jendrowiak, 'Die Sogenannte "Urtrommel"; Unerwartete Einblicke in die Genese der *Blechtrommel* von Günter Grass', *Monatshefte*, 71 (1979) esp. 177–80.

13. *The Child's Conception of the World*, trans. Joan and Andrew Tomlinson (New York: Harcourt, Brace, 1929) p. 133.

14. Alexander Gelley, 'Art and Reality in *Die Blechtrommel*', *Forum for Modern Language Studies*, 3 (1967) 117, links this sentience of inanimate things in the novel to the German romantic notion of 'Tucke des Objekts', as well as to fairy tales and folk stories.

15. The term 'Objektzwang' was applied by Klaus Wagenbach, 'Günter Grass', in *Schriftsteller der Gegenwart: Deutsche Literatur*, ed. Klaus Nonnenmann (Olten und Freiburg: Walter, 1963) p. 123. Idris Parry, 'Aspects of Günter Grass's Narrative Technique', *Forum for Modern Language Studies*, 3 (1967) 108–12, associates Grass's treatment of objects with science, photography, and the modern writer's desire to 'seek infinity through the infinitesimal' (p. 110). Lore Ferguson, 'Die Blechtrommel' *von Gunter Grass: Versuch einer Interpretation* (Bern und Frankfurt: Lang, 1976) pp. 41–87, offers an elaborate analysis of how objects dominate the lives of characters and emblemise situations.

16. Ralph Manheim's English version, of course, reads 'the Black Witch' for 'the Black Cook', and one can only sympathise with that heroic translator's dilemma. By turning 'die schwarze Köchin' into a witch, he made her recognisable to non-German audiences, but only at the price of separating her from the elaborate system of cooking and repulsive food images that is one of the novel's notable features.

17. Gelley, 'Art and Reality', notes, '. . . the novel as a whole becomes a cirtique of art, an allegory of its problematic life in this age, and a search

for what is still possible' (p. 123). The critic likens *Die Blechtrommel* in this respect to Hesse's *Das Glasperlenspiel*. Gide's *Les Faux Monnayeurs*, and Mann's *Doktor Faustus*, with the notable exception that *Die Blechtrommel* is not the retrospective of a long-seasoned artist but the first novel of a writer still in his early thirties. See also Ann L. Mason, *The Skeptical Muse: A Study of Günter Grass's Conception of the Artist*, Stanford German Studies, 5 (Bern: Lang, 1974) pp. 85–6.

18. Grass as quoted in Tank, p. 62.

19. As the present study is prepared for press, I discover that John Flasher, in his general review of Volker Schlondorff's film of *The Tin Drum*, also hit on the term 'grotesque hero' as an appropriate description of Oskar: 'The Grotesque Hero in *The Tin Drum*', in *Holding the Vision: Essays on Film*, Proceedings of the First Annual Film Conference of Kent State University, ed. Douglas Radcliffe-Umstead (Kent, Ohio: International Film Society, Kent State University, 1983) pp. 87–93. Other critics have commented on Grass's use of the grotesque, with Theodor Wiesser, *Gunter Grass: Porträt und Poesie* (Neuwied: Luchterhand, 1968) pp. 34–5, linking it to the author's early training as a painter. Anne Campbell, 'The Grotesque as a Critical Concept: a Question of Cultural Values', *Seminar*, 15 (1979) 251–61, perceptively sums up the difficulties of defining the term, but without solving the problem very convincingly in her analysis of the eel-catching episode.

20. Michael Hollington, *Günter Grass: the Writer in a Pluralist Society*, Critical Appraisals Series (London: Marion Boyers, 1980) pp. 23–9, discusses Grass's use of the grotesque as an attack on classical art and a means of upsetting the reader's usual expectations. See also Mason. *Skeptical Muse*, p. 26.

21. Silke Jendrowiak, *Günter Grass und die 'Hybris' des Kleinbürgers* (Heidelberg: Carl Winter, 1979) pp. 170–80, analyses the tensions between Hamlet and Yorick in Oskar's role as an artist.

22. On the other hand, Frank-Raymond Richter, *Günter Grass: Die Vergangenheitsbewältigung in der Danzig Trilogie*, Abhandlung zur Kunst – Musik – und Literaturwissenschaft, 244 (Bonn: Bouvier, 1979) pp. 40–1, sees the antithesis as being between Beethoven the revolutionary and Hitler the reactionary.

23. Irene Leonard, *Günter Grass*, Modern Writers Series (Edinburgh: Oliver and Boyd, 1974) pp. 18–21, sees the drum as an instrument of protest in religion, politics, and love.

24. The publication of John Reddick's superb study *The Danzig Trilogy of Günter Grass* (New York: Harcourt Brace Jovanovich, 1975), has done much to correct the initial misapprehension of Oskar, see esp. pp. 63–82.

25. Vladimir Nabokov, *Pale Fire* (New York: Berkeley Medallion, 1962) p. 211.

26. An eloquent case was made for this view by Andrew Field in *Nabokov His Life in Art* (Boston: Little, Brown, 1967) pp. 312–14. Less convincing is his argument that Shade is the primary character in *Pale Fire* and creates Kinbote as a mad extension of himself. This conclusion is reached by the strange route of considering the poem as a separate

work under the rubric of Nabokov's poetry (pp. 106–13), and then discussing the rest of the novel in a completely different section of the study. That makes about as much sense as treating *The Murder of Gonzago* as an autonomous Shakespearean play rather than as a part of *Hamlet*.

27. Marilyn Edelstein, '*Pale Fire*: the Art of Consciousness', in *Nabokov's Fifth Arc*, eds J. E. Rivers and Charles Nicol (Austin: University of Texas Press, 1982) pp. 214–23, approaches the novel through three kinds of consciousness, the author's, the artist's, and the madman's.

28. Lucy Maddox, *Nabokov's Novels in English* (London: Croom Helm, 1983) pp. 21–2, discusses the similarities between Kinbote and Gogol's clerk.

29. Nikolai Gogol, *The Diary of a Madman and Other Stories*, trans. Andrew R. MacAndrew (New York: Signet, 1960) p. 28.

30. John Haegert, in what seems to me an inappropriately literal-minded approach to the novel, questions the 'reconstruction' in Kinbote's commentary and its status as a conscious work of art. Instead, the critic stresses Kinbote's 'real' function as a misreader and misinterpretor of texts. 'The Author as Reader as Nabokov', *Texas Studies in Language and Literature*, 26 (1984) 405–24.

31. Samuel Beckett, *Watt* (New York: Grove Press, 1959) p. 126.

32. Eric P. Levy, *Beckett and the Voice of Species* (Dublin: Gill & Macmillan, 1980), discusses Watt and Sam in terms of mirror images (p. 36), and sees all Beckett's fiction as told by a universal narrator, 'the voice of species which is constantly looking in a void for the certain relationship between subject and object that once made life intelligible' (p. 125).

33. John Harrington, in 'The Irish Landscape of Samuel Beckett's *Watt*'. *Journal of Narrative Technique*, 11 (1981) 1–11, discusses the 'literary, cultural and geographical dimensions' of the Irish setting of the novel.

34. G. C. Barnard, *Samuel Beckett: a New Approach* (New York: Dodd, Mead & Co., 1970), studies the prevalence of schizophrenic behaviour in all Beckett's major drama and fiction, suggesting that the writer's interest in the illness dates back to his visit to Bethlem Royal Hospital and his acquaintance with Lucia Joyce (p. 7). In his discussion of *Watt* (pp. 16–27), Bernard sidesteps the problem of the relationship between Sam and Watt and the schizophrenic world of the novel by making Sam the narrator only of part three and situating the rest of the novel in Watt's mind. That is attractive, but ignores the references that Sam makes to himself elsewhere in the book.

35. *Interpretation of Schizophrenia*, 2nd edn (New York: Basic Books, 1974).

36. Arieti, p. 264. See also Laing, *The Divided Self*, p. 175.

37. 'The Personal System – Samuel Beckett's *Watt*', *PMLA*, 86 (1971) 255–65.

Chapter 5: THE ART OF DECADENCE

1. 'Symposium on the Question of Decadence', *Radical Perspectives in*

the Arts, ed. Lee Baxandall (Harmondsworth, England, 1972) pp. 225–39.

2. Oscar Cargill, *Intellectual America* (New York: Macmillan, 1941) pp. 176–310, contains a lengthy discussion of decadence from Poe and Baudelaire, through Dada, to Pound, Stein, and Cummings. See also: Matei Calinescu, *The Faces of Modernity: Avant-garde, Decadence, Kitch,* (Bloomington: University of Indiana Press, 1977); C. E. M. Joad, *Decadence: A Philosophical Inquiry* New York: Philosophical Library, n.d.); Patrick Brantlinger, *Bread and Circuses: Theories of Mass Culture as Social Decay* (Ithaca, N.Y.: Cornell University Press, 1983); and Suzanne Nalbantian, *Seeds of Decadence in the Late Nineteenth Century Novel* (London: Macmillan, 1983).

3. 'The Fascination of Decadence', *Time* (10 Sept. 1979) p. 86.

4. 'A Theory of the Grotesque in Southern Fiction', *Georgia Review*, 26 (1972) 425–37.

5. James F. Light, *Nathanael West: an Interpretive Study,* 2nd edn (Evanston, Ill.: Northwestern University Press, 1971) pp. 138–42, notes the influence of Spengler on West. O'Connor, in a letter to a friend on 5 Aug. 1961, says she had never read Spengler; elsewhere in her correspondence, she shows a secondhand familiarity with his ideas, however (*The Habit of Being,* ed. Sally Fitzgerald [New York: Farrar, Straus and Giroux, 1979], pp. 294, 334, 447). She certainly read West, and his influence on her work is analysed in Frederick Asals, *Flannery O'Connor: the Imagination of Extremity* (Athens, Ohio: University of Georgia Press, 1982) pp. 22–4.

6. *The Decline of the West,* trans. Charles F. Atkinson (New York: Alfred Knopf, 1926) I, 353.

7. *The Complete Works of Nathanael West* (New York: Farrar, Straus and Giroux, 1957) p. 51. All further references to West's novels are from this edition.

8. In *The Day of the Locust,* Fay Greener and Tod Hacket have a similar reaction to the wretched Homer Simpson: 'His helplessness was extremely irritating' (p. 369).

9. *Nathanael West,* University of Minnesota Pamphlets on American Writers, No. 21 (Minneapolis: University of Minnesota Press, 1962). Victor Comerchero, *Nathanael West: The Ironic Prophet* (Syracuse, N.Y.: University of Syracuse Press, 1964) pp. 99–100, endorses this reading in a psycho-sexual analysis of all four novels.

10. *Nathanael West: the Art of His Life* (New York: Farrar, Straus and Giroux, 1970) p. 187.

11. Comerchero, p. 151.

12. 'Nathanael West: a Particular Kind of Joking', in *Nathanael West: a Collection of Critical Essays,* ed. Jay Martin, Twentieth Century Views (Englewood Cliffs, N.J.: Prentice Hall, 1971) p. 156.

13. Warwick Wadlington, 'Nathanael West and the Confidence Game', *Nathanael West: The Cheaters and the Cheated: A collection of Critical Essays,* ed. David Madden (Deland, Fla.: Everett Edwards, 1973), discusses art as revenge, asserting that in *Balso Snell* 'art is a deceitful act of

aggression fulfilling the ulterior needs of performer and viewer . . .' (p. 306).

14. *Mystery and Manners: Occasional Prose*, eds Sally and Robert Fitzgerald (New York: Farrar, Straus & Giroux, 1971) p. 34.
15. Kathleen Feeley, *Flannery O'Connor: Voice of the Peacock* (New Brunswick, N.J.: Rutgers University Press, 1972) p. 29. Carol Shloss, *Flannery O'Connor's Dark Comedies* (Baton Rouge: Louisiana State University Press, 1980) pp. 38–57, discusses the grotesque in O'Connor's work, largely in terms of the author's own remarks.
16. *The Complete Short Stories* (New York: Farrar, Straus & Giroux, 1971) p. 450.
17. Preston Browning, 'Flannery O'Connor and the Grotesque Recovery of the Holy', *Adversity and Grace: Studies in Recent American Literature*, ed. Nathan Scott (University of Chicago Press, 1968) p. 135, cites O'Connor's antipathy to a world 'in which the intellectuals are positivists and the nonintellectuals are positive thinkers'.
18. *Flannery O'Connor: the Imagination of Extremity*, p. 67. Asals discusses the relationship between the grotesque and the sacramental in O'Connor's work.
19. *Wise Blood*, in *Three By Flannery O'Connor* (New York: Signet, n.d.) p. 12.
20. Jonathan Baumbach, *The Landscape of Nightmare: Studies in the Contemporary American Novel* (New York University Press, 1965) p. 99.
21. Marshall Gentry, 'The Eye vs. the Body: Individual and Communal Grotesquerie in *Wise Blood*', *Modern Fiction Studies*, 28 (1982) 487–93, uses Bakhtin's ideas to stress the positive notion of the grotesque in O'Connor's fiction, with particular reference to Hazel Motes.
22. New York: Bantam, 1964, p. 310.
23. Quoted in Calinescu, *The Faces of Modernity*, p. 164.
24. *Gravity's Rainbow* (London: Picador, 1975) pp. 490–1. In quotations from the text, unspaced periods reproduce the three dots that Pynchon uses as a stylistic device. Spaced periods, as usual, indicate an ellipsis.
25. Melvyn New has a splendid discussion of Vheissu as a paradigm for the entire novel in 'Profaned and Stenciled Texts: In Search of Pynchon's *V.*', *Georgia Review*, 33 (1979) 395–412.
26. Raymond Olderman, *Beyond the Wasteland: A Study of the American Novel in the Nineteen Sixties* (New Haven: Yale University Press, 1972), p. 132, observes '*V.* is everything symptomatic of our century, and that all the symptoms point toward a communal dream of annihilation.'
27. Josephine Hendin takes a very different view of the character, in whom she sees female serenity, the clean, eternal balance of emotional control. 'She absorbs the force of war, of all male thrusts, as erotic curios and returning them when as mother she abandons, as protectress she corrupts, as lover she murders, as transvestite priest she damns.' 'What is Thomas Pynchon Telling Us? *V.* and *Gravity's Rainbow*' in *Critical Essays on Thomas Pynchon*, ed. Richard Pearce, Critical Essays on American Literature (Boston: G. K. Hall, 1981) p. 43.
28. Richard Pearce takes a very different view in 'Pynchon's Endings',

Novel, 18 (1985) 145–53. He argues that the last chapter is a parody of an epilogue and must not be taken seriously. 'Stencil's father may have been killed by a wild waterspout *and* a mischievous narrator may be playing with our expectations and needs' (p. 150).

29. Arnold Cassola, 'Pynchon's *V.* and the Malta Connection', *Journal of Modern Literature*, 12 (July, 1985) 311–31, sorts out Pynchon's historical and fictional material about the Malta of both 1919 and 1565, the year of the Turkish siege (311–15).

30. Steven Weisenberger, in 'The End of History? Thomas Pynchon and the Uses of the Past,' in *Critical Essays on Thomas Pynchon*, pp. 140–55, combines astute criticism with literary detective work to give a fascinating account of Pynchon's use of historical material. Like Cassola and Weisenberger, David Marriott has tried to stalk Pynchon's tracks through history and research libraries: '*Gravity's Rainbow*, Apocryphal History or Historical Apocrypha?', *Journal of American Studies*, 19 (1985) 69–80.

31. One cannot help having such misgivings about Douglas Fowler's massive *A Reader's Guide to* Gravity's Rainbow (Ann Arbor, Mich.: Ardis, 1980). I can think of few critics who have lavished so much labour on a single modern novel outside the Joyce canon, but when he divides the book into scenes (as I do with one episode below), he may be allying himself with precisely what the novel singles out as the major fault in Western thought. Besides, inevitably his book is not a guide but a reading – a good, interesting reading, but only one of many possible. If all literature were like *Gravity's Rainbow* (which it is not), then the post-structuralists would be right (which, mostly, they are not). It is no accident that some of the best criticism of this novel approaches it from a post-structuralist perspective. For an excellent discussion of the modern and the post-modern in *Gravity's Rainbow*, see Brian McHale 'Modernist Reading, Post-Modern Text: The Case of *Gravity's Rainbow*', *Poetics Today*, 1 (1979) 86–110.

32. See Khachig Tölölyan, 'Seven on Pynchon: The Novelist as Deconstructionist', *Novel*, 16 (1983) 165–72. The critic uses a review article to assess, like McHale, the situation of a novel built on premises about language and literature similar to those of deconstructionist criticism.

33. Mark Siegel makes the 'creative paranoia' of the narrator the key to his study, *Creative Paranoia in Gravity's Rainbow* (Port Washington, N.Y.: Kennikat, 1978). The narrator's paranoia, in contrast to that of the other characters, is 'creative' because it is controlled and self-conscious, constructing tentative fictional patterns (p. 47).

34. Just to make sure no one gets the wrong idea, Pynchon sets a trap for the reader later in the novel. Waxing lyrical about the names of towns caught in the war, the narrator seems to be inviting another lament like the evensong. But he suddenly turns nasty and mocking, telling us that the only thing the towns share in common is being located on the edges of time zones. The reader is then banished as a 'sentimental surrealist' (pp. 695–6).

35. For a good account of the Zone as a way of looking at things, see James Earl, 'Freedom and Knowledge in the Zone', in *Approaches to*

Gravity's Rainbow, ed. Charles Clerc (Columbus: Ohio State University Press, 1983) pp. 229–50.

36. Tony Tanner, in *Thomas Pynchon*, Contemporary Writers (New York & London: Methuen, 1982) pp. 80–1, divides the setting of the novel into the System and the Zone, with many characters inhabiting one or the other, or gravitating between them.

37. Richard Pearce discusses energy and motion in *Gravity's Rainbow*, as part of a wide-ranging study of movement as both theme and technique in modern fiction: *The Novel in Motion* (Columbus: Ohio State University Press, 1983) pp. 96–101.

38. Sherill Grace has argued convincingly that Fritz Lang's influence on Pynchon extends both to themes and structure in *Gravity's Rainbow*, 'Fritz Lang and the Paracinematic Lives of *Gravity's Rainbow*', *Modern Fiction Studies*, 29 (1983) 655–70. The influence of Burroughs on Pynchon's writing has been noted by several critics, but this subject is worth closer examination.

39. In his essay, '"Beasts Vaulting Among the Earthworks": Monstrosity in *Gravity's Rainbow*', *Novel*, 17 (1984) 158–72, Terry Caesar asserts that the monstrous opens into the miraculous and *is* life in the novel. 'Monstrosity becomes a form of language by which the novel speaks of things which have no name, and indicates a category of experience which has no pattern but its own strangeness' (p. 168).

40. Mark Siegel devotes a chapter of *Creative Paranoia* to the narrative viewpoint, and observes, 'We are always seeing reality through the eyes of the narrator and are meant to be aware of that fact' (p. 34). He discusses the characters as projections of the narrator in the chapter following (p. 44–72).

41. In *Sophie's Choice* (New York: Random House, 1979). Peter L. Cooper makes the distinction between 'Neorealists' and 'Counterealists' in modern fiction in his study *Signs and Symptoms: Thomas Pynchon and the Contemporary World* (Berkeley: University of California Press, 1983).

42. Anyone who saw the late Gerhard Stolze as the Captain knows just how unnerving this grotesque role can be.

43. For a good discussion of Enzian's search for the 'absolute centre' and the 'Second Firing' see Thomas H. Schaub, *Pynchon: The Voice of Ambiguity* (Urbana: University of Illinois Press, 1981) pp. 83–88.

44. Josephine Hendin, in 'What is Thomas Pynchon Telling Us?' asserts that Blicero 'dives straight into the flames of the rocket launch' (p. 49). I can find no indication of this in the text, even allowing for the very loose meaning the word 'evidence' must have with regard to this novel. If she were right, the parallel would be not to the *Liebestod* as she suggests; rather we would have a brilliant parody of Brünhilde's immolation scene.

45. Fowler, *A Reader's Guide to* Gravity's Rainbow, notes the parallel (p. 200), but does not give it the significance I think it warrants.

46. For a very balanced assessment of Pynchon and well as an interesting study of his erudition, see David Cowart, *Thomas Pynchon: The Art of Allusion* (Carbondale: Southern Illinois University Press, 1980).

47. Michael Begnal apparently felt the need to mount an apologia for

Benny, but the defense is based upon the assertion that Stencil is the narrator of the V. chapters, while the narrator of the Profane episodes is 'Pynchon himself' (!). 'Thomas Pynchon's *V.*: In Defense of Benny Profane', *The Journal of Narrative Technique*, 9 (1979) 61–9.

48. John O. Stark, in *Pynchon's Fictions: Thomas Pynchon and the Literature of Information* (Athens: Ohio University Press, 1980) p. 39, points out the necessity of distinguishing between Pynchon and his characters, a point that should not need making but does, to judge by some Pynchon criticism (see n. 47 above). Stark goes on to examine Pynchon's complex but methodical ways of organising the vast amounts of information he makes use of in his fiction.

49. Cf. Siegel, *Creative Paranoia*, who sees the narrator as a modern individual trying to construct a self from a broad range of materials (p. 124).

50. David Leverenz, 'On Trying to Read *Gravity's Rainbow*,' in *Mindful Pleasures: Essays on Thomas Pynchon*, eds George Levine and David Leverenz (Boston: Little, Brown, 1976) pp. 229–49, gives an account of initial exasperation and final enthrallment that many readers will recognise as their own experience of this novel.

51. Gabriel García Márquez, *One Hundred Years of Solitude*, trans. Gregory Rabassa (New York: Avon, 1971) p. 12.

52. For a stimulating overview of recent Márquez criticism see Gene H. Bell-Villada, 'The Marquez Industry', *Novel*, 18 (1985) 281–4. The critic calls for 'a synoptic work that would . . . read Garcia Marquez for the synthesis of seemingly contradictory forces he is' (p. 284).

53. Roberto Gonzalez Echevarria, '*Cien anos de soledad*: the Novel as Myth and Archive', *MLN*, 99 (1984) 358–85, offers a very different interpretation. The skin of the child is like the parchment of the manuscripts and the dead infant becomes representative of both them and the novel itself. 'The novel is a monster, engendered by a self-knowledge of which we too are guilty, to which we add our own pig's tail of reading and interpretation' (p. 378). Grotesque!

54. Márquez himself said that the struggle to write the novel was a search for the right narrative stance: '. . . it is necessary to tell tales simply, like our grandfathers. Tell it in an intrepid tone with a totally foolproof calm so that nothing can alter it even though the world were to fall . . . as if those old men knew that in literature nothing is more convincing than your own conviction'. Quoted in John Ferguson, 'Gabriel García Márquez: a Study of *Cien Anos de Soledad*, Diss. Florida State University, 1971, pp. 114–15 (my translation).

55. The best comment I know on this aspect of Márquez work comes from one who is most intimately familiar with his fiction, English-language translator, Gregory Rabassa: 'In many ways García Márquez has fended off his critics and analysts by always doing what is right, not thinking about what is right. This trait of his writing seems to have a touch of magic about it, and yet it always rings true, so real, hence magic realism. But it is not that: it is reality in its several dimensions, the ones we are hard put to explain without recourse to naked formulas. He has returned to the roots of reality, which are the roots

of the novel as it was conceived by Cervantes. But he has gone even deeper and given us the Roc once more. That is the nature of his ancient art'. ('Beyond Magic Realism: Thoughts on the Art of Gabriel García Márquez', *Books Abroad*, 47 [1973] 50.)

POSTSCRIPT

1. Harpham, *On the Grotesque*, discusses the paintings under the coined term 'grotto-esque'.
2. *The Masks of God: Primitive Mythology*, pp. 309–10.
3. Jakov Lind, *Counting My Steps* (London: Macmillan, 1969) p. 206. Lind was himself an avid creator of grotesques in his small, very strange body of fiction.
4. Nadia Khouri, in 'The Grotesque: Archeology of an Anti-Code', *Zagadnienia Rodzajow Literackich*, argues that the distinction between the grotesque and the monstrous can only be made in terms of the prevailing ideologies of a period. She concludes: 'In a global perspective, however, this introduction to the grotesque should lead to the fundamental problem of critical theory: that of the dynamic interaction between the empirical world and aesthetic expression and interpretation, that of art and literature as products and extensions of organised, controlled, selected, distributed and changing systems of social discourse' (p. 24).

Index